A REBEL HISTORY
of RURAL LIFE

BRIAN BRETT

TRAUMA *Farm*

GREYSTONE BOOKS

D&M PUBLISHERS INC.
Vancouver/Toronto/Berkeley

Greystone Books
An imprint of D&M Publishers Inc.
2323 Quebec Street, Suite 201
Vancouver BC Canada V5T 4S7
www.greystonebooks.com

Library and Archives Canada Cataloguing in Publication
Brett, Brian
Trauma farm : a rebel history of rural life / Brian Brett.
Includes bibliographical references.

ISBN 978-1-55365-474-2

1. Brett, Brian. 2. Brett, Brian—Family. 3. Authors, Canadian (English)—
20th century—Biography. 4. Farm life—British Columbia—Saltspring Island.
5. Natural history--British Columbia—Saltspring Island. I. Title.

S522.C3B74 2009   C818'.5409   C2009-904051-4

Editing by Nancy Flight
Copy editing by Barbara Czarnecki
Jacket and text design by Naomi MacDougall
Jacket illustration by Michael Kelley/Getty Images
Printed and bound in Canada by Friesens
Printed on acid-free paper that is forest friendly (100% post-consumer
recycled paper) and has been processed chlorine free.
Distributed in the U.S. by Publishers Group West

We gratefully acknowledge the financial support of the Canada Council for the Arts,
the British Columbia Arts Council, the Province of British Columbia through the Book
Publishing Tax Credit, and the Government of Canada through the Book Publishing
Industry Development Program (BPIDP) for our publishing activities.

The author would like to thank the Canada Council, the British Columbia
Arts Council, the Haig-Brown House, and the Writers' Trust for their support.

This book is dedicated to Sharon and the children...

and the children of the children...

* * * * *

the eagerness of nineteen-year-olds...and Beverly

and Mike Byron—teachers and mentors.

CONTENTS

· · · · ·

A FARM IS BOTH theory and worms. Once it was the bridge between wilderness and civilization; now it has become a lonely preserve for living with what remains of the natural landscape—a failing companion to a diminishing number of hunter-gatherer societies, a few parks, and the surviving wilderness. There is a science to farming, but one of its by-products is the terrifying logic of the factory farm. There is also a history of traditional practices, some delicious and others scary. Those traditions, along with the small farms remaining, are being crushed by regulation and globalization.

Yet, if anything, the small, mixed farm is a hymn to the lush achievement of our complex world and to ecological entropy—the natural process that creates diversity. Tradition and science and ecology wrapping around each other like a multidimensional puzzle. It's nighthawks celebrating the dusk with their booming dives, the fields turning gold in the late afternoon light, laughter in the face of the absurd, a bright Spartan apple peeking from behind a green leaf, and the need to produce good food for the community.

We moved into our four-thousand-square-foot log house on a cold January afternoon, eighteen years ago. The shake roof leaked, skylights were smashed, snow drifted through the laundry room, the plumbing was split from freezing. Two of the outer doors were completely gone. Lost. Who would take someone's doors? You could see outside through the gaps in the log chinking. The sole heat was provided by a pair of wood stoves, both working inadequately. The woodshed attached to the barn contained a forlorn, punky chunk of alder. The kitchen stove hadn't been cleaned in a year because the caretakers didn't realize that ashes needed to be hauled from cookstoves. The chimneys were thick with creosote.

I was still in good health then, and Sharon was, and still is, tireless. We were fools for work. We brought our younger son, Roben, nineteen years old and a silent tiger when it came to labour. He was accompanied by a changing cluster of anarchic nineteen-year-old friends, eager for adventure in our world outside the city—Joaquin, Seb, Paul, Gerda, Lenny, Jason. The farm was a romantic escape for them, as well as a way to keep out of trouble, and they crashed in various spare rooms in the house and barn (which had a guest room). The group changed regularly. A few women drifted into the barn, but it was mostly guys, except for Gerda, who became a master gardener and sculptor. Sebastion, easygoing and affable; Paul, brilliant though he kept his genius hidden; and Joaquin, the vocal rebel who questioned authority. They were the most regular. They still whine about how hard they worked for so little. I tell them that's farming.

We could have probably taken the more economical route of hiring farmhands, since the boys ate like horses and had a tendency to break furniture and tools, but we achieved an enormous amount of work and I loved relearning the world of the young. I like to think we gave them some good directions about living in the world. They all spent varying amounts of time on the farm, working for room and board and wine. There was lots of partying, and very little cash. When we look back now at those first six years, none of us can believe how much we accomplished.

As the initial building, fencing, and rebuilding years drew to a close, I recognized I would eventually write about the farm, but some instinct demanded I find a way to tell its story within the natural history of farming itself. The question is, How do you write the natural history of a farm when such histories tend to follow a linear logic? A farm isn't logical, as anyone who's had a foot stepped on by a clueless horse or watched the third crop of peas fail to sprout will tell you.

I realized the only way I could write this memoir was by association—a walk through a summer's day—the June day of the solstice. A walk that simultaneously remembers winter snows, sunflowers, the dinnertime song of the sheep, history, and the taste of acid soil—a sublime landscape framed by laughter and absurdity and shock—an eighteen-year-long day that includes both the past and the future of living on the land, tracing the path that led hunter-gatherers to the factory farm and globalization. Just as we have learned to respect the educational and social fountain of Native teaching tales and their great resources, it became obvious to me that the tradition and science of farming could also be told through the magic of story.

Rural living is an eccentric pursuit, in the same way that beauty is an eccentric pursuit—an exercise in nonlinear thinking as much as a series of rational steps. It's both a logical and an intuitive act, like running an obstacle course; it seems easy until you attempt to make a machine that can do it.

Although our business name is Willowpond Farm, we came to refer to this land as Trauma Farm, because we soon realized beauty also demands a little terror and laughter, and that this story would have to follow the form of the farm and not the romantic or scientific myths we inflict upon it.

Farming doesn't have a long history by evolutionary standards. The earth is approximately 4.5 billion years old, whereas Emmer wheat was first utilized around nineteen thousand years ago. Its systematic cultivation began a mere twelve thousand years in the past, closely followed by Einkorn wheat. That's when the small farm began. These two exquisite grains remain in cultivation, though mainly in small pockets in Ethiopia—and in North America, where seed savers are attempting to protect endangered grains. Rice, although the genus appeared 120 million years in the past, wasn't cultivated until ten thousand years ago.

The discovery of seed collecting marks a paradigmatic change in human evolution toward what we optimistically call civilization. Cap this with the invention of record keeping, and suddenly, in the five thousand years since writing began, the rest of the planet is in trouble. Estimates of our population in 10,000 BC average around 5 million people. Today, we are 6.5 billion individuals on an endangered planet. The historian Ronald Wright notes our recorded history equals the combined lifespan of only seventy people, counted from slashes in wet clay, around 3000 BC, to the billions of binary codes in the hard drives of today.

Modern economics and simplistic thinking have made farming even more cruel and dangerous than it has been historically—thousands of pigs clamped screaming into sterile environments; fields flooded with contaminated sewage sludge; frog genes crossed with tomatoes; potatoes that are also pesticides in the brave new world of genetic modification.

Fortunately, a new generation is reconsidering the concept of the modern farm, inventing new methodologies and building on traditional knowledge.

AS SOON AS WE arrived at the farm, I recognized it was what I'd always dreamed, even as a child—a forlorn kid fantasizing in the back of my father's truck full of potatoes he'd bought from a farmer, while we drove from the country to the homes of suburban wives, who would sometimes buy our potatoes merely because they had nothing else to do. Being a peddler gave him freedom, and he loved the land, especially in the morning. My earliest memories are of lying on those potato sacks, with a few filthy burlap bags pulled over me for warmth as we drove the ice-puddled frost roads of the Sikh, German, Chinese, or Japanese farms of the Fraser Valley and Steveston in British Columbia—the richest, most temperate farmland in Canada, now covered

5

in apartment blocks, malls, and subdivisions. Father and these elders showed me the real world, and their teachings eventually caused me to lure Sharon to Trauma Farm.

At dawn the canvas flap would snap in the wind while the truck bounced and picked up speed, and through the open window in the back of the driver's cab Father would yell far-fetched stories. He was excited like a puppy, ready to begin the adventures of the day. We sold bootleg potatoes, unapproved by the government regulators of a byzantine protectionist bureaucracy. Potato-board inspectors would hunt us down and arrest us and seize our potatoes, but my father had a knack for dodging the inspectors and the police, and they seldom caught up with him as he unconsciously encouraged the rebel in me. Both my childhood with my adventurous father and this farm taught me that the world is fluid, and that our compulsive need for regulation could simultaneously be beneficial and dangerous.

Born with a rare genetic malfunction that made me middle-sexed, Kallmann's syndrome, I was a troubled and difficult left-handed child, regularly thrashed by my teach-ers who wanted to make me right-handed, though there was a lot more help I could have used. So I learned to be ambidextrous and would switch back and forth just to drive them crazy. One teacher used to give me the strap because I'd look out the window and weep at the beauty of the world—bad form for a twelve-year-old "boy," and he tried to beat the beauty and the weeping out of me. "Be a man!" he said, as the leather strap hit my girlie-boy's out-stretched hand. It was a popular phrase in that era, and I began to understand its real ramifications only when I started receiving treatment in my twenties for this disorder that disables the pituitary gland and causes numerous side effects, including the inability to produce male hormones. The doctor who diagnosed the condition shortly after my twentieth birthday predicted I wouldn't make it to forty. That was thirty-eight years ago. It took a long time to accept he was wrong—and his comment merely another incident in the absurd circus of life. As luck would have it, he died, and I lived beyond his prediction. Though I will never awake to another day without pain in my body.

These experiences taught me to always look over the wall, to enjoy traditional knowledge, yet never trust authority. And that's why I am writing these stories in this non-Euclidean form—stories within and alongside other stories—as elastic as the world around us, a web in every direction. It is the way we actually live, despite our attempts to regulate the world—a stroll told backwards and forwards, all the way from Babylon to the exotic archipelago where my island farm exists today.

Milan Kundera long ago discussed how we see the history of a life. Each of us spends our existence walking through a fog, but when others look back on our stories, they see only the missteps, the great leaps, the retracings—they don't see the fog. History, real history, needs to run with all of it—numbers, dreams, and the fog.

Not only have Sharon and I lost money every year since we began farming, like all small farmers we are also in conflict with the mighty tentacles of agribusiness. Given a bad year or two we could even be forced to sell. It took us only a few years to realize we couldn't make it financially. Every one of our naturally grown free-range sheep cost us $25 when we sold them last year. We paid our customers for the privilege of spending a year growing their lambs. Now that's farming. ·

Yet we're unwilling to sell the farm. Debt used to terrify me. Farming today is learning how to accept debt—a spiritual exercise in humility. Like the seasons, you live with it. The small farm hasn't got an ice cube's chance in hell. But we've made our rebel decision. That's what makes the fight so beautiful. Farming is a profession of hope. You will not meet a farmer without hope even when you encounter a flock of them drinking coffee at the local café, lamenting their lot, bankers, pests, fuel prices, seed costs, weather— hoping they can harvest the low field before it turns to mud, or the rain won't split the cherries, or they can get the livestock to market before the prices crash again.

I like to tell the story of the government inspector who showed up at a farmer's door claiming he'd heard there was a man cheating his hired help, and was it him? And would it be possible to talk to the workers? The farmer doubted the culprit was himself. "I've got a hand here who I pay good wages, and I cover all his benefits. You can talk to him until the cows come home, but it won't do you any good."

"Anybody else?" asked the inspector.

"Nope." Then he thought for a moment. "Maybe you mean the local idiot who I pay fifty cents an hour and feed a bottle of whisky every payday."

"That's the one I want to talk to—the idiot."

"You're talking to him."

It's a comic occupation.

The numbers vary depending on who they come from, as it's complex trying to calculate what is rural, suburban, or urban, but it's generally accepted that in 1790 almost 90 percent of Americans lived rural lifestyles. By 1900 the number had fallen to 60 percent. Yet rural skills remained strong. During the Second World War, according to Michael Pollan in a *New York Times* article, 40 percent of American produce came out of Victory Gardens. When the recent century expired, around 2 to 4 percent of North Americans lived on working farms. The farmland has been accumulated by multinational agribusinesses, and the leftovers, the land that once circled the cities, have been swallowed by subdivisions named after the landscapes they destroyed. Hazelnut Grove, Meadowlands, and Orchard Valley have become tacky comments on our vanished landscapes.

But you must recognize that as soon as you start talking numbers you have already made a judgment. The issue of local farming versus factory farming has been a victim of the same dissemination of false statistics as the cigarette wars and the climate change debate—too many of the numbers depend on the point of view of the number cruncher. Lewis Carroll knew what he was talking about when he said, "If you want to inspire confidence, give plenty of statistics—it does not matter that they should be accurate, or even intelligible, so long as there is enough of them."

Both sides of the debate are guilty of twisting statistics, but this story is not about statistics, it's about the glory and joy and terror of living on the land. That's why I've decided to treat all statistics as stories. I've sought the best numbers I could find, but the reader, like me, should regard them as what they are—stories. This is a story of stories, not of statistical leveraging. Distrust all authority. Suspect all statistics. Although I have abandoned the practice of footnotes,

1

GREY HOUR,
THE BIRD GOD

• • • • •

*T*HE NIGHT UNLEASHES the sudden cry of the peacock, perched on the maple outside our bedroom. When he's in season Ajax considers it his duty to warn every sheep and leaf to stay away. Our tom, Wu, has ignited him. Wu is so strong the cat door is beneath his dignity, and he prefers to launch himself into the house from our second-floor bedroom deck, parachute through the four-foot-high window, and land with a triumphant thump on the floor—a mouse still alive in his jaws.

In the shadows the ancient game resumes—the high-pitched screams of Wu, the skittering and squeaks of the mouse—until boredom or mistakes lead to the fatal crunch. But tonight there's a loud *squeeeeeeee* fading across the deck. The mouse got out through the cat door! I know that Wu, despite his intrepidity, will be sitting in the dark like a dummy, staring at the door that betrayed him, and I can't help smiling. I lie back in bed, thinking mouse thoughts. Terror and freedom. They live side by side. My eyes are now wide open.

I question the world, which means I sleep like the spring on my water pump—ready to work as soon as the switch level is too low or too high. When I was wild and twenty I fashioned words on a diet of Southern Comfort—raw on the belly and harder still on the nerves. I often wouldn't fall into bed until four in the morning, catching only a couple hours of sleep before I went to work. Now my body has reversed itself, and I sleep early, waking often, fevered, eager to begin each day—one less sunrise to witness in a lifetime. I'm hot under the comforter. I slip out of bed while I listen to the soft bubbling of Sharon's breath. She will sleep for hours yet, waking momentarily, perhaps, if she senses I'm going downstairs—to call for tea, which I will bring up, steaming, and leave to grow cold on her night table, since she will have already faded back into the luxury of sleep.

When I open the mud room door a dog rouses. It's Olive, our Labrador-Rottweiler cross, unwinding out of her Japanese/Thai/raincoast-fusion doghouse, one of the more absurd structures I've built over the years. She's short-furred, large, black, and muscled like a bodybuilder on steroids. Jen, the border collie, our herd dog, stirs beneath her doghouse. Jen prefers hidey-holes and ungratefully sleeps under the deck and the house I built for her. She slithers out and arrives like a dart, eager. They expect raccoons—the opportunity to prove themselves in the protection of the farm—but tonight we're only walking. I step into my gumboots. They're stagged—cut off at six inches high because that makes them easier to pull on, and as anyone who wears gumboots knows, if you stick your feet into mud deeper than six inches, it's going to get messy whatever you're wearing. I close the door softly and take the path behind the house with the ease of a man long-lived in his home and on the land he's worked. I'm a raincoast boy, in my element. I walk this landscape one or two nights a year. Depending on the season and my mood, I might heat a mug of hot milk or run a glass of cold water and slice lemon into it. I find my way to our back road where the cedars are six feet thick—the dogs panting at my side, wondering what's up. Nothing. Only the night, only the lovely darkness.

I dislike clothing because my syndrome made my skin so sensitive every touch almost burned me until I was twenty and the treatments began. Years of steroid injections have blunted that raw barrier, so sometimes I relish small delicate contacts, like the damp, humid air of a summer night. Now I want to feel the world on my skin, especially when the world is tender. That's why, on these special occasions, I enjoy walking naked in the forest. This was once common to the human species. Today, it is so rare that most people regard it as kinky, or even disturbed, which is only more evidence of the growing separation between us and the wilderness that was once home.

I live in a temperate island climate. That makes it easy to slip out from under our goose-down coverlet on a night like this—the shortest of the year. The solstice. The plants are gearing up for summer while washed in the silver moonlight. Everything looks like an old science-fiction film. The tomatoes already want to flower, the snow peas are extending their green tendrils. The ferns are Jurassic.

Walking among the cedars I feel as if I'm also made of quicksilver, cool and pale. The moon, peeking between branches, is actually a dark landscape, one of the least reflective objects in our planetary system. Its intensity is equivalent to only a quarter of a burning candle—hard to believe when witnessing this spray of silver and shadow across an X-ray landscape—shaded thus because the human eye's receptors can't receive all the wavelengths of light from the moon at that low level. This makes me wonder if we perceive moonlight the way the honeybee sees flowers. Its colour perception is weighted toward the blue end of the spectrum.

Olive, blacker than the night, pants alongside me, her oily fur glowing. This makes me remember the varieties of darkness I've seen. Prairie dark, near-Arctic darkness, darkness in the high mountain country, the total blackness of jungles, and the luminosity of nights at sea. Most of all, there's the darkness of my homeland, the raincoast. When there is no moon the Gulf Islands have a darkness you can almost breathe. It's a cloud forest, and we can live for weeks inside clouds. Sometimes, you'd swear the rain erupts from the ground. Rain showers strike when there isn't a cloud in the sky. That's when they say the devil is kissing his wife. Standing at our window I'll watch clouds appear miles away on Swanson Channel and drift inland, and the rain will hit our house on the upswing. It can also be drizzly for months, yet warm, a temperate climate at the end of the Japanese Current. I am so born into our weather, my forgetfulness, and the usual neighbourhood visits, I often spend weeks trying to figure out where I left my jacket.

Night walking has its disadvantages. A few summers after we moved to the farm I was awakened by the dogs.

14

The chicken coop again. I jumped into my boots and rushed outside. When I reached the coop it was locked tight and quiet, the hens muttering softly. The night was island dark and the dogs were running strange—this wasn't a coon chase. Their hackles were up, and there was a nervousness in their circling. I moved around to the back of the coop, curious. Then I heard a branch break under the big rock maple. Something was moving between me and the field.

A deer? Since hunting season was approaching, I decided to investigate, despite the bad light. There were stinging nettles between me and the intruder, who was drifting stealthily away. Stinging nettles are no fun for the bare-assed. Yet I couldn't resist the opportunity to follow, albeit cautiously. This is the lot of the hunter. I instinctively went into mode, almost inhaling the hunt, while circling the maple. Intelligence-challenged Olive, meanwhile, had finally caught on that I was following prey. She circled onto the back road, trapping it between us. I moved faster in the darkness, still unable to see what I was pursuing. Another branch snapped, and then our prey started to run, swiftly. It had to be a large buck, the way its feet struck the ground.

That's when it hit the page-wire fence concealed by another clump of nettles. A bloodcurdling scream erupted, and I realized I'd done a very bad thing. It was a cougar, and it was pissed—and I was right behind it, wearing nothing but my gumboots. I froze. Brave Olive ran for the house, while I needlessly yelled for both dogs to get back, the border collie cravenly glued to my ankle as I retreated.

We all know how, in a moment of fright, the hackles on our neck can stand up. Well, I was so scared I could feel my chest hairs straighten out.

"The pigs!" I thought. The cougar wasn't interested in the chickens; it was going for the young feeder pigs I had in a pen beside the lower field. Having backed up close enough to the house, I ran inside and began fiddling with the locks and double locks on the gun cabinet that the laws of our time dictate. I was looking for a howitzer, but I settled on a shotgun and lead slugs. A better tool for close encounters in the dark. By the time I returned, armed, dressed, waving the powerful hand lantern, the forest was quiet again. I flashed the pig yard, where they were calmly browsing amid the stumps. They looked at me with an intelligent curiosity that made me recall an old farmer who remarked, when I was dallying on some job, "Don't just stand there like a pig shitting in the moonlight." The stinging nettles rustled softly in the wind, and the dogs moved cautiously, sniffing at a trail into the forest. The insouciant pigs made me feel guilty for my silliness and bravado and panic. Beauty had slipped by in the night. I was grateful for not stumbling into a confrontation with such a sublime creature as a cougar.

The next morning the only trace I could find was a large, perfect paw print beside a puddle on the back road.

ASIDE FROM THE ODD thrilling encounter, the truth about darkness is that it's gentler than daylight, when we, the most dangerous creatures on the planet, set in motion our endless slaughter of animals. But maybe I should not say that anymore—the multinational slaughterhouses now work around the clock.

I feel safer in the saturated darkness of our farm than I do walking into a 7-Eleven store in an urban ghetto in Salt Lake

City or Winnipeg and asking for directions while the neighbourhood kids size me up. The dark of the wilderness is a relatively safe country, which is why many animals prefer its embrace. At night, I occasionally shine my flashlight across our field. The green eyes of the sheep and maybe a nervous young buck will focus on me like a pattern of fireflies, accompanied by the nervous sigh of the horse. I love the music of the night. Then I feel guilty for disturbing them.

WE HAVE BECOME LIGHT-LOVING urbanites, creatures of custom, acclimatized to our war on darkness, which accelerated with the invention of artificial light and our rapidly increasing technological achievements. After the gaslights, after the electric lamp, our fear of the night increased. What's stranger still is that so many urbanites now sneer at the rural world. It's Hicksville. Those of us who live outside the urban streets are an anachronism, quaint, irrelevant to the roaring train of civilization and its luminosity spreading like an erratic, feverish infection across the nights of the planet.

A friend used to rent out his cabin. It was very beautiful, wall-to-wall windows overlooking a pond and the cedar forest beyond. Serene and private—a hundred yards down the driveway from his home. A Los Angeles couple rented it on a misty fall evening. They were delighted with the cabin, but later, about ten o'clock, there came a knock at the man's door. Opening it, he saw the headlights of their car idling in his driveway. The woman was holding the key to the cabin. "I'm sorry. Your place is so lovely, but we come from Los Angeles and we're not used to such darkness. We feel too insecure, so we're leaving. We don't want our money back,

of course, but we just can't stay." She handed my bemused
friend the keys and was gone. Later, he heard they'd stayed
at a cheap motel in Ganges—the little town that supplies
our island's basic needs. There was more light there.

DARKNESS CAN ALSO TEACH us about the way we look at
the world. A decade ago a friend erected a full-size canvas
teepee at the south corner of our upper pasture; then, being
a typical islander, he took a few years to haul it down. So
one evening, Sharon and I decided to try it out before he
retrieved it. A night in a teepee sounded romantic. We collected a pile of bedding and cushions and a lantern, and
hiked down. It was another moony night. All three cats
followed us. Since they were domestic cats they didn't
appreciate the change in sleeping arrangements. This was
too far from home. They cried out their displeasure, which
led to some disciplinary adventures. The cat who had figured out complaining wasn't going to do him any good
slept on a heap of bedding at the other end of the teepee,
while his two friends were terminally booted out. With
that ruckus settled, we proceeded to cavort in the teepee,
discovering that the flashlight made great shadows on the
white canvas walls. We had a riot.

It was only after we were settling into sleep that I began
to consider that flashlight. I woke Sharon and told her to
stand up and turn the light on; then I crawled outside and
discovered the first rule of teepee living. Unless they have
liners, canvas teepees perform like old-fashioned lantern
shows. Everything that had occurred inside during the
last two hours was not only clearly visible—it had been

18

magnified. Our house is far back on the pasture, but the teepee was near the public road, and very evident to anyone out for a moonlit walk, a common occurrence on Salt Spring Island. I had to smile. Sharon was not amused.

Later, with the moon down and starshine filling the sky, I crawled out of the teepee to take a leak. Immediately, I became nervous, even before I pushed the flap aside and saw the ram gazing curiously at me, ten feet away. They were all here, the whole flock, circling us, equally spaced apart, staring at the teepee. It was like a vision out of a primitivist painting. Directly in front of the flap, four long legs pointed at the sky, was Stonewall Jackson, the black horse, sound asleep on his back during his self-appointed guard duty. And I returned inside, dodging the cats and the snoring dogs, comforted by the knowledge we were surrounded under the stars, guarded by the curious animals of the farm.

Now, another fevered night comes to a close, and there's a freshness in the air as a breeze rustles the sword ferns. The dogs begin to make wider circles when I come up from the bottom field's gate beneath the first lily pond. The grey hour is arriving, and the bird god is about to unleash its opera, a chorus of songs rising from the forests, the ponds, and the fields. The peafowl will soon float out of the maple, 150 feet above the field near the house, gliding to the ground like water bombers. Everyone starts singing, even the peahens with their goofy, honking dawn call. And I am walking naked into the morning.

2

MORNING IS A COMMUNITY

. . . . .

*A*PPROXIMATELY 100 MILLION years ago a tentative wave of song began rotating around our planet without interruption, following the dawn, travelling at eighteen miles a second across the equator in an oral celebration of approaching sunshine. In the temperate landscape of Trauma Farm the song surf of the birds is spectacular, and the grey hour, now peaking, is my favourite moment of the day. It's when the earth, bursting with the energy of the dawn chorus, flexes its muscles, the hope and desire for life singing strongest in the shrubs. *Hayom harat olam,* "Today the world is pregnant," goes the opening line of the Rosh Hashanah liturgy. Birth always inspires us. At first, only a few tentative, pensive notes and insecure rebel yells drift into the air. Then the drab Swainson's thrush calls out its haunt upon the farm. A ghost in the trees, this bird wears all its colour in its song, possessing the most lingering bittersweet refrain I've ever encountered.

Although the thrush is endemic to North America, the Swainson's defines the raincoast, its distinct song identified with the Gulf Islands—lingering, plaintive, echoing in the evergreens, replaced only by the mighty vocalizations of the raven in winter or the punky yap of the gulls in the saltchuck. Every landscape has its song. One of the crimes of our time is that most of us no longer know the birds of our region—so many ears are stopped with the headphones of personal music devices.

Though evocative, the Swainson's thrush is no vocal athlete and its song is simple and pure, whereas the hermit thrush is reputed to have twelve thousand songs. Its songs generally last less than two seconds, using forty-five to a hundred notes and fifty pitch changes. The hermit thrush sings with both sides of its syrinx simultaneously, its minute muscles controlling the volume of air and its position in the bird's throat and beak. That this feat of engineering evolved out of chance mutations is a wonder of the world. As a result of these mechanics, the bird sounds like an angel. The biologist Don Kroodsma describes the hermit thrush song as "Oh, holy holy—ah purity purity—eeh sweetly sweetly."

The thrush is not the only Olympic athlete of song. Bewick's wrens learn songs from their fathers and translate them into the songs of the other males whose habitats they pass through, combining and recreating local traditions. Marsh warblers also steal the songs of territories they touch upon during migration.

21

TRAUMA FARM ENJOYS SEVERAL waves of sound and many small cacophonies. The most impressive one struck in the first months after we arrived. We came to call it "the wall." The *krek-eks* of an impressive throng of tree frogs— now endangered in other locales. Here they rule the dark hours in the spring, their roar impressive despite our thick log walls, which dampen outside noise more than stud-wall homes. When we first moved onto the farm Sharon would catch herself whispering to me at night—overwhelmed by their thunder.

We accidentally made the landscape-shifting decision of introducing sheep to replace the long-gone goats of the original owners. The sheep ate the tall grass. Sheep have no interest in frogs, but the loss of cover lured the frog-eating herons, and the slaughter began. Soon there was hardly a peep from the ponds, and to our horror we realized the enormity of what we had done. Thus I found myself fencing back the sheep and planting willows, wild iris, and swamp grass to provide a safer habitat. The roar began to build again, though it still hasn't reached the level of our first years. Such a significant change in a soundscape because of a dozen sheep was one of the first events at the farm that helped me to recognize that an ecology may appear simple but it's difficult to reconstruct.

Our frogs fade out by dawn, though a few sometimes emerge in our sunroom or attached greenhouses, nestled among the tomatoes and the bougainvillea. They are difficult to spot and often croak amusingly at odd moments, as if announcing they are lost.

22

SUNRISE BRINGS THE DEWBOWS, fogbows, halos, rainbows, and sun-rains of our temperate coast that enhance the opalescent greens of the landscape. There's something about our local misty greens that enchants me more than the gaudy tropics. Each of us carries within us the homeland of our dreams, and this is mine. As Dorothy discovered in *The Wizard of Oz,* my heart's desire is in my own backyard.

All the hope of the day is singing in the shrubs surrounding our farm while I make more tea and move to my desk. In the animal world, apart from humans, birds are my first love. I have lived with the African Grey parrot, Tuco, in my study for twenty-three years. He is very good at correcting me when I lose contact with the natural. He may have fewer brain cells, but they're all turned on, unlike mine at various points in the day, and he does delightful double takes when a lost frog croaks. He sits on my shoulder while we communally sip our tea from my mug, and he stares at the endlessly fascinating computer screen before he turns to me and says, "Whaddya know?"

In odd ways birds have shown us how intelligence works. It was commonly thought we were dealt all our neurons at birth, until a team of researchers investigated the canary's brain and discovered that learning new songs created more neurons. Yes, music makes their brains grow. Now we have evidence of the same with the human brain. Those who teach our children music in schools advocated this idea long before science proved them right. Experience is often ahead of science.

The mind invents itself with song, though not always. While the canary might be making a different music with its tunes, the chickadee is a three-note wonder, and it sticks to those notes until it can drive you mad in your backyard. Like many birds chickadees are constant in their song. Other birds are also obsessive. The red-eyed vireo wins the gold medal for intrepidity—one demented individual was recorded singing 22,197 songs in a day. That said, the intelligence of birds constantly surprises me. Ravens are so smart they can make your jaw drop with their tricks and tool uses. I like to think our pair of resident ravens are the real owners of our farm, blithely strutting about, supervising the day.

Mike Byron, the seventy-seven-year-old farmer down the road who, along with his wife, Bev, taught me so much about the small farm—even though I originally assumed I already knew enough to get along fine—once told me that in his childhood he'd owned a flock of guinea fowl. They might be good eating, and great alarm birds, but they're also obnoxiously noisy and usually regarded as stupid. However, one of his hens hatched twenty eggs. Shortly after, the young hen, apparently fed up with the demands of her large flock, went down to the creek and crossed it via a narrow log, the chicks dutifully following. A chick fell off and was swept away by the rushing water. At the other bank the hen turned around and came back, losing more chicks along the way. She repeated her journey several times while Mike stood agape, paralyzed by this combination of murderous intent and intelligence. She whittled her flock down to one and then returned to the barn with the surviving chick blithely following.

Peafowl, in contrast, are known for their ferocious mothering, and at Trauma Farm they provide, along with the geese, our best early warning of trouble in the fields. They drive Sharon mad because of their love of dust baths in newly planted seedbeds and their addiction to tender garden greens, especially brassicas and mustards. Yet they work at keeping the ravens and eagles away from the chickens, maintaining a hundred-yard safe zone around the house. They are so obsessive they will spend all day driving starlings off the lawn.

There was a morning I was at my desk nursing my tea, wondering what words I could put together that would make enough meaning in my life to prevent me from becoming a victim of it, when suddenly the dawn became even noisier than usual, with a great honking of geese and wild ducks, joined by the warning blat of a peahen. Then I heard an eerie *kiee-kieee* cry I recognized immediately. Eagle. I strode out of my office and onto the deck of the adjoining second-floor greenhouse, where I had an overview of the fields. An eagle, obviously young and enraged, was striding along the shore of the top pond, screaming at the ducks and Chloe, the goose. He'd obviously muffed a dive at the mallards (eagles around our neighbourhood are far too cowardly to take on a fully grown goose), and now that the mallards had seen him, they were safe and would just dive if he tried again. They were swimming in circles, a few feet away, tormenting him, squawking out a duck's version of "Nyah-nyah, you missed me," as he strutted along the shoreline, powerless.

Meanwhile, the white peahen, Adona, at the lower pond with four chicks, was growing more stressed by the eagle's refusal to depart and equally enraged by his hubris—turning his back to her and ignoring her warning cries. While the frenzied eagle screamed again at the ducks, she rushed him from behind, covering the thirty feet in seconds. She jumped onto his back, grabbed his white neck feathers, and began beating him with her wings. The terrified eagle tried to leap into the air, but she hung on and rode him like a bucking bronco as he ran across the field, her powerful beating wings preventing him from extending his own and flying away. His gut-wrenching screeching echoed across the field. Feathers were flying, and she must have ridden him a hundred feet before he finally rodeo-tossed her with an impressive jump kick, his beak striking the ground. Then he fled into the sky. I never saw that eagle again, or at least I didn't recognize him. Adona harrumphed back to her chicks, while the ducks, the geese, and I froze temporarily, filled with silent awe. I returned to my office, knowing that Trauma Farm was secure in its madness, and began to write.

AS SOON AS WE bought the farm we began creating a sanctuary for local wildlife. Over thousands of years, ever since the first grain seeds were collected and stored for the following spring, farms have provided an environment for wildlife, often despite the farmers' attempts to eradicate every unwanted living creature within trapping or hunting range. Our planting of bird "sanctuary trees" impenetrable by cats and other small predators—and shrubs that provided fruit and seeds all year around—was rewarded, within a decade, by a growing community of birds, including more quail than you could shake a stick at. When the quail returned to the farm, after being driven off initially by our cats and dogs, we thrilled at their cuteness, the multiple

26

parenting of their young—the "alarm" males standing sentry on the fence posts. Quail have a very structured society.

Then one day Sharon was planting peas. She turned around and discovered a row of quail picking out the pea seeds behind her. She'd become a Pied Piper of quail. We decided to create a less quail-friendly habitat. But when you provide for nature it also provides for you. Soon after, before we could do anything, a Cooper's hawk showed up, perched every morning on the high crossbar above the garden gate. The quail and, sadly, the Steller's jays disappeared at a stunning rate. We began to call him Coop, short for Cooper's hawk, and also after Gary Cooper, because he had the silent but determined gunslinger look of the actor in *High Noon*.

The ecology, because of its very nature, explodes around its barriers, like a river, always flowing in the path of least resistance. Although the first grains were harvested as long as twenty millenniums ago, it was almost another ten millenniums before mixed farms truly began to find their form and spread across the planet. Small animals, birds especially, learned to use the borders, the woodlots, the untilled land along the roads and trails surrounding these farms as habitat, allowing many of the migratory songbirds to flourish. These "margins" are now perhaps, along with diminishing marshlands and jungles, the richest sources of bird and mammal life in the temperate regions.

With the human populations expanding in Europe and Asia, the large predators and undomesticated ungulates gradually withdrew into the few wild pockets of today. Smaller animals and birds were hunted, and their populations also diminished. Plates of baked nightingales

27

and skewers of deep-fried sparrows replaced roasted deer and boar. During the past century in North America, as thousands of small farms were swallowed by corporate agribusiness, or devolved into landscaped suburbs, their margins have also been lost.

Once people began moving into cities and suburbs in accelerating numbers at the beginning of the twentieth century, the phenomenon of birdwatching appeared, and within a hundred years it emerged into its current status: the fastest-growing hobby in North America and Europe. Now that we no longer live with the hens and the hawks we have to go looking for them. The planet is rapidly being converted into a collection of zoos, tourist hot spots, and little islands of endangered species we need to visit and view before they become extinct. The increasing rareness of birds makes them even more attractive to the strangest kind of enthusiasts—life-listers, birders who number their bird sightings. It's the body count that counts, and the more endangered the bird, the better.

To have a unique bird show up in your yard can turn your life into a chaotic invasion of privacy, as numerous victims of "birder stampedes" have testified. I often laugh at the poet and novelist Jim Harrison's bogus threat to shoot a rare little tweety bird at his ranch because so many birders were lurking in the shrubs, hoping for a sighting and driving him crazy.

Birding is a benevolent fresh-air sport that inspires a need to protect our depleting wildlife, and I can understand the desire to chance upon a rare grey owl or motmot, yet the life-lister's compulsion to rigorously count sightings is symptomatic of the way we affect the earth—it's the

28

linearity of their fanatic hearts that sometimes makes the counting more important than preserving the endangered birds.

EXPERIENCING THE PRIVILEGED STATE of being middle-sexed in my younger years, like Tiresias, I saw the world while drifting between the female and the male condition. I've spoken with both their voices, the testosterone-pushed "voice of blood" and the intuitive female voice, watchful and communal.

In some ways these bipolar voices mirror human history on the planet—the demands of our male and female natures, the hunters and the gatherers, each with its blessings and dangers. Wendell Berry talks about our schizophrenic nature as comprising the exploiter (hunter) and the nurturer. Together they can make a lovely marriage but also a potentially toxic combination, depending on whether they balance each other or not. Men hunt and women gather. Skewed cultural slanting of these tendencies can lead to an endangered world—the dominance of those who hunt like heroes and berserkers, or of those who protect our nest with all the implacable compulsion of a psychotic mother.

Hunter-gatherer cultures based on sharing survived for hundreds of thousands of years. Many of them were matrilineal, giving slightly greater power to the feminine side, but history has shown us that men gravitate toward technology. The word, the plow, the potter's wheel—all changed our social structures. Once tools and record keeping reach a critical stage, sharing becomes a lesser trait—until this century, in the developed world, where the

29

power of the feminine principle has finally begun to rise again in everything from writing to tool use. Women now run tractors and pottery wheels, drive trucks and program computers. This is going to make for interesting times, and new possibilities for cultural change as our species faces the increasing threat of an environmental endgame.

The naturalist Bernd Heinrich believes that "our well-being is tied not so much to the structure of our society and the politics that determine it, as to our ability to maintain contact with nature, to feel that we are part of the natural order." While it's dangerous to generalize too much, occasionally it's impossible not to when you are living close to the earth. It's my belief that, because of the miracle of writing, which allows collective memory to be retained beyond oral tradition, we haven't evolved as quickly as our tools, and thus accidentally separated ourselves from that natural order. That's why I find myself in the odd position of attempting to write myself back into the landscape where I live.

But not on this eighteen-year-long day in the life of our farm. I shut down the computer and stand up. Tuco flies back to his cage. Outside, the morning is fresh with promise. LaBarisha, the Arabian mare, lets out a loud snorting neigh by the paddock. For her it's always breakfast time, and when you are a beauty of the world, as she believes she is, breakfast should come regularly, which unfortunately it doesn't always if Sharon is at the hospital, where she works as an emergency nurse, and I am locked in my room. The sheep are moving down from the field behind the house, which they find more comfortable in the dark. Since I've opened up the cross-fencing between the two largest fields, they've developed a routine. Spend the night behind the house, with the dogs standing sentinel; then drift down to the dewy grass of the lower field for a leisurely morning, and finally move up to nap beside the ponds, tug for a while at the hayrack, and wait for dinner.

Most farmers do their chores early and return to the house for breakfast, but my best writing hours are in the morning, so I do only the essentials, such as feeding the animals or opening their shelters, before breakfast (more honestly, Sharon usually does them) and then return to write until my office grows hot in the afternoon. That's when I work the farm.

The dogs are ready as soon as I pick up the horse's feed bucket by the greenhouse. Jen, the older border collie, glances at me with her knowing eyes, as if to say, "I'm ready to organize the farm, Boss. What should we do first?" The feed bucket is the giveaway. They bolt down the walkway; Bella the puppy, eager in the morning, deflects off a fence post and misses a turn—sliding hockey style into the page-wire fencing. But she is so young and thrilled with energy she hardly notices this spectacular crash. The dogs brake at the pasture gate, staring up at the horse, who studies them with contempt. She's interested only in her breakfast. I dump the feed into her bucket, hung on the fence, and toss a couple of carrots in, which she crunches triumphantly.

Returning in the cool, freshened air, surrounded by the dancing dogs, it's hard to lose heart. I glance over at the koi pond by the back door and notice the empty insect shells. The dragonfly nymphs have already climbed up the stalks of the iris and cracked open like science-fiction monsters, allowing the blue or orange adult dragonflies to emerge

31

and unfold their lustrous wings to dry—leaving their transparent, hollow exoskeletons still attached to the leaves when they leap into the air and begin to hunt. Everywhere there's a magic show, and I've stepped out of the dawn into the day, ready to let the tricks of life unfold.

3

FOWL PLAY

. . . . .

I PASS THE KOI pond and walk around the back of the house to the chicken run's gate, which we leave open for the dogs to patrol at night and for the chickens to free-range during the day. The gate is only for emergencies. Then I unlatch the ramp to the coop. I love the thump of the hinged door with its little wooden steps when it hits the ground, and the fluttering exodus of the chickens, cackling excitement and joy. Every morning the chickens know delight. I wish I did.

As the birds rush toward the field a ruthless cock leaps onto the nearest hen, and she crouches dutifully, wings spread and trembling. The hens that escape the sex-mad roosters of the morning sometimes won't stop for a hundred feet. I don't blame them.

I open the side door and check the feed and the water. When I'm raising layers I carry a woven collecting basket that makes me feel like Little Bo-Peep.

There it lies in the straw. As fresh as it's going to get. The egg. Despite its current sorry state in factory farms the egg remains one of history's great cultural icons. From the cosmic egg to the primordial egg to the golden egg laid by that doomed goose, this marvellous creation has long inspired our imaginations. "Whiter than an egg...," Sappho said twenty-six centuries ago. This phrase, quoted from a rare Greek text known as the *Dinner of the Learned,* is all that remains of a poem written by a long-dead woman with a fondness for young girls. It's taken on its own beauty over the years. Kenneth Rexroth called the fragment a supernatural gleam and a delusion. When I first encountered Sappho I was shocked by the evocative simplicity of this phrase, and the shock has remained with me for forty years. An egg can hardly be called white, but it's a phrase that means more than it means; it can also describe a cooked and peeled egg, as firm and white as a young Greek woman's thigh. It evokes purity, the qualities of whiteness, the mythology of eggs.

How lovely the egg—within it all the miracles of creation. Besides white, you can find brown, blue, speckled, grey, and even the legendary black eggs of a mysterious bird, possibly a honeycreeper, in deepest Central America. Pablo Neruda once talked of encountering eggs in the jungle that shone like a shotgun barrel.

Eros, that libidinous symbol of Greek mythology, was born from the egg laid by Nyx, the goddess of night. Leda met her swan, and the twins Castor and Pollux were born of her eggs. A multitude of cultures—Phoenician, Egyptian, Hindu, Japanese—insisted the world was either egg-shaped or hatched from an egg laid by the creator of the land. According to the Dogon people of Sudan and

Mali, the cosmos is represented by the Nommo, a gigantic egg with two placentas. The Russians have a cruel wizard named Koshchei the Deathless, who can be killed only by destroying a magical egg in which the needle of his soul is buried. The Egyptian sun god hatched from an egg. And Sun Hou-zi, the divine ape of China, was also born of an egg, impregnated by the wind. The serpent-circled egg was a key symbol of the ancient cult of Orpheus.

GALLUS GALLUS, THE RED jungle fowl, and its variant, the grey jungle fowl, strode out of the Indus Valley into backyards at least five thousand years ago, and was more famed originally for cockfighting than for its eggs or meat. Black-chested and black-legged, it has red-brown neck feathers that shine deep mahogany. The hen lays clutches of six to eight brown eggs, an impressive number in the wild-bird world, though some birds can produce more. The partridge can clutch up to seventeen eggs. The chicken is so prolific the world is now eating more than 78 million tons of chicken a year.

The original bird was noted for the brilliant red comb on the cock. The hen was combless, unlike the majority of modern varieties. I had a combless Rhode Island Red hen for several years—combless only because, when she was young, she was struck by a marauding Cooper's hawk that ripped the tip of her head off. Instead of a comb, she grew back a punky tuft of feathers and had a cute, thuggish look.

A real chicken can fly like the wind, melt into the jungle, and crow at unexpected moments. The scrawny, two-to-three-pound wild fowl so won the hearts of fight enthusiasts that even today, in Java, a phenomenon known as "deep play" exists—where fanatical cockfighters will stake more money than they can win on their birds.

The chicken enjoyed pride of place in the land of the pharaohs 3,500 years ago. Egyptian lords stepped aside when the cock strutted about the court, and its cry was a conversation stopper. We can only imagine the aristocrats pausing in dilettantish delight at the crow of a great rooster before it shat on the marble floor and strode off.

The chicken is impressively attractive to human culture. Biologists have estimated its diffusion rate across the planet at approximately one to two miles a year. It made it from Asia to the Americas a hundred years ahead of Columbus. Before the electronic age the transfer of technologies and ideas moved at a similar speed. I like to imagine a scholar publishing a text in Düsseldorf and the ideas reaching Paris at the same time as a new variety of chicken from the same city.

⁕

36   WHEN I RAISE EGG layers, I prefer a mixed flock. Bantams are the best brooders. Their broody hens will stubbornly hatch anything short of dinosaur eggs. If you place a smooth round stone under one, it will try and hatch that too. Leghorns give white eggs. The luminous-feathered Ameraucanas have blue-green eggs.

Rare, unusual varieties like the black-skinned silkie or the Polish chicken add an amusing diversity to the flock. The Polish chicken has an extravagant tussock of feathers that falls over its eyes like the furred helmet of medieval Polish soldiers—hence its name. It's also an extraordinarily

Traditions passed from farmer to farmer also impart healthy, nontoxic methods for controlling pests. For instance, mineral oil on the coop's perches will reduce or eliminate mite populations because the bugs transfer between birds at night and the oil smothers them. Lately we've been summer-raising meat birds—letting the fields fallow in the winter, which kills any pests or diseases that might have arrived with the commercial chicks of spring—but I miss my layers and the exotic pleasure of sliding a hand under a hen and pulling out a warm egg while she clucks morosely.

Since before recorded history people have lived with birds. Not only do birds entertain and comfort, but they feed us. Brillat-Savarin, the nineteenth-century French epicure, noted: "Poultry is for cuisine what canvas is for painters." However, in North America, after the Second World War, the taste of both the chicken and the egg changed when agribusiness discovered how to keep several laying hens in a single cage and then stack the cages in "batteries." Within a short while the majority of hens (the cocks were all destroyed at birth) were confined in cages. They never saw the sun, living out their lives in cages as small as twenty by eighteen by sixteen inches, five birds to a cage, in block-long buildings holding up to ninety thousand chickens fed on processed high-protein pellets, the cage floors slanted to allow the eggs to roll out onto conveyor belts. Their beaks were melted off so they wouldn't cannibalize each other (cannibalism always appears among tortured animals), their feet growing into the cage wire as they choked on the dust, their bodies spattered with manure, forced to undergo artificial moulting using regulated illumination cycles and starvation; and then, before they were two years old, every chicken was recycled for "chicken products." Battery chicken production escalated, along with the production of confined broilers in the 1950s, following the discovery of nicarbazin—the breakthrough drug that diminished diseases common to overcrowding. Undoubtedly, Brillat-Savarin is rolling over in his grave. *Bon appétit!*

By the eighties the manufacture of poultry feed (like that of most livestock feed) began to be calculated in computerized control rooms—where specialists studied shipping tables of carloads of raw materials, calculating against costs the necessary proteins, enzymes, fillers (and so on) that made up a standard pellet mixed from different grains (soy and wheat and corn and barley), alfalfa, canola oil, enzymes, minerals, rendered animal (cattle, pigs, chickens) by-products, fish (sometimes from fishing beds polluted by heavy metals—mercury, cadmium, lead), and high-protein excrement recycled back into the feed.

Consider putting five teenagers in a room not big enough for one of them to fully stretch; then pull out their teeth, feed them powdered meal made from dead animals and excrement and pesticide-laced grains on conveyor belts, and put them under constantly increasing light levels. Now imagine what you'd find when you opened the door. The world of the battery hen.

Animal rights groups and the general public gradually became aware of these conditions, and the resulting outcry has led to some changes being instituted in this hideously cruel industry.

Continuous antibiotics are no longer permitted in Canada, but low-level antibiotics remain common in the United States, and the chickens are still sprayed in broiler sheds by huge rollers blasting out pesticides and antioxidants and arsenical compounds that enhance growth and egg production. These practices and their variations are slowly being banned in North America and Europe (Britain banned forced moulting in 1987) even as they are being revived in Third World countries.

Also, because of the uproar over these inhumane conditions, nervous processed-food manufacturers like McDonald's and KFC have created minimum standards (for instance, the cages are bigger) that are slightly less horrific. The mistreatment of livestock has fed a growing rebellion, and many countries are banning animal and fish by-products altogether in feed. A new, gentler regime is arising. This can be affirmed by the confusing variety of eggs we encounter in the more conscientious big-box grocery stores. However, despite the labels depicting radiant little farms or cheerful chickens, it's still a grim world for poultry.

Since 1955 the average flock size in a laying house has risen to eighty thousand birds. But between 1986 and 2002 the number of major American egg producers declined from 2,500 to 700. Globalization and corporate consolidations led to the construction of ten "farms" that each raise more than 5 million hens. Another sixty-one producers keep more than 1 million hens each. These are U.S. Department of Agriculture numbers from 2002. This is the Goliath that the small farm with its little flocks of fifty or one hundred or two hundred clucking hens in the yard is competing against, yet almost everywhere the small farms can't keep up with the demand for real eggs from humanely raised chickens. Sometimes, when I'm trapped on a reading tour, and I gaze at those pathetic runny, pallid, thin-shelled eggs served in a dismal franchised restaurant, I can only think we've broken the primordial egg in order to make an evil omelette.

WE RESCUED OUR FIRST batch of chickens, red rocks, from a small commercial layer facility. We had only just moved to Trauma Farm. I had grown up as a child among farmers, and my father had gifted me with much knowledge about animals without my even knowing it. To catch the chickens I brought along our resident flock of nineteen-year-old skateboarders and anarchists.

Me and three of the boys arrived at this last local, small-scale egg factory in the evening, when the birds were settled down, and I set the boys loose in the semi-dark shed. The first question was from Joaquin: "How do you catch a chicken?" This caught me off guard because I'd assumed they'd know, taught by their father, as I was. But it's a different world for their generation. Describing how to hold a chicken is more a matter of showing than of explaining. There were soon a few feathers flying and Charlie Chaplin routines, but we safely rounded up thirty chickens that escaped the soup pot to be housed in our old-fashioned coop.

Because commercial birds are given an enriched diet under intense light to keep them laying, they burn out fast, but they can be reclaimed. I bought them for a dollar apiece. These were so-called free-range chickens, which meant they still had beaks and were kept in a shed, not a cage. They are usually slaughtered in their second year, yet a chicken can easily live a decade, even if it's a little grungy by then and

41

won't lay much. We moved them to our coop, where they received only natural light, and weaned them onto grain. Battery hens, like children raised on fast food, will spurn real grain at first, but gradually they return to their natural appetites and learn how to scratch as well. After they went through their moult they started laying again.

That first night, about three in the morning, I was suddenly awoken by an elbow in the ribs. "What's wrong?" I asked. Even the frogs had grown creepily silent.

"Listen!" Sharon said. "Our rooster is crowing." She was born in Thunder Bay and had never lived on land larger than a city lot. She was thrilled.

I groaned and turned over. "You'll get used to it."

"I love the sound, but why is it crowing in the dark?"

"Something disturbed him. He's protecting the hens. He'll soon go back to sleep, and that's what I want to do."

We named the rooster Charlie, after a rooster my father's family used to keep. It slept in their basement rafters. The original Charlie was so mean the postman refused to come into the yard. Our version of Charlie was a big, white, lovable goof. He'd strut around the yard pompously, guiding the hens to bug nests with much clucking, guarding against dog and raccoon scares; and after the first eagle left a big pile of hen feathers on the grass, topped by a gory-looking gizzard, he sent the hens fleeing every time a plane flew overhead.

There was also a feisty hen who decided she liked our house better than the coop. She took to sneaking into the mud room and laying eggs in my toolbox. Sometimes she'd sleep there if we didn't catch her. Despite our reaction, she was graced with a streak of stubbornness and kept coming back, so we christened her Gertrude because she reminded us of a Scandinavian housekeeper with her own mindset. After we put a door on the mud room she'd often sleep in the trees, which corrupted a growing number of hens, and I would have to go out every night near dark and shake the chickens (with a great deal of squawking) out of the cedars and send them scurrying into the coop.

This soon earned me the nightly query, "Have you shaken the chickens?"

IT'S RELAXING TO WATCH chickens. I can sit with them for hours, observing the dynamics of their behaviour. They live in a more restricted social world than ours. Any chicken that moves beyond its station will soon be attacked, and often gang-attacked—including the rooster on rare occasions, despite his guard-duty strutting.

City children are often afraid of chickens at first, but within a few days at the farm they are striding out there and grabbing the hens by the neck to raise them up and look for eggs, until I tell them to be nice to the birds or the hens won't give any eggs. Then they settle into a good relationship. I've also found that most children accept death more easily than adults. They will suddenly look up and see a dead rooster hanging from a winter tree and say: "Why is that rooster hanging in the tree?" After I gently explain that it's for dinner, they will usually say, "Oh," and go about exploring the hens for the real treat—the egg. They know a gift when they see it.

We hired a young university student, working her way across the country, to help in the garden, but when she learned I was going to be slaughtering chickens she begged to assist me. This seemed a little twisted at first. Although

I slaughter animals, I've never enjoyed slaughtering, unlike some sadistic farmers I've met. She explained that she loved eating meat, and that, like me, she believed it was two-faced to eat meat without having at least once participated in the slaying of a living creature. So I said okay, curious about how this lovely, city-raised, idealistic student would deal with the passion play of death.

Over the years I've developed a simple system with minimal stress for both me and the chickens when I am slaughtering. It's more complex and much sadder now that I'm forced by regulations to drive them to the slaughter-house an island away.

I gather the chicken up, holding it until it's calm, loop the baling twine around the legs, and hook the twine over a nail in the rafters of the woodshed. Then in a swift move I slide the killing blade into its brain through its beak and let the chicken drop and hang, killing it instantly.

Few people witness real, violent deaths today. Our knowledge of death is mostly a product of Hollywood films, where the standard victim clutches the heart, or the wound, and keels grandly over, dead. Those deaths are one in a thousand. When almost all creatures die they release their natural electricity, especially upon bleeding out. The bird is already dead, but around ninety seconds after its death it will convulse and shake wildly. As soon as I kill the brain I cut the throat or sometimes cut the head right off. When the electric death throes begin, the convulsing headless chicken will usually just shake and go still, but the occasional chicken will flip so hard that it will leap right out of the baling twine and run around, somersaulting and shivering in the ecstatic dance of the death of the nervous system.

The first chicken I killed with my helper watching did exactly that. I was so used to the death convulsions I didn't think anything about it; then, to my surprise, the girl began performing the same dance. She suddenly started screaming and strutting a weird, high-stepping ballet in front of the convulsing chicken. It was completely physical, unthought, visceral, a kind of communion with death and a simultaneous rejection. The guttural noises coming out of her matched her spastic ballet, which echoed the chicken death.

I had no idea what to do. "Are you all right?" I asked when she finally slowed down. A dumb question under the circumstances.

"Yes...yes...," she gasped. "No...no...that was extreme....Oh man, I had no idea....Oh, that was awesome...." She finally choked back her shock and smiled shyly at me, embarrassed. "Wow, I had no idea it would be that real."

"Well, of course. Death is always real."

WITH LAYERS WE OCCASIONALLY found ourselves renewing the flock, slaughtering them for soup or stewing birds, then bringing in fresh chicks. Chicks need a hen and a rooster to guide them through both diets and dangers. If it's a whole new flock, we take those roles, scaring them when we see eagles or luring them to food. Sharon is brilliant at this. She collects worms and beetles and bugs, and drops them into the brood under the heat lamp. At first they are frightened. But there's always a brave one. A first tentative peck. Then a chase and, before long, a chick fleeing with a worm while being pursued by the rest of the flock darting for the worm. It's a sight.

Chickens raised by hens often have an aversion to sowbugs. Someone once told me the birds find them sour tasting. I've never eaten a sowbug myself, so I have no idea, but we discovered that we could feed the bugs to young, undiscerning chicks and they would eventually show a real appetite for them, which gave us a laugh and was useful too, because the sowbugs are a menace to seedlings in the garden.

Here, now, standing beside my coop, I'm comforted listening to the clucking hens who always keep one eye to the sky and one eye to the ground where, with soothing conversations, they direct their little chicks to grains and grasses and insects. While I know the bureaucrats are diagramming scenarios for the elimination of all domestic fowl from the open air and the raising of commercial poultry in sealed "biosecure" environments, I also know all is still right with the world when you can stand in the meadow, even if temporarily, and admire the birds living their lives with their fullest attention.

46

Distantly, down by the pond, the peacock cries merely to honour the sun, and the heron spreads the canopy of his wings, sunning himself like an ancient pope blessing the fishes. The sheep stand a few feet away with a kind of awed, dumbstruck gaze. And I think that somehow in the shade-dappled highlands of the remaining forests of Bolivia or Uttar Pradesh—after we and our chicken factories have all faded into dust and smoke—in that last jungle of the world, there will be the distant crow of the rooster of celebration, and the dynamic flock will begin rebuilding itself again.

4

BREAKFASTS FOREVER

* * * * *

*F*ARMERS TEND TO eat their breakfasts late. Livestock are eager for the dawn, and if you have a cow in milk, she'll be calling. First light is the time to open the corrals, check there's hay in the bins, release the chickens, confirm no deer have broken into the vegetable garden, fix the overflowing water trough, and so on. There's always a couple of hours of work in the morning on most farms, though since we've designed Trauma Farm to be less schedule intensive, I can write in the morning, and others can farm-sit easily when we're away.

When I'm not writing or there's an emergency repair in the morning I find that breakfast after a few hours' labour has more joy than just stuffing the stomach within a half-hour of waking up, and rushing off to work. Besides, as the French say—hunger is the best sauce.

I BOIL A RIDICULOUS mush. We even have a spurtle—a carved Scottish stick designed to stir mush, which you are supposed to stir clockwise with your right hand or you'll invoke the devil. Living on the bounty of the raincoast economy I make a show-off breakfast cereal for my health-fanatic friends and family. It consists of rolled and quarter-cut oats, cracked wheat, barley and wheat berries in various stages of cracking and baking (like bulgur or kasha), quinoa, pumpkin seeds, cracked flax and millet, sunflower seeds, and amaranth in small quantities. If it's a grain it's in there. Then later, when the grains are cooked, I add raisins and chunks of apple. It's so rich that Sharon practically goes cross-eyed trying to digest a small bowl. I tell her that's because she doesn't eat it standing up with a bone spoon, the way a good Scot should. When I eat my mush with brown sugar and heart-clogging milk and butter, I almost feel guilty, remembering the boring quick oatmeal porridges of my childhood. Also, I know what I jokingly refer to as my "death porridge" is a symptom of globalization. I might be poor by the standards of my wealthier neighbours—fighting to pay the endless debts of a poet—but I'm also pillaging the world, and if I had any real moral qualities I'd be eating my flatted oats cold and plain with water, as a health-conscious friend does, to my horror. Actually, I have several friends who have dodged the standard quick-fix cholesterol medications just by cutting out the fats and sticking to porridge in the morning. It scours the stomach clean.

Generally, we lean toward a Western breakfast, yet I sometimes veer into a version of the dawn meals I ate in the cheap hotels in Beijing, where I was served a boiled millet, cooked all night in enormous pots and flavoured with

48

a weak broth, alongside thin-sliced preserved vegetables that resemble miniature, pickled kohlrabi mutations but are a form of mustard stem, and a flat lump of fried dough. Sharon glances at this meal and flees the kitchen. It looks and sounds disgusting, yet the combination of flavours is exquisite. Its origins are ancient.

If I describe this breakfast to North Americans they invariably react with the same suspicion as Sharon, but I have different food values. I'm still notorious for too enthusiastically hurling a box of Froot Loops out the kitchen window while the startled kids watched in horror. Even the crows wouldn't eat that cereal, and it took days to decay in the backyard. I've become a little calmer over the years, and now I figure you can eat your strange food if I can eat mine, but I still wouldn't wish that stuff on children.

I had the unfortunate experience, several months ago, of visiting a superstore while I was in a small city on Vancouver Island. I thought I'd renew my millet supply. To my shock, no one knew what millet was, and the store certainly didn't stock it. Such is the fate of one of humankind's earliest crops—breakfast, lunch, and dinner for millions. Finally, on my third try with the staff, an elderly store clerk's eyes lit up. "Oh, you mean food for birds."

"No," I said. "I mean food for me."

She gave me a suspicious look and politely got rid of me. It was apparent I had to find the sole organic-grain supplier in town.

BREAKFAST WAS ONCE A sip of water at a stream and some scratchy grasses from the south side of a hill. Since then, it's evolved, like the rest of our inventions—faster than we have. Early hunter-gatherer societies picked at leftover grains and roots scooped from their leather storage bags or chugged down a few seeds when the day began. After we stopped dragging chunks of burnt meat from the fire and nibbling on barely washed roots, breakfast evolved into leftover mushes and gruels in the first subsistence farming communities, whose breakfasts were equally boring.

One can only wonder how many generations of farmers glared at their cold barley mush until someone said, "I need an egg." Thus began the evolution from those first taste-less quick gulps before a day in the hardscrabble field to the Dutch seventeen-course breakfast that would probably give an Afghani farmer a heart attack. A statistical study shows that what's now regarded as the traditional breakfast by a middle-class Swedish family involves so many trade and food miles that the earth must be circumnavigated every day in order for that family to sit down to eat.

That ancient, leftover gruel has changed hugely and often for the worse. The world's poor have even less to eat, and in North America the Walmart generation eats a different cereal altogether: immense quantities of grain are now boiled, beaten, and dried, then pressed into nutrition-free ornamental shapes—the taste provided at the end of the manufacturing process by an artificial flavour factory in an industrial park. North Americans are also eating on the run, either at home or idling in the drive-by at the local fast-food franchise—pumping artificial flavour, sugar, fat, salt, and a spike of caffeine into their bloodstreams.

50

HISTORICALLY, LOCAL CROPS MADE for a great diversity of breakfasts that became even more diverse during the era of exploration and world trade that began in the Renaissance. But free trade and the globalization of the multinationals during the past fifty years is now shrinking breakfast fare. Still, breakfasts around the world demonstrate the magic of local produce supplemented by imported foods. Oh, what strange breakfasts we have grown and still eat. There's falafel, the deep-fried fava bean or chickpea mashes of the Mideast, wrapped in *khubz* bread and slathered in yogourt. In Africa it's cassava or corn gruel with coconuts and bananas. Cornmeal gruel, *uji*, is often mixed with ground peanuts. In Madagascar you might snack on *kitoza*—dried beef grilled over charcoal—along with your gruel. And in Cameroon you can eat an omelette confected with beans, sardines, and eggs.

West, across the Atlantic, you can drink *tascalate,* hot chocolate with ground pine nuts, sugar, and vanilla. The magnificent *huevos rancheros* are eggs with fried tomatoes; *huevos motulenos* are refried beans, scrambled eggs, ham, peas, and cheese wrapped up in a corn tortilla. Costa Ricans eat *gallo pinto,* or spotted rooster—fried rice and black beans served with sour cream and fried eggs. In Bolivia there's the *salteña,* a pastry filled with chopped hard-boiled eggs, raisins, olives, peas, and meat. Farther south you can have a *submarino*—steamed milk rich with a melted bittersweet-chocolate bar.

Mushy rice has colonized Eurasia and spread to Africa and Spain. Wild strains exist on every continent except Antarctica. The breakfast of the Chinese farmer usually revolves around leftover rice congee or noodles. I love rice slightly burnt brown in the pot, soaked overnight in a weak chicken broth and eaten, warmed up, with soy sauce in the morning. The same for the gooey noodles. The Japanese sometimes top their breakfast rice with green onions, salmon, ginger-pickled fruit, or roe, flavouring it with chicken stock or miso, as I do. They call this *okayu*.

Soybean milk-soup. Turnip cakes. Century eggs. Parma ham. Injera (a flatbread). Steamed buns stuffed with sweet red beans. I've made tofu French toast for vegan friends. Fermented soybeans. The halva of Pakistan—a sweet made from semolina. *Alloo cholay*—a spicy chickpea and potato curry with nan bread. Garlic fried rice. Pork *tocino* (caramelized). Marmalade, fried green tomatoes, waffles, pancakes (flour or potato). Cooked sugar-beet spread. Nut butters. Muesli. Granola. Thousands upon thousands of jams and jellies. Our hunger for diversity is as great as our hunger.

Knowing all this, I am almost embarrassed to admit that Sharon and I often succumb to a simple Western-style breakfast. I try to make my own bacon and have a smoker for that purpose. The same with bread. There's nothing like home-baked whole wheat or rye bread, still warm, with butter and handmade jams. Throw in some spiced Yukon Gold potatoes and tomatoes and soft-boiled eggs, along with the home-smoked bacon, and we're in heaven. Sharon eats earlier than I do, yet we still manage to meet for a quick sit-down breakfast a few days a week. Companionship is a fine spice.

Every second year I make marmalade, but the making of marmalade has become such a lost art that Seville oranges appear at our local market for only a few days. You need a sixth sense to know when they have arrived, so you can beat the last marmalade fanatics to the oranges. One year Sharon stumbled upon them and decided to make her own marmalade because mine was always too lumpy and dark.

Hers was light and runny, which horrified me, so I rushed out and managed to rustle up the last scungy oranges. Naturally mine came out even darker and lumpier and more unspreadable than usual. So now we have Mama and Papa Bear marmalades, and in truth, the best would be the combination of the two. Still, we aren't stuck with the flavoured sugar-water that passes for marmalade these days.

I KEEP RETURNING TO the egg. Maybe because it's so central to my North American diet. It's my local food, and the other breakfasts are merely an exhibition of my need for exotica. With the egg, I have undergone a lifetime quest for its use in every meal. Since I was a child and had six hens in the backyard, I've studied the behaviour and breeds of the chicken and still attempt different methods for growing a proper egg. How do we address the egg? Over thousands of years humanity has learned to put hard-boiled eggs in curry, fry up chicks half grown, or whip whites into desserts. Oh, the banana cream pie with its lightly browned meringue! Egg-drop soup. Cakes. Eggs scrambled with truffles. Egg breads. Scotch eggs. The egg is a paintbrush used to illustrate the enormous range of the human diet. Like tofu, it has the ability to absorb the recipes it's cooked with, and unlike tofu, it is coveted in almost every culture.

Cooking an egg is a way we judge ourselves. We say of a poor cook, "He doesn't know how to boil an egg!" Although boiling an egg is an art and a trial, especially when you have eggs of such diverse density, shape, and size as today's varieties. Consider the histrionic excesses that people will put into boiling a "just right" soft-boiled egg—a near-fetish

53

object in Western society. It's a lifelong trial for Sharon, who has a knack for cooking every variation except soft-boiled. I usually cook a good egg, but I'm so absent-minded that I tend to forget they're ready, which always earns me a snort of contempt at breakfast because Sharon is so competitive about the eggs. Even a hard-boiled has its demands. Here at Trauma Farm our eggs are too fresh to peel. So we plan our hard-boiled dishes like potato salad a week in advance. The interior air pocket expands with age, and the protective skin between the egg and the shell dries, allowing the egg to be peeled aesthetically when it's several days old.

You can't make an omelette without cracking an egg, and a real egg is a lovely creation. I can tell what a chicken has been eating and how it's been raised when I break an egg on the frying pan. The best yolks are a deep orange, almost red. A good yellow yolk derives from corn, which is included in hen scratch. Factory manufacturers generally add dye to food pellets to yellow the yolk. And you have to keep a wary eye out for today's "organic" factory eggs, because some feed manufacturers jazz up the mash with enough canola oil, high-protein alfalfa, and soy meal to give both the chicken meat and the egg a fishy smell and taste.

Orange yolks come from eating lots of insects, which chickens love. That's why the rooster will cluck when he finds a treasure of bugs, and the hens will come a-running. Interestingly, if hens discover something delicious, they will eat silently—greedy-gut girls that they are. Chickens are scavengers and will eat almost anything. I've fed them the intestines of livestock I've slaughtered. They go wild over that, as do traditional Inuit, who balance out their meaty diets with the stomach contents of caribou.

An unfertilized egg is a single cell. An unfertilized ostrich egg is the largest single cell on earth. The white is thick in a fresh real egg and doesn't slime all over the pan like the store-bought ones—especially since the white becomes thinner as the egg ages. A good diet, freedom, and the sun make both the yolk and the white firmer and more nutritious. We also feed our chickens crushed oyster shells scavenged from the beach and mixed with their grain. This provides calcium, which makes thick, protective eggshells. Sometimes they get a maggoty or wormy vegetable or fruit. They relish compost—every ruined dinner or mouldy green discovered in the fridge is always greeted with the refrain "Happy chickens!"

A homegrown egg that's fresh will sink if you put it in a bucket of cold water, a test we use when we're suspicious of any eggs discovered in toolboxes or on a woodpile. Perfectly fresh, it will lie on its side on the bottom. Slightly older ones will stand on end. A dangerous one will float. Don't crack that egg! Occasionally, we get forgetful or fooled by a broody hen clever at egg-hiding games. Every farmer is eventually caught off guard and cracks one of these skunky things on the frying pan's rim; the egg will explode over the others and drive everyone retching from the kitchen, especially Sharon, who has such a keen sense of smell. When this happens I hurl the pan right out the door and onto the lawn, to hose down later. Despite the mythologies about the charms of rural life, cooking an egg can have its thrills.

That said, usually we don't wash eggs for our own use. They are covered with a natural protective bloom. If you keep your nests clean with fresh hay and collect your eggs often, they won't get soiled, and if they do, we prefer to wipe them with a dry cloth. Eggs for sale we are forced by the law to wash, improving their chances of spoilage, because washing destroys this protective coating. The factories heavily wash their eggs and then spray them with a mineral-oil seal, which causes enthusiasts like me to claim this makes them taste worse. Factories have to treat their eggs because they are so notoriously infected with salmonella and other dangerous bacteria that health agencies now warn everyone to assume cracked eggs are diseased.

Breakfast has become so dangerous that some American states have considered banning sunny-side-up eggs. I assume it won't be long before the factory system, with its attendant troop of health Gestapo, bans the serving of any meal with raw eggs, including favourites like steak Diane and the original Caesar salad. I've never contracted salmonella from our birds—the chances are slim compared with the toxic possibilities of industrial eggs—and I don't know anyone who has picked it up from free-range, traditionally slaughtered animals, though it certainly can happen. If the birds are treated well and intelligently they will give you beautiful eggs.

56

TAKE AN EGG AND crack it on a bowl. Out will slide one of the richest treasures of the animal world. Cooking an egg is an exacting business. In the film *Big Night,* after a traumatic all-night drama, a man brilliantly cooks up a pan of near-perfect scrambled eggs (apart from the mistake of not heating the frying pan first) for his ruined older brother, which they eat together, almost weeping, arms around each other. The cooking of those eggs was such a masterly production of scrambled-egg technique that I haven't met a chef who's seen the film who doesn't go into orgasmic ecstasy at the mention of it. I spent almost a year imitating that actor's egg-cooking technique.

We use a flat steel crepe pan for scrambled, and for sunny-side-up I use heavy cast-iron fry pans I salvaged in 1972 from a garbage dump on Texada Island, maybe a hundred miles north of us. I discovered a lifetime supply of these pans because everyone was throwing them away in favour of the toxic nonstick Teflon fryers that were the fad of the era. You can rescue a misused cast-iron frying pan by curing it in a bonfire. Then oil it up and season it in an oven. It comes out better than new. One of the joys of a cast-iron frying pan is its ability to be reborn again. A frying pan was almost all that a friend recovered from the charred remains of his house after a fire.

We forget what a treasure food is, especially the lowly breakfast, which has been so brutalized in North America. Like Sunday dinners, weekend breakfasts used to be an extended feast and gossip festival, a chance for the commu- nity of the family, and sometimes neighbours, to reunite and bond.

More than thirty years ago, when I lived in a ramshackle log cabin on Texada Island, I knew three brothers. They were big, hairy, farmy-biker-looking guys, yet tender and generous. It always seemed to work out that one would be away logging while the other two survived on unemployment insurance, renovating their family farm until they got a new job. They were the most amicable trio of brothers I ever met, and they considered it important to gather together on Sunday for breakfast—an open house where islanders could show up for a chat, a meal, a beer, or coffee.

They'd start eating early and really be cooking by late morning. There'd be piles of homemade sausages, pancakes, waffles, eggs (scrambled or fried or hard-boiled), and bowls of porridge, cream of wheat, or oatmeal. All performed with minimal hassle. I'm sure they lived off the leftovers for the remainder of the week. One of them would wander into the kitchen and soon reappear with another heap of sausages or pancakes. I never understood how we could put all this food away, as well as the cases of beer. It would take too long to recount the down-home amiability of the conversation, which flowed from gardening to cabinetmaking...to fishing...to logging...to motorcycle repair...to relationships with women (who would often be present and wolfing down the pancakes). The brothers never got angry, even if the beer unexpectedly disappeared and desperate measures were needed to replenish the stock. As many as fifteen people would casually drop in. It was an endless feast, and everyone was welcome. Even lost tourists looking for directions would suddenly find themselves at table, plowing into the homemade sausages.

These rough, hairy lads served a local breakfast—the classiest I ever pulled up a chair to join. Thirty-five years later I'm suspicious that I've romanticized them, as memory tends to do, but the hope in me wants to believe in those boys of the morning who understood the meaning of breakfast in the country.

5

WALKING THE LAND

• ○ ◆ ○ ○

*I*T'S A GOOD habit to walk the land every morning after breakfast, checking the fences, the livestock, meditating on the past and the future. I don't do it enough. We bought the farm because of its landscapes. It includes a forest grove of cedars with up to six-foot-thick trunks, pasture land, and classic Gulf Island rocky knolls. It also has a half acre of swampland, which we've nurtured with ponding to protect the marshy edges against the changing climate and to give us water for irrigation and waterfowl—wild and domestic.

The house is entered by a long cedar deck with herbaceous borders. To the left the middle of three lawns is currently owned by the puppy, Bella. This is where she discovers the world at night and in the early hours of the morning. Her most coveted possessions are littered around its central Turkish fig tree—a broom head, a crumpled peacock's tail feather, two shredded teddy bears (she's been raiding the grandchildren's toy box again), our garden twine in a big jumble, several gnawed plant pots and a deer antler, an ancient lead toy soldier (where did that come from?), and the remains of a slipper. Carnage. Is this how we learn the world, by chewing on the relics?

The Turkish fig has its own story. I was given a cutting from a much-admired shade tree on Hornby Island, also north of us. We rooted our cutting and planted it in the middle of our lawn—protected from the deer by the dogs and the high fences. It never occurred to me that it needed protection from us until Olive, demonstrating her best black Labrador characteristics, decided to eat it. Fortunately, this was in the fall, so I trimmed the tree back to the ground, mulched the pathetic little stump, and erected a protective fence. The fig shot up in the spring, and I kept it shielded another year, until Olive was older, and I decided to release it before we held one of our "pig parties," where we cook a pig on a spit and invite a hundred or so friends and family to spend the weekend on the farm. I was watching from the greenhouse when our first guest arrived, overloaded with unassembled tenting parts, and as she walked by the fig whip, she neatly cut it off at a foot high, without even noticing what she'd done. Back up went the fence. I started worrying about this tree.

Today it stands fifteen feet high and provides large, sweet brown figs yearly. It will soon be a fine shade tree. Poor Olive is so arthritic she will probably not see another summer. She is looking toward the stones under the willow tree that mark the history of our dead in this eighteen-year-long day.

MY WALKS USUALLY BEGIN at the Chinese-style moon gate beyond the deck, then follow the dirt road around the barn into the cedar forest, which is dark and serene and needle-carpeted. Like most stable temperate rain forests it's quiet, because most birds and animals prefer the margins where the shrubs thrive with food and protection. Despite the silence and their invisibility, I know life is about. Ravens in the treetops; deer, raccoons, mink in the salal; the smaller animals tucked into rotten logs. A red-shafted flicker swoops between the trees, and sometimes I see a gaudy tanager. This is the night territory of the barred owls who disturb our sleep and make the chickens tremble. The dogs love the forest and race after its mysterious scents. We reach the gate to our lower field, and I survey the split-rail fencing that borders our neighbour's pasture. Among her horses she has a young stallion our ancient mare, LaBarisha, finds irresistible; she knocks down the rails to get at him, despite our neighbour's sturdy horse fence on the other side of ours.

A mare in flush is not a sight for the faint of heart. Her vulva pulsates and drips gallons, occasionally squirting. Her "heat" is almost alien in its energy. I pile the rails back into place, then return uphill through a grotto of maple and cedar to the top pasture and the ponds.

AT THE WEEPING WILLOWS beside the main pond the world is all rhythm, the breeze-rocked branches like jelly-fish tentacles in a current. The mallards and the pintails are muttering, circling in the water. Under the largest willow is a clutter of stones marking the lost animal heroes of the farm, the dead we've accumulated over the years. It's a good place to go to ground. The willows make a soothing swoosh above the graves.

Willow is a proto-Germanic word, derived from the word for "flexible." Not only are the limbs flexible but so are the uses. We grow osier willows for the ornamental pussy willow market and special varieties for basket makers. We also sell the fasciated Sekka willow, which grows at eccentric angles and is much loved by ikebana enthusiasts and florists during catkin season. Our Chinese curly willow is another "stick" used by flower arrangers. Cutting and bundling them makes for a hectic month before Valentine's Day; then the market loses interest.

I love our market willows best in early spring, before they leaf. Their branches can be mottled or each one a different colour: scarlet, tangerine, maroon, yellow, brilliant green, black, displaying an assortment of narrow or fat catkins, also multicoloured. The willow is striking in every season. It is early to offer pollen and nectar to the honeybees, as well as important riparian habitat for songbirds, which hide and nest among its branches and feed on the buds. Willow water, derived from cuttings, is an excellent rooting compound. I often pour it on seedlings and struggling plants. Out of the bark comes salicylic acid—Aspirin—long known to Native healers as a treatment for rheumatism and fevers and pain relief. Florists toss an Aspirin into their rose displays. Some willow fanatics claim its water is also an aphrodisiac. Up by the house, Olive is always headfirst into the bucket of cuttings, sucking up the willow water, as if her body knows it's good for her arthritic bones.

Willow roots yield a purple dye once used for colouring

Easter eggs, and the wood has found a multitude of uses over the centuries: clogs, wheelbarrows, flooring, firewood, lumber for boats and houses, chariot-wheel spokes, brake blocks for railway cars, washboards in mills, Gypsy clothes pegs, coracles, sweat lodges, cricket bats, and, most importantly, wickerwork. There's hardly a person who hasn't sat in a wicker chair or held a wicker basket. In human hands willow has become lobster and eel trap, clothes hamper and beehive.

The willow is an antique creation—pollen has been found that's 135 million years old. The ancients loved their willows. Orpheus carved the sound box of his lyre from willow, and ever since he carried the tree's branches underground, the wind in the willows has been regarded as the song of poets. In Psalm 137, Jeremiah and his people hung their lyres on the branches of the willow trees (though authorities suspect they might have been poplars) and sat down beside "the rivers of Babylon" and wept, before he endorsed the dashing of Babylon's children against stones. Thus the weeping willow came to be carved on tombstones. Some have thought that the name Wicca derives from wicker, as the willow was associated with witchcraft. Homer's Circe kept a riverside cemetery planted with willow, dedicated to dark Hecate and the moon magic she controlled. The branches continue to be used for divining rods and witches' wands. Those born in March are known as "willow people," and they are said to be beautiful and melancholy. Willows were also placed in coffins. Along with protecting the dead, willow nurtures the infertile, and sterile women lay branches in their beds. Willow is about as multipurpose as you can get.

Beyond the willows, amid the orchard, are the farm's two hives, and the bees are making their first forays into the day as the sun warms the hives.

"THEY'RE SINGING THE QUEENLESS song," the old bee-keeper said. A tall, thin man who doesn't appreciate fools, he's known by islanders as the "honeyman" of Fulford Road. Once, he was a mathematics teacher, but the bees snatched him. These days he's a swarm of advice, educated in many things, and his knowledge makes him cranky on occasion. I go to him for instruction. After he's finished lecturing me about the failures of my generation, the secrets spill out— he's generous despite himself as he tells the stories of a lifetime among insects. They've spoken to him for so many years I think he's become ashamed of his own species.

My initial hive was troubled. Even an amateur like me knew it, so I stuffed the entrances with foam and bound it with the bungee cords he'd given me, humped the hive onto my pickup, and drove it to his cluttered yard. As soon as I dropped the tailgate and we stood listening, he knew she was gone. A hive is always talking to itself. This one was humming grief. There was no queen, and all the lar-val cells were too old to convert into a queen—the hive was doomed, its last survivors wandering mournfully on the empty combs without purpose. A sick hive can even smell different. The odour of the combs, their colour, and their density constantly vary—red, thick and blackish, pale and fluid, or even crystallized like sweet amber. Resting my hand on the lid, I felt a low, sad thrumming. A healthy hive is aggressive if disturbed, and a couple of guard bees will immediately leap into the air. If I bang the hive an angry mob will kamikaze toward me.

When a bee stings, the exquisitely designed barb, its tip composed of two lancets jabbing alternately, sucks itself under the skin until the apparatus snaps off at a breakaway point and remains in the flesh, venom sac attached, shouting an olfactory war cry, as the bee stumbles off and dies, self-eviscerated. The released scent of the sting directs new warriors to the ambush site. Meanwhile, after seven minutes the venom sac reactivates and pumps in another shot. I've watched this often; the intestines act like a thinking organism.

When I approach a hive, even if the advance guards do not sting they will seize me with their mandibles and dab me with a volatile odour that will lure other guards, who will decide if I am worthy of the sacrifice, since every sting means suicide. Only the queen can sting repeatedly. Bee venom is a miraculous substance, composed of seventy-six chemicals, which interrelate in a way that amplifies their effects—a tiny stinger slightly thicker than a pin can kill people with sensitive immune systems.

"Deadly poisons," according to Ovid, "are concealed under sweet honey." But a poison is only a medicine delivered in the wrong dose. Bee venom has been used for centuries to treat diseases like arthritis and, more recently, multiple sclerosis. Some api-therapists have suggested that acupuncture originated from studying the effects of bee stings on various parts of the body. I have a neighbour afflicted with MS. Every two days his wife uses tweezers to place live bees on the key acupuncture points of his spine. He showed me his back once—symmetrically inflamed by the healing stings. Paralyzed down one side when the disease first struck, he now fast-walks past my gate every morning, with only a slight numbness remaining in two fingers. The effects of bee-sting therapy vary wildly, and the disease can return. Others report that it merely helped them wiggle their toes. For someone with MS that is encouraging news. Hope is huge in the world.

What first drew me to the bees was my arthritis. I stung myself for several weeks. It was a curious experiment. Since Sharon is allergic, I kept a jar of bees in the spare bedroom in our barn. I'd lift a bee out of the jar with tweezers and hold it against my skin. The rush was brutal, especially by the time thirty barbs hung like tiny fetishes from my knees. The adrenalin would speed up my metabolism, pounding my heart against my chest, my skin alive with sensitivity, and I'd leak an awful-smelling sweat that enthusiasts claim is the body's toxins oozing out. Then, in several minutes, the stings would deliver their second poison-injecting pulse. After fifteen minutes I'd remove the stingers. They slid out easily if I got the angle right. I'd sit and gaze at the water jar where I crushed and drowned the doomed bees (a bee doesn't die quickly after releasing its sting), and I'd feel overwhelmed with the sadness of the world. During the next days my sweat ceased to stink, and I found myself more energized. I lost weight. The pain in my knees went away. However, after six blessed weeks, the arthritis returned, so I ended the treatment, but I decided to purchase some bees anyway. I guess you could say I'd been stung.

For too many people today bees are scary. There is something about tiny, crawling, stinging creatures that instinctively repels us. Seals are cute; bees, spiders, wasps—we squash. Yet through a microscope, or in a close-up photograph, they are lush, brilliant, seductive creatures—as beautiful as tigers and flamingos.

The life of the hive, like much of farm life, is female. Males serve for stud service or slaughter. In the hive, every worker can become a queen—if she is fed royal jelly—but one suffices. Multiple drones hatch in the spring. Big and useless, they roam around like bumbling bachelors, enjoying the run of the combs, living in luxury, sometimes moving unrestricted from hive to hive, awaiting their glory moment. The young queen will make several preliminary flights, scouting her kingdom, perhaps to remember it for the dark years within the hive that lie ahead. Then one day she will leap out of her hive and take to the air, releasing a jet trail of pheromones, emitting a *chip-chip-chip* sound as she lunges for the sun. So loud is her cry, so strong her odour, males will find her from ten miles away. Those that fly the highest and fastest will reach her in the "drone zone," a hundred feet above ground. Obsessive beekeepers claim they've heard the snap of their tiny genitalia as they break away from the queen and tumble to the ground, ripped apart by their one act of copulation. Sex and death with altitude.

Once is not enough for a queen. She will accept several drones, ensuring the genetic diversity of the hive, each one having to lunge higher and harder in the ecstatic nuptial flight, lushly described in Maurice Maeterlinck's *The Life of the Bee,* perhaps the most romantic passage on natural history ever written. After the nuptial flight, she returns triumphant, trailing her lovers' genitalia like streamers, and the failed drones revert to their old bachelor mode, mumbling about the hive while the female workers grow more annoyed with them until, in what's known as the "summer slaughter of the drones," they are evicted. Some will fight bitterly, uselessly, as the relentless females shove them out of the hive, suicidally stinging them to death if they resist, heaping up clumps of bodies on the landing and tumbling them down into the waiting mandibles of wasps.

For thousands of years the Americas thrived without the honeybee. Pollination was accomplished by bumblebees, mason bees, carpenter bees, stingless bees, and other insects. Mesoamericans learned how to extract some honey from varieties of bumblebee. Then, only a few centuries ago, Native Americans gazed in horror at a sky full of "stinging flies." The arrival of a honeybee swarm meant that white colonialists were not far behind, eager to seize and change the land.

Now in this new world, small farmers like myself are also endangered. Modern agribusiness spends more money on chemicals than on machinery or seed. Their pesticides are poisoning millions of bees, already suffering from other introduced pests, such as foulbrood—a bacterium that eats bee larvae from inside out—varroa mites, tracheal mites. The wild European honeybee is approaching extinction, the large commercial apiary operations floating in a plethora of chemicals. Our islands, until ten years ago, were the last in North America to produce organic honey, but the mite was illegally introduced by an ignorant beekeeper, and now we have to use chemicals also, merely to keep our bees alive.

Yet I stubbornly continue to learn the world of the singing bees, who teach me small new lessons every day while going about their lives. Civilization, communication, progress—these are the myths we tell ourselves. I don't have faith in them anymore, but what's left of the natural world, though it's often brutal, I can still love. Resting my hand on a hive, I feel the thrum of the bees' conversations, and I dream about the mysteries they are discussing inside. Sometimes, on my better days, I think that language is just another word for the poetry of the earth.

ONE OF THE GLORIES of living on the land is the freedom to fertilize it, and the need is suddenly upon me. I've always felt a secret enjoyment pissing beside a tree when the body makes its demands. I avoid the smaller plants because I don't want to feed them too much concentrated nitrogen. Elimination outdoors used to be common for our species, but as we move away from the land, it's become unusual. I love watching the expression of bliss on Sharon's face when she suddenly drops her pants and squats in the woods. Maybe we just recognize the growing repressions of culture, and there's a special pride in regaining our freedom. Though, after a while, I've found I've become so used to freedom I sometimes catch myself looking for a likely tree in the city, 69 and realize rural life has created dangerous habits.

SURROUNDING THE HIVES, the orchard is in full leaf, seeds and fruit already swelling. I stride past them, followed by the dogs. Pecan, almond, quince, pear-apple, hazelnut. The apples are the most diverse—heirloom varieties: Wolf River, king, Cox's orange pippin, Lodi, Gravenstein, Boscoop. I shut the field gate and pass the white hawthorns, newly planted to shade our driveway. I've nearly come full circle, heading toward the barn, the moon gate, and the house.

The sun never sets on this land. In winter it's a grey ball permeating the mists. To the west a hill blocks the luxurious coastal sunsets. East, we look upon the United States, across the blue, metallic skin of the Pacific Ocean—more islands, the glaciers of the coast range, and a volcano, Mount Baker, coughing up a spittle of steam. Beyond that a continent vibrating with life and urgency. We live at the edge of the ring of fire—the volcanic Pacific Rim. Streaky clouds unfold over the coastal mountains, reflecting off the strait between Salt Spring and Pender Island. Standing in the driveway above the garden, looking down beyond the low field between two maples, I watch a ferry, as big as a cruise ship, slide between the islands.

The garden rail fence is lined with mulberry, kiwi, winterberry, climbing rose, and eucalyptus whose branches we sell to florists. Close to the house, in a fit of whimsy, we planted bananas and palm trees, so very un-Canadian, but they're surviving in our temperate climate. The queasy acknowledgement of this menagerie haunts me on occasion. I remember when we arrived, pulling up with a five-ton truck filled with trees and shrubs. "You're bringing trees to the Gulf Islands?" my friend said, laughing. These islands are known for their lush, unique flora and fauna, and the first thing I did was introduce strange trees, fool that I was.

Within only a few years I recognized the consequences of our appetite for gathering original companions around us.

"WHAT'S THAT?" I YELLED. "Stop the car!" In the road was a sprawling, twitching, brown-green creature the size of a dinner plate. I climbed out of the passenger seat and walked back. It was a giant frog, one side of its face swollen

and its eye blood-red. I scooped it up and took it back to
our car. We were going to visit the grandchildren, and I
thought the little ones would be mighty astonished by it.
Sharon was. We released it in their small pond, but after
the afternoon party the frog appeared less stunned, almost
healthy, aside from the bloody eyeball. I didn't want it to
eat the children's goldfish, so we collected it and returned
to the lake near the road.

Although this monster was the size of a small chicken,
and I'd heard somewhere that it had a bad reputation,
I let it go. There was an odd sense of fair play in me that
demanded giving it a fighting chance. That was five years
ago, and I've regretted the decision ever since. It was as surprised as I was when I liberated it in the reeds. It hovered
there a second, and then kicked off.

The American bullfrog, *Rana castesbeiana,* is a species
introduced to southern British Columbia by delusional
entrepreneurs in the 1930s who thought they were going
to corner the frog-leg market for French restaurants. When
the frog farms failed they released the frogs, and their numbers have been increasing since. Now they are swallowing
endangered red-legged frogs whole, along with rare sala-
manders. Not long after the incident I saw a video of these
frogs sucking down a flock of tiny ducklings, one by one, as
they paddled behind their mother. There have been reports
of attacks on kittens. This is one mean creature. And it's not
alone. Whether it's gypsy moths, starlings, zebra mussels,
or Himalayan blackberries, we are introducing an increasing quantity of alien creatures into ecosystems where they
can cause untold harm.

If you fly over my island in June, the hills are yellow
with Scotch broom flowers. Broom seeds can be "banked"

71

in the soil for thirty years. A single plant can, theoretically, produce eighteen thousand seeds every year. Captain Walter Grant of Sooke, a homesick Scotsman, brought twelve seeds in 1850. Three survived. The invasion of Vancouver Island derives from the offspring of these three seeds. Broom will overwhelm entire fields in a few years, driving out native plants, and it has no North American predators. Its oily branches can suffer tip die-off, making it one of a few plants capable of spontaneous combustion—a real hazard in our dry summers—and we've got it forever.

A line of broom follows our snake fence alongside the gravel road leading to our home. A neighbour has suggested, several times, that I remove it. I keep intending to, but on a farm, one never has enough time to reclaim an environment under constant threat. After an acquaintance mentioned how beautiful all the yellow blooms looked from the air, I began to wonder what other invasive species there were on our ten acres. Reading the available material I was shocked to learn how much our species is changing the world's environments. British Columbia's original grasses (before colonization) now cover only 2 percent of their native habitat.

The number of invasive plants and species across North America is astronomical. Only in the last few decades have we begun to restrict the traffic in animals. Meanwhile, brown snakes, insects, and diseases like West Nile virus are hitching rides everywhere. When I tried to look up Canadian government regulations for introducing plants and seeds I realized that, except for a few specific disease watches, most of the guidelines are *voluntary*—the bureaucratic term for "anything goes."

Lately there's been a ban on importing certain potted plants from the United States, out of fear of oak root fungus, and plant soil must be fumigated. Some disease outbreaks are recognized and the plants sprayed. Otherwise, the nurseries are wide open. My horticultural friends tell me the oak root fungus is already here and the government inspectors are just going through the motions so they will look good. Every day the skies are filled with planes airlifting exotic orchids and plants from all over the world, along with their insect or disease hitchhikers.

On Salt Spring the cornucopia of plants at our nurseries is a lush Eden—bulbs, seeds, rare species from the Himalayas or the deserts of New Mexico. Most people are not aware of how dangerous these plants can become in a new location. The history of farming and gardening is the history of infecting landscapes with beautiful plants that turn into monsters in another habitat—like the kudzu "mile-a-minute" vine that grows a foot a day and can overwhelm a parked car in a week. A few years ago I decided to plant milk thistles for their healthy seeds (good for the liver). I missed a few flower heads at harvest. Five years later, milk thistles are still appearing. We now have them under control, but the experience made me realize how quickly an alien plant can escape. That's why Canada's fields are plagued with so many varieties of thistle.

Today's walkabout set me counting, as it has done on other occasions. Despite our vigilance, there are several dozen introduced noxious weeds on the land that arrived before us. They'd come in via the wind, bird droppings, the fur of wild animals. Then there were the other introductions—mine. The pecans, the bananas, the artichokes, the

73

hawthorn, the dogs, the chickens, the domestic sheep—the list seems endless. Even the colourful willows. Who knows how many alien insects and fungi and introduced diseases lurked invisibly around me?

The Global Invasive Species Database list is chilling: giant African snails, Asian tiger mosquitoes, the crazy yellow ant, Eurasian milfoil, blue crabs, a crayfish plague, walking catfish. What a roll call of monstrous species! With a growing horror my thoughts return to the potentially dangerous material I have introduced. I consider myself an ecologist, yet surrounding me, on what had been wild land only a hundred years ago, is an increasingly alien landscape, and I am the most dangerous alien invader of all.

6

LIVING INSIDE
THE SOIL

$\mathcal{E}$NTERING THE MOON gate, I see Sharon is already headfirst in the flower bed, tossing onto the lawn behind her a growing pile of thinnings, trimmings, weeds, dog bones, and surprising bits of detritus from the entrance walkway, discarded by guests and puppies, who seem equally casual about what they chuck. Sharon looks cute from my perspective, face first under the camellia, butt in the air, hurling the rejects into the pile, but I refrain from wit because I know she's in her own world when she's weeding. Even Bella, the puppy, gives her a wide berth, and returns only when Sharon waters everything and Bella has her chance to play her favourite game with the hose, chasing water and never catching it, as Sharon joyfully uses the jet of water to lead her into some impressive acrobatics.

My earliest memory comes out of the ground. Was it my first day of school? I'm scooping up mud and pea gravel outside the classroom window where my teacher is watching with horror. I whip around and hurl the mess at the bullies taunting me. Then I am hauled into the principal's office while the bullies move on to a new victim, and the kindly principal informs me there are better things I can do with earth than throw it around.

My next teacher of the uses for soil was a Japanese farmer in the delta of the Fraser River—perhaps the most fertile farmland in Canada, forged from a temperate climate and millions of years of river silt. The old farmer and my father were negotiating the price for several tons of potatoes that my father would sell door to door. More to distract me than for any other reason, the farmer nodded to my father and said, "Tell the boy to take a cabbage home."

I was gone—a pygmy among the rows of Goliath heads. These cabbages were so large they seemed as tall as I was. I can't remember my age. I was always a little child. I yarded on a monster head I could barely get my arms around. The roots were deep. I punched my tiny fist into the earth. Elbow deep, my fingers clutching the narrowing root, I yarded again and it snapped underground. I rolled backwards underneath a cabbage as big as a medicine ball, and it was just that—a medicine ball—the gift of a memory of when the ground was rich and a Japanese farmer had the talent to put more into the earth than he took. I lugged my prize to the truck while my father and the farmer watched, bemused. Fifty years later, I wonder how many children would prize a cabbage.

Today that farm grows apartments. The town councils of the delta committed one of the largest transgressions against nature in Canada by paving that lush earth, justifying their crime with the need for a tax base and income for their friends in the business community; yet the tax base is probably worse now than it was fifty years ago because of the infrastructure all the development required. When I look back on that lost farm, and its black, good earth, I recognize that's where I found my roots.

Roots need their nurture. Mine were watered by my Italian grandfather's garden. In Vancouver he used to follow the horses of the milk wagon with a bucket and a shovel, treating the manure like the treasure it was. Once, manure was gold for the garden, composted in small piles and recycled back into the land, but when we shifted to industrial farming the unnatural volume converted manure into toxic waste. Modern industrial farms produce three tons of manure for every North American. That's a lot of shit condensed into so few factories.

Afterwards, Grandfather moved to the country, and his garden expanded by a couple of acres. Not long ago I realized I'd spent my adult years attempting to recreate his garden. There was no front lawn, only paths between flower beds. His gladioli won fat ribbons at the local fairs. Out back there was a strip of lawn large enough for bocce games and for laying out tables for Sunday dinners alfresco. Beyond were the garden rows, the raspberries fat and sweet, the plum and apple trees.

IN A GARDEN YOU learn the value of time. Weeding, like farming, is never accomplished. It's an activity, not a result, so a good gardener learns not to fret about finishing a job. It's all in the doing. Otherwise, the quack grass will drive you insane. After a while you learn to go into the "zone" and just work. Beautiful work. You work until your mind runs free. There's a Ch'an (Zen) story about the monk who was hoeing all day. The dinner gong sounded suddenly, and the monk threw down his hoe, laughed, and happily strode off to the temple. "That's it!" exclaimed his ancient master. Enlightenment. The glorious complexity of rural life soon teaches us how to think simply—when you listen to it. Dinner becomes dinner. Dirt becomes dirt.

OUR PLANET IS A soil-creation machine. All the elements come from galaxies created at the advent of time, far away and long ago. When I first read William Bryant Logan's *Dirt: The Ecstatic Skin of the Earth,* and his reference to all life on earth as "the dust of ruined stars," I suddenly understood how big the issue of dirt was. It made me think of the rock singer Roger Daltrey, an obsessive gardener who, ruminating on an epic, ongoing garden project, remarked wisely, "Nothing lasts forever. Nothing," he said. "We're just pushing dirt around." More or less—like your average beetle or earthworm.

We took up the cause with great gusto at the farm, and between Sharon's unrelenting devotion to the flower and vegetable beds, my tendency toward megaprojects, and our clan of inherited young friends and helpers, we moved a lot of dirt.

VOLCANOES SPEWED GREAT CLOUDS of dispersed particles, which mixed with the oxygen in the air, then precipitated upon the planet. Wind and freezing rain crumbled the rocks heaved up from the planet's molten core. After several million years the stone-dust of the earth broke into its chemical basics, and the first compost hesitantly formed in the organic broth of what Darwin suggested was some "warm little pond"—out of the muck and into the slime of birth. Decomposition and composition. Existence is the child of death. I'm convinced the decomposers outnumber the creators. Once the plant world began, the compost supply increased rampantly, along with the rich underground civilizations that now inhabit the soil that breeds us. We are the garden, and we are healthiest when we live in it. Farm children are the least susceptible to the immune diseases crippling modern urban society.

Yet when was the last time you saw a bug on produce from a supermarket? Imagine the chemicals and the pesticides needed to keep those millions of beetles and trillions of other creatures out of your food. We're no longer eating bugs; we're eating the chemicals that kill the bugs. They're in our air, our soil, our bodies—swimming through the cellular universe of our blood. About 125,000 tons of toxic chemicals were used in the First World War. The results were so horrifying that finally, in 1993, the United Nations outlawed their use in warfare. Yet 500 million tons of chemical poisons were dumped on North American soil in 2001 alone. The noxious insects don't show any sign of surrendering. If anything, they are increasing, while the good and the beautiful are dying all around us.

All life is born in the alchemy of earth, some creatures in impressive quantities. A possibly apocryphal story claims that when the eminent evolutionary biologist J.B.S. Haldane was asked what evolution had taught him about God, he speculated that God "must have an inordinate fondness for beetles." There are over 350,000 varieties of beetles on the planet. Yet they are merely one of millions of creatures thriving upon the dirt under our feet. However, nature actually isn't especially fond of beetles—it prefers compost-ing, and beetles are merely one of its tools. When I dip my hand into the soil of our garden, I am scooping up trillions of micro-organisms. There is more biomass beneath than above ground. This provides rich feed for plants, which have evolved innovative root systems for utilizing its nutri-ents. An intrepid agrologist with time on his hands teased apart the mazy roots of a single rye grass. Finishing his cal-culations, he concluded that this lone plant had more than 6,800 miles of root and root hair.

Our small farm, like every other small farm, is built upon the empire of the underground. When I hold my handful of dirt in front of me I can only wonder at the pro-cesses that took millions of years to make the flesh of that hand out of the earth. And the earth my hand is holding? The most diverse ecosystem of them all. Fungi, bacteria, protozoa, nematodes, mites, microarthropods, amoebas, flagellates, classes and subclasses of each other, maybe a fat earthworm or an ugly (to a gardener) cutworm. Then a tiny beetle rushes out of the dirt and skips off a finger, back to its source.

Farming is all earth, or at least real farming is. The factory farms, ignoring ecology, are attempting to cre-ate nutritious soil with basic chemicals and minerals, and maybe a few squirts of liquid manure that fools the farmer more than the soil. Life is about relationships, and the closer the relationships between the land and our belly, the better the food. This is the task Sharon and I set for ourselves from the beginning, building a circular relationship with our soil, feeding on its products and feeding it more in return. We have our differences, of course. I tend toward philosophy. I see systems. Sharon sees weeds and stalks them with an unrelenting single-mindedness.

At Trauma Farm our fastidious horse, LaBarisha, politely craps in the same general area each day, providing manure. The sheep waste hay, pulling it recklessly from the racks in their sheds and shitting on it. This provides another excellent compost. Mixed livestock is part of a real farm's complex structure. The animals produce manure, fibre, feathers or down, hides, meat or dairy products, eggs, labour for the fields, management of grazing land, and thus protection against fire. As the proportion of livestock on a mixed farm diminishes, small farms lose their most important element—that circularity.

Earth is the great decomposer. Here before me, in this handful of soil, I'm witnessing the creation of life. I don't want to spray it or poison it, because to work with soil is to praise and nurture it. Real science, real culture, real understanding goes so much deeper than the narrow, linear, reductionist methodology of the factory farm. Our planet has always been polycultural. That's why the permaculture movement is becoming popular—these are gardeners who believe in creating self-sustaining environments centred on perennial plants rather than the annuals that have become the mainstay of gardens and cultivated farms.

Gardeners are also relearning traditional cultivating techniques from Europe, Africa, the Orient, and what many aboriginal communities long knew. For instance, Native tribes, from Mexico to Maine, grew corn with beans and

squash. The Iroquois called them the "three sisters." Corn
and squash are heavy feeders, but beans are a nitrogen fixer,
and their compost and the decayed leaves of the bean plants
and squash helped fertilize the corn and squash. Like the
Iroquois, we replace any missing nutrients by digging seaweed and the remains of our fish dinners into the soil, along
with ashes from our fire for potassium. The scratchy leaves
of the squash plants also keep raccoons away from the corn.
Balanced crops can coexist happily for hundreds of years,
and even increase the wealth of the soil. If you grow only
corn, using artificial fertilizers, you will gradually strip
your land of life, as many farmers have belatedly discovered
after damaging their soil so badly it will take centuries to
heal. Our three sisters grow proudly every year in the garden, messy yet rich.

One of the intentions of Trauma Farm is political—to
create while leaving only a small footprint. It's an argument against the modern mythology of agribusiness that
believes we can control the gorgeous organic complexity of
the planet. The small farm is a dying anachronism in our
age, but it is here that some of us are taking a rebel stand,
returning to the traditional knowledge that grew good
food for thousands of years. This is why we have tried to
make our farm as circular as possible. We purchased this
land not only for its fine soil but for its natural wealth of
water and sunlight, two of the most important ingredients
in a farm. I can irrigate the garden from our biggest pond
and the excess water will drain back down to the pond
below, where it can be pumped back to the garden. All of
our compost is recycled into the gardens or the chickens.
The chickens recycle their grain and the compost and the

grass and bugs they harvest from the field, and they provide us with chicken manure, the major nutrient for our garden. Even the water from our septic system filters through the soil for a safe distance and eventually seeps down to the lower ponds so that our well water is not wasted.

THE FINAL INGREDIENT OF a good garden is labour. A gardener needs "a cast-iron back, with a hinge in it." It often feels like I am either leaning exhausted on a shovel at the end of a row or wrestling with a bucking bronco of a Rototiller that wants to go wherever I don't want it to go—usually seeking garden netting to snarl in its tines. But then when I look upon the rich rows of earth, I feel the comfort of knowing we have made something well. Lately, we've divided up our labour because of my hectic schedule. I always complain I get the short end, the heavy mechanical business, while Sharon has the thrill of seeding and the flower beds, though she also inherits too much of the dreaded weeding.

In February Sharon organizes the seeds, and the greenhouses fill with trays of tiny seedlings—the hairlike onions, the slow and delicate peppers that take so long to sprout even on a heated soil tray. When the winds of March brush the moisture from the earth we can cultivate the high, dry sections of the garden.

All our vegetable planting is wide-bed. We till the four-foot-wide raised beds and then dig a trench or path around them, heaping that dirt atop the beds. After they're raked out and their corners staked, they're never stepped on again. Trampling and compacting the soil is as bad as not weeding

83

it. That's why my grandfather laid down ten-inch-wide cedar planks between the garden rows. If I ever stepped off a plank and onto the earth, I got my ears boxed or pulled until they grew as red as his Spartan apples.

Despite my admiration for his garden, I know our wide beds work better. The Chinese have used wide beds for centuries. I first saw them in the Chinese farms I visited with my father when he was buying potatoes for peddling. I remember one farm with soil so healthy you could practically serve it up for dinner. I've seen soil as healthy as that only in Cuba, where—because of the American boycott—the lack of chemicals and the organic local farms have created a rich earth and plants that glow electric in the Caribbean light. You can easily see the physical and colour differences between plants grown healthily in healthy soil and plants grown in maltreated soil.

Several women were always working in that soil-rich farm I visited with my father, their wide-brimmed basket hats dipping as they weeded. Today I know they must have been indentured labourers, but to a child they looked lovely in their commitment, and I admired them. For a while that prolific little ten-acre farm produced most of the summer lettuce for the city of Vancouver. Then cadmium and other heavy metals from the city dump across the highway leached under the road, and they had to shut the farm down because its priceless soil had become toxic—so they put a subdivision over it.

Those women flowed, yakking, down the rows of lambent mustards, lettuce, and choi, their fingers flicking like scissors as they plucked weeds with unrelenting energy. After watching them in action I had no trouble

84

understanding Voltaire's famous phrase when I encountered it years later: *Il faut cultiver notre jardin.* "We must cultivate our garden." A cultivated garden produces more and costs less labour. If you leave the weeds too long, they become difficult to remove and stunt your cultivars. All gardeners eventually learn this unusual natural law—the more often you weed, the less you have to weed.

When we weed at Trauma Farm, we throw the weeds in the rows between the beds and then cover them with canary grass or straw, which won't reseed. Big stuff might go into the compost dump, but everything else goes into the rows, except for dangerous, stem-or-root-reproducing weeds like morning glories or quack grass, which are thrown into a big empty plant pot to dry up and die. In autumn, preparing the soil for our winter-crop greens (along with garlic, shallots, and fava beans), we heap the now composted material from the paths onto the harvested bed and dig everything in with ashes from our wood stove to supply the necessary potassium. We often also lay down several bags of slow-releasing rock phosphorous and dolomite lime, and include any extra compost, horse manure, and seaweed we can scavenge— mixing this mélange with our chicken manure, which we "cure" in a pile at the end of the garden.

Chicken manure—like a select few manures such as llama and rabbit—is the richest shit, far more nutritious than cow or horse manure. It's the gold that enriches our garden, providing ample phosphorus and more potassium and nitrogen. We still collect the horse and sheep manure, but that's mainly for texture and colloids to sweeten the soil. As you may imagine with a regime like this, the garden grows wealthier every year and even more abundant, especially since we rotate our crops of peas and beans to fix the nitrogen in the soil. A surprising number of gardeners aren't aware that if they don't manure but use only chemical fertilizers, they can lose up to an inch of soil a year; their gardens turn to sand and dust. Farmers have destroyed some of the great soils of the world with bad practices that led directly to erosion and salinization. The plow can be a weapon of mass destruction, depending on how it is used.

Over the years I've met a few gardeners who seem to irrationally believe that seeds contain everything necessary to grow the entire plant. I like to think of the seed as a trigger for a process that thrives on water and minerals, millions of organisms, and organic matter, all powered by sunlight. Gardening is a technique for turning sunlight into carrots, and once you eliminate a participant in the process you begin the inevitable destruction of your garden. Bad irrigation practices are the main reason why the Garden of Eden (which became the green fields that once surrounded Baghdad) is now a salinized wasteland that will take thirty thousand years to recover. We are working toward the same fate in factory farms around the world.

LIFE IS COMPOST—A PROCESS that goes back to ages before the first mutant child now called *Homo sapiens* squirted out of the womb. Yet we obviously caught on to compost long ago in the history of the garden. Most impressively, our mothers even discovered their placentas will feed not only the child in the womb but the garden after the birth, and thus began another time-honoured fertility rite—the burial of the placenta.

As soon as our hunter-gatherer ancestors stopped moving, they had to think about compost. In the beginning, it was natural gaps in the forest—burn-downs, decayed windblasts—that could be used a few times before exhaustion. Then some genius discovered that you didn't have to wait for lightning. You could "slash and burn" the forest or the grasslands yourself, and the soil was temporarily rich. Shortly afterwards, an old corral or coop sprouted richer greenery than the land surrounding it, and we discovered manure.

This year I noticed unusual size patterns among our garlic. We make our beds about twenty feet long. One of these beds contained three circles of enormous garlic heads. Early in the fall, I had dumped my wheelbarrow loads of chicken manure on those spots and then got distracted (small farming is all about distraction). I never managed to dig it in until planting time. I rushed the job and did a poor tilling before we planted. The nutrients remained in a cluster, creating my prizewinning garlic bulbs. Those fat bulbs, and their runty neighbours, were a lesson in nutrition. Like Thomas Jefferson, I might be growing into an old man, but I'm still a young gardener.

HISTORY—IF WE ARE NOT approaching the end of it—will remember our era as the Oil Age. It's a short era among the many eras of our species. It began around 1850 and it should last until 2050, two hundred years. After that, all bets are off. Maybe before then. These hydrocarbons took more than 500 million years of creation in the long song of the earth. Currently, we are consuming them about 2 million times faster than they were produced.

The polyculture and permaculture we naturally practise at Trauma Farm have been displaced by industrial mono-culture. Vast amounts of energy are now spent on both the production and the ingredients of oil-based fertilizers and pesticides and their distribution. It's so strange when you realize this frenzy of energy and labour is merely a danger-ous, complicated replacement for old-fashioned livestock manure and good garden management.

During the early days of the garden our species needed only human energy and common-sense husbandry to grow food. In what we think of as the small farm's historic gar-den, it's been estimated that 100 calories of food were returned for every energy calorie that went into producing it. Now in the globalized greenhouse production of plants such as iceberg lettuce, the process has been reversed, and it takes as much as 127 calories of energy to produce a single food calorie. The system has become so insane that lettuce produced thousands of miles away can be sold in our local market for less than it costs Sharon and me to grow lettuce four miles from the market. The purchaser pays for the real, hidden costs with government subsidies to factory farms, increasingly toxic environments, and less nutritious and often unhealthy food.

Now that we have become oil consumers, or necro-phages—eaters of the dead, our civilization based on the fossilized lives of earth's history—we have lost our knowledge of the local. Oil, in an odd way, has made trans-portation too easy, and its child, globalization, has separated us from contact with the soil and moved us at an accelerat-ing rate into cities. And city people no longer understand rural life, speeding up its rush toward extinction.

Though it can be difficult in this absurd era, I am relearning how to live and act locally. When the Oil Age inevitably ends we are going to see the failure of globalization, as the transportation system collapses under escalating costs. The captains of industry, along with the rest of us, will be forced to discover a unique formula for earning our keep—creating the kind of land where a child can drive his fist into soil up to his elbow. If we don't—well, then we're facing a big collapse back into a hunter-gatherer civilization. Long, long ago, a woman emerged out of the forest with a digging stick, and we could meet her again.

7

RUNNING DOGS AND FELLOW TRAVELLERS

. . . . .

*B*ACK IN THE house, the dogs loll on their cushions as I make tea. Three dogs, two of them border collies, are too many. I regret the day we decided to keep Bella, though she's a beauty and I love her—she's a born troublemaker. Jen, the older collie, is a control freak and keeps everyone in line. Olive—the gentle, bullheaded Labrador-Rottweiler— is in rough, arthritic shape these days, since she broke her back climbing up a tree after a raccoon.

It's thought that the first domesticated animals were dogs. A tiny puppy skeleton was discovered in the hand of an elderly woman in a 12,300-year-old burial site in Israel, so we can assume our relationship goes back further. Skeletons of domesticated dogs in North America date back to 8500 BC, suggesting that they moved around the world quickly, probably alongside us.

Domestic dogs were soon used for hunting—sight hounds for spotting distant prey, scent hounds for tracking, and "catch dogs for the kill"—though they probably began their domestic careers as alarms against predators and for comfort in the cold. A North American Native description for very cold weather is a "three-dog night." In the Arctic and a few other regions they found a place as sled or pack animals. When agriculture appeared, people became less nomadic, and dogs were relegated to more specialized uses—herd dogs and fighting dogs, retrievers, guard dogs and lap pets. When we consider the varieties of domesticated dog, from the wolfhound to the chihuahua, our evolutionary manipulation over maybe fifteen thousand years is impressive indeed. Dogs have been bred for both useful and distinctly non-useful purposes. For example, Pekingese were bred to resemble miniature lions (until the bored ladies of the Chinese court reputedly discovered an alternative use for that flattened nose and little tongue). Some dogs, such as the much-maligned pit bull, have been bred to kill dogs or valiant animals merely for sport.

We try to keep a herd dog—a border collie—for the sheep, and usually a Labrador to guard against raccoons and marauding dog packs. Dogs are helpful and sometimes necessary allies on a small farm.

Goats and sheep and pigs soon joined the dog in the human fold, quickly followed by the cow and an increasingly exotic menagerie, ranging from the yak to the guinea pig, the silkworm, the camel, the cat, and the turkey. The art of domestication rapidly grew more complex. At the same time the grains and rices and fruits and vegetables began to transform under our guidance into a stunning array of varieties. You only have to consider the *Brassica* genus—mustard, cabbage, broccoli, canola, and a myriad of other cultivars—to recognize what diverse characteristics we are capable of breeding into the world. The history of domestication is mainly the history of the small farm, which tended toward a balanced mixture of horticulture and livestock that suited the local environment.

I've always bonded quickly with animals, despite the livestock and game I've slaughtered and despite the number of times I've been kicked, bitten, and trampled. Wherever I've been, all my life, animals have come to me, even so-called ferocious dogs, schizoid cats, or twitchy horses. I also lean, instinctively, toward physical contact with animals. I brush against them, rest my fingers on a shoulder. Simple gestures in the middle of hard tasks. I love their physical world. They recognize that, and they come forward to be touched. If you are unafraid and open with animals, you will learn how much they want to like you. I've been chased around a few trees by bulls and horses, and I slammed more than one gate just in time on a charging dog while peddling with my dad when I was young, but I've also stopped stampeding livestock and vicious dogs in their tracks. You have to trust yourself in the world, and learn when to run and when to stand. I've never been bit while offering my hand slowly to a slavering German shepherd, though I've met a couple of dogs who've kept me in my vehicle.

Dogs on a farm, like livestock, tend to find the most impressive ways of injuring themselves or sickening. Fortunately, on our island, we have a good vet. Malcolm has what is known as "the touch." When he returned to Salt Spring after many years away, he performed emergency operations in his home while building his hospital. I much preferred it in the house. You'd go there, and Malcolm and his wife, Stephanie, would wipe down the kitchen table and he'd start operating. Afterwards, with the dog kennelled or in a basket by the fire, we'd clean off the table and maybe have a glass of wine and swap lies about farming.

Our first Lab, Tara, got an ear shredded by a vicious raccoon. Malcolm stitched it up and we returned with her a week later to have the stitches removed. We were sitting around in the kitchen, chatting, and Malcolm patted the chair he was sitting on. Tara walked right up to him and sat down with her head between his legs. He took his tweezers and slowly began pulling the stitches out of her ear while she trembled, unrestrained. I've never seen so flagrant a "touch" in a vet before and such trust from a dog.

Afterwards, he told her to go lie down, and she curled up in the big basket in front of the fire in the living room. We gossiped on, then got into a disagreement, mostly because Malcolm, like many farmers, is a flamboyant conservative (though he'd deny that with some vigour), and I'm definitely not—so we usually have much to argue about. It was late in the evening by then and, after finishing our wine, Sharon and I left. We were a mile down the driveway before we realized we'd forgotten the dog, who was happily snoring in front of the fire. Most times when you take a dog to a vet it cringes and shakes and looks hopelessly at you as soon as you turn up the driveway. But not at Malcolm's place. The dogs look forward to visiting his farm. And if they are good, which they usually are, they get a biscuit.

However, when you work a farm, you also have to deal with your own problems. Like the time old Tom Grundy brought his equally ancient but much-prized Highland collie, Cap, over to act as stud for our first border collie, Samantha. Tom has obviously spent many years hard labouring and walks with a ninety-degree stoop. Cap was so geriatric that Tom had to bring a bale of hay for Cap to jump on to get into the pickup. Samantha was a young, choice virgin, and we were all eager to see how this was going to turn out. We introduced the suitor to the virgin and it didn't take long, even though Samantha was not sure about it all.

Suddenly everything went south. They stuck together. Old Tom was horrified. "It'll kill him," he moaned. I didn't think so. I suggested a bucket of cold water. I'd seen that work before. This doubly horrified Tom Grundy. "That would surely kill him." So we phoned Malcolm, who immediately volunteered that this was his funniest phone call of the week. I was all for letting the dogs solve the problem, and so was Malcolm, but Tom was fretting about his aged dog.

"There's only one other thing you can do," said Malcolm, "and that's stroke Cap off. Then the knot will go down and he'll fall out." At this point I was starting to suspect the much-delighted Malcolm was having us on.

Sharon and I looked at each other and said simultaneously, "I ain't doing that."

This even gave Tom Grundy pause. Fortunately, while we were discussing solutions, nature took its course, as it usually does, and Cap flopped out of Sam. Sam ran for cover, having experienced enough of this sex business, and Cap staggered away as if he was going to keel over from exhaustion.

After Tom had settled down from the crisis with a cup of coffee, he and Cap returned to his old pickup. Cap climbed onto the hay bale and into the back of the truck. I threw the bale in after him, and Tom lifted the gate, but it wouldn't close. He kept shutting it, and it fell with a crash each time. Finally, I slammed it up. That locked it. Tom slowly walked around and climbed into the cab. Sitting behind the wheel, he gave me a long, baleful look and said, "Old man...old dog...old truck..." Then, shifting into gear, he slowly motored down the driveway.

THE BIRTH OF THE pups was almost as stressful. Sam practically had a nervous breakdown as they began arriving. I'd been watching her all morning, but every time I left her she'd start to panic. She shredded her bed in minutes. I moved her to the attached greenhouse and went to get a coffee. By the time I returned she'd almost eaten her way through the exterior door. I phoned Sharon for help, but she was too busy with other traumas at the emergency ward where she was working that day.

Eventually, I had to lie down with Sam and console her. Once the puppies started popping out, she tried to run away, so I restrained her until she naturally shifted into mothering mode and licked the blood and caul off them, warming and drying them, before suddenly trying to escape as each new one appeared. After an hour of this I was a basket case. Fortunately, Sharon arrived home and took over. Once the birthing was done, Sam became a magnificent mother.

Jen's first batch of pups arrived several years later, and both Sharon and I were lucky enough to be home. We'd built her a covered hay nest in the barn, and she seemed to think it adequate, but we still kept a close eye on her. We were in the library watching a movie about raising camels, which included a birth scene that Jen watched wide-eyed. Border collies are smarter than some people I know, and I'm convinced she understood exactly what was going on. It's only human stupidity that causes our failure to recognize animal intelligence. Whether it's the cats and dogs or Tuco the parrot, watching videos with our gang can be a riotous experience. Tuco always growls at bears and furry critters and cheers the reptiles and the birds in the movies, and he adores rampaging dinosaurs, scantily clad women, and noisy science-fiction wars.

Being so near to term, Jen had a weak bladder and needed to relieve herself. Sharon unthinkingly let her out and started making some popcorn. By the time she opened the door again Jen was long gone.

We searched for an hour and then just as I returned out of the rainy night I heard a squeak like a newborn puppy might make. Only it was under my feet. Jen had slithered into the crawl space beneath the mud room. The entrance at the other side of the house was so tight I was forced to dig it out so I could crawl inside. Wearing my headlamp, I had to exhale deeply in order to slide under each joist. Talk about claustrophobia!

Worse, it appeared that the cool, dampish earth of the crawl space under the rear addition was also a graveyard, containing the fossilized skeleton of a cat, probably killed by a raccoon long before we bought the farm, a dead sparrow, and a dead mouse. It was ghoulish, and now there was more squeaking, multiple squeaking. I turned the corner beneath the laundry room. It was still too black ahead, even with the headlamp. I kept crawling as the squeaking grew louder. Finally, I saw her huddled in the corner. Four pups.

Obviously more to come. She was in a panic. I crawled up to her and took the first four pups, one at a time, and placed them behind me. Then I grabbed Jen by her chain-collar and started gently dragging her on her back. I couldn't leave her there, in case she developed problems.

So I lifted the pups a foot ahead, dragged myself, then dragged her. I couldn't let go now because she'd crawl straight back to her damp hidey-hole. Cursing and sweating in the dark, I retreated a foot at a time until we rounded the corner and I saw Sharon's flashlight at the entrance. She called out to Jen, and the dog broke away and ran into her arms, while I slowly wormed forward with the pups. Once outside we leashed Jen and carried the pups to her fancy, hay-lined, blanket-adorned birthing lair, where she finished the job, locked in. I returned to the house and showered off a half pound of mud, dirt, and dead things.

WE RASHLY KEPT THE patch-eyed pup and named her Bella. She's a classic working dog, schizoid and brilliant. During dinner preparation she's permanently parked under the breadboard, so we now call her Bella Breadboard. She also quickly figured out the dishwasher and licks all the dirty dishes as soon as our backs are turned while we're cleaning up after dinner—including the knives, which gives me the hair-tingles when I catch her doing it. So we also call her Pre-wash.

Living on a farm, you soon learn not to be squeamish. We often put down our dirty, burnt pots and dishes to let the dogs scrape them clean before we wash them. That raises eyebrows, but I've always felt the need to live in a slightly contaminated world, and besides, I figure anything

97

that survives the soap and our extra-hot water is going to
get us anyway. The growing cultural fetish with sterility
might be our death. I have eaten more than my share of
dirt, that's for sure, and I ain't going to get all rankled if I
accidentally receive a big tongue slurp in the mouth from
an over-happy puppy, or worry about the dogs licking the
dishes clean before I wash them.

A farmer I know, Harry Warner, an expatriate Irishman,
tells a great story of hosting a crowd of Korean students for
a weekend during a cultural exchange. They were city kids
and had never met a live chicken, so Harry gave them the
royal tour. After they finished dinner that night, he put all
the plates on the floor and let the dog lick them clean. Then
he picked them up, stacked them, and put them straight
back in the cupboard to the wide-eyed horror of the Korean
tourists. He tells me it took close to an hour of explaining it
was just a joke before they settled down.

TARA, A BLACK LABRADOR, was the first dog to die at the
farm, and the second to be buried under the willow trees
because I'd brought the ashes of my first dog, Tlell, with us.
Tara had been having small strokes, and one day, after we'd
been given a bottle of fine Ontario maple syrup, I cooked
up a stack of waffles and drowned them in syrup. Naturally,
I'd overdone it, and there were a couple of little puddles left,
so I gave Tara the treat of the year and put the plate down
on the floor for her. She took a lick and you could see the
delight in her eyes. What a sugar junkie!

I know giving even a small amount of syrup to a dog is
bordering on maltreatment, but she was old and had been

having those mini-strokes. Her time was near, so I wasn't worried about obesity. I hadn't taken into account an overdose of ecstasy. Tara's head suddenly snapped up, and she turned to me with a look of absolute fear and ran toward where I was sitting. She collapsed and skidded on the floor up to my feet. I fell to my knees beside her, trying to hold her head, the fear still in her eyes, and then she went into convulsions and was dead, her bowels loosening.

Now she's out there under the willow, beside Tlell, and Sam, who soon followed her. Olive will not be far behind. Farming inevitably builds up a history of lost animals like Tara—whom I probably killed with my stupidity—all of them loving life until it ends.

Among Sam's gifts was her ability to smile. You could say, "Give us a smile," and she would break into a beaming grin. Olive soon noticed that this behaviour got Sam a reward and decided to try her luck. One day, as I was encouraging Sam, Olive broke into a huge grin. However, what is cute on a border collie is a little different on an enormous tank-headed Lab-Rottweiler cross. When she exposes her fangs it's a real sight, which I delight in showing to our friends. It does not always enchant visitors, however, to encounter a pack of dogs at the gate, Olive flashing her fiendish grin. They usually stay in their vehicles until I come out and hush the dogs and let my guests know they are safe.

Since then, Bella, in her puppy glory, has taken to dancing about us and yodelling in the morning. Naturally, this brings her much affection and praise, so Olive is now attempting to talk to us, which can make it spectacularly noisy when we let everyone in at dawn.

Witnessing that interaction, I sometimes think of how it

99

8

TAKING STOCK

· · · · · ·

*S*OMEHOW WE DODGED owning a goat at Trauma Farm, though there were a couple of close calls— gifts that we missed or deals that fell apart as we worked our way through the general history of domesticated livestock. While it might be rash not to discuss goats much in a history of rural life, every farm exists in a different universe, and there's no possibility of exploring all those intermingling universes even in this nearly two-decade-long day at Trauma Farm. Besides, what's missing in a farm is as important as what's there.

Likely the next animal to be domesticated after the dog, the goat is a clever creature. I love its wise eyes and mischief. Goats will also escape almost any fence you can build. A friend was so annoyed with his goats standing up and chewing his fruit tree branches that he erected a rail fence around every tree. The goats were momentarily checked by these fences, before they climbed up onto the top rails and continued browsing the trees, higher than before.

Goats were a natural for domestication—multiple-use, self-sustaining creatures providing goatskin water or wine holders, leather coats and gloves, meat, milk, and cheese. Their hair made the finest wool: cashmere (pashmina) and angora. Handy livestock for a rudimentary civilization on the move, they've also proved merciless grazers. Innumerable landscapes have become near-deserts because of goats. Feral goats are particularly intrusive.

Trauma Farm was originally a goat ranch and supported a large herd before it collapsed and we arrived. The trees show the damage. I find myself, this morning, standing in front of a giant cedar that's shredded, its bark embedded with chicken wire that had been nailed to it in a useless attempt to protect the tree.

Maybe that's why goats made us nervous. It's a myth that goats will eat everything, but they might try. Goats will sample and experiment, unlike sheep, who have a fussier sense of smell. That's why outlandish objects have been discovered in the stomachs of goats. I've met a few goats with a predilection for trying to eat the pants off me. This can be a big surprise if you are not paying attention. And whatever you do, don't bend over. With a few goats, for some reason, that makes you a target.

While we avoided the goat, we did end up with a few horses. Our first was the aptly named Tie Me Down. A neighbour informed me he had just the horse for us. A beauty. A brown gelding with a white blaze on his chest and forehead. Small, but in his glory—a quarter horse who didn't quite make the track. Our neighbour was selling this wonderful horse for a song, and was so sure we'd love him, he asked us to try him out for a couple of months. It's been said you should never look a gift horse in the mouth, but I soon learned why this horse was called Tie Me Down. For a start, he didn't have much affection for the saddle. As I cinched it he tried to bite my hand. Then he did a half somersault and a sort of triple roll in my direction, and as I skittered sideways he kept rolling past me, trying to shake the saddle.

Mean-minded horses will bloat their stomachs to avoid a tight saddle. If you aren't aware of this trait you could find yourself hanging upside down from the horse's belly. Tie Me Down could bloat like a pufferfish. I hadn't fully cinched the saddle before he went into puffer mode, so after about his fifth roll he managed to slide the saddle back and kick it at me like a jet projectile. I ducked as it flew past my head.

This performance brought out the stubborn streak in me. I've been around horses, off and on, since I was a child. They are beautiful, wilful, sometimes sly animals that can develop deeply emotional relationships with their companions. These relationships can be loving, workmanlike, or occasionally toxic. I'm the first to admit I'm no expert horseman, but I had enough brains to recognize this horse was going to need some work. I maybe exaggerate. Tie Me Down was as docile as a lamb—as long as you didn't enter his field. I saddled him up again, this time cinching the saddle tight before he started rolling around. After about fifteen minutes of trying to eject the saddle, he settled, exhausted. I climbed aboard. He was quiet and gentle, and we looked lovely together. Such a pretty horse. Sharon took a photograph to prove it. Since I was smoking then, I lit up a defiant cigarette.

We trotted around the field for several minutes. Everything was terrific. Then we set off at a gallop. When I pulled him up I thought, "This horse is not so bad." On a farm, one never should think things like that. We turned and I steered him toward the gate at a slow trot while lighting another cigarette. Talk about overconfidence. Halfway across, Tie Me Down suddenly braked, bucked, and fell to his front knees, flipping me in a full somersault over his head. I landed on my ass in a cloud of dust, choking on my cigarette butt, the horse standing behind me, waiting for another go.

After I spit out the butt and ashes and regained my calm, along with the feeling in my legs, I climbed on again.

This time I was ready for him and we went down together. Somehow I hung on, which really annoyed him, so he started rolling with me atop him. Every time he rolled I climbed off, between his flailing hooves, and climbed back on when he stood to his feet. By the third roll he gave up and just stood there trembling. I urged him back to the gate. That was enough for today. In fact, that was enough for good. I could tell by the look in his eye that he would take me out as soon as I was off guard, and there was no way Sharon was ever going to ride this horse. We gave him back a few days later. Eventually he found his way to a horse whisperer, a woman who brought out the best in him.

From the behaviour of Tie Me Down you would never know that the horse has been domesticated for six thousand years. At least that's what the experts claim, based on some worn molars on a skeleton in Eurasia. As with the donkey, the horse's first known uses were to pull chariots, domestic and war, although there's a good argument that they were ridden first because the date of domestication barely approaches the era of the invention of the wheel. Maybe once the horse arrived, a pretty little cart became compulsory. Our knowledge of the wild horse goes back to thirty-thousand-year-old cave art. Most of the feral horses were hunted out, and it's assumed the only survivors were those that had been domesticated. There were no survivors at all in the Americas, and the horse didn't return here until the era of the conquistadors. The last known member of the wild species, the Tarpan, perished in the nineteenth century.

Although quickly recruited for battle, they blended in seamlessly on farms, both for carriage and for labour. The Amish have clung to the working horse, and local-farming enthusiasts are determined to bring the old breeds back. Occasionally you see the fancy ones at farm fairs, and they're stunning to watch. A show pair of working horses can wear $25,000 worth of livery at the drop of a horse-shoe. This year at the Saanich farm fair I witnessed a pair of Percherons pulling a sumptuous hack. It was so beautiful it was kind of sad, like watching a reality television show about leather-and-silver fetishists who happened to enjoy horses.

A riding horse is a lovely creature, but owning one is similar to owning a boat; only instead of being a hole in the water into which you pour money, the horse is like a constantly demanding teenager into which you pour money. Hobby horse farms, unfortunately, are buying up the land from working farms. On Salt Spring, once the home of the most famous lamb in North America, the pastures of gambolling spring lambs are now becoming occupied by horses. Recently, the owner of our feed supply store lamented to me that he was selling more horse feed than sheep feed. These hobby farms are another symptom of the sickness overwhelming our landscapes. The horses, usually ridden a few hours a week, dot the fields like expensive living lawn ornaments overlooking mowed fields and pseudo-forests too divided up to ever become contiguous natural forest. Ecologists regard these estates with the same jaundiced eye they cast upon single-species tree farms— they're all green concrete, and they lead to unbalanced predator and prey populations.

"SHE HAD AN EXPRESSION on her face," Mike Byron said, "like a horse eating a thistle flower." He was describing a pompous shopkeeper, and it cracked me up—especially since I'd seen my horses eat their share of thistle flowers. When we bought our farm it was riddled with thistles. Sheep don't eat thistles, but horses do. In fact, they take a certain masochistic delight in gingerly deflowering the thistles with their rubbery lips. They eat only the flower, but this gradually eliminates the thistles from a field. Upon being offered our next horse after Tie Me Down, a twenty-year-old semi-retired show horse, we decided to do the charitable thing and give him a retirement home while reducing our thistle nightmare and supplementing our desperately needed manure.

Stonewall Jackson stood eighteen jet-black hands high. He was a beautiful, stubborn, and affectionate creature, with a tendency to mug any strollers on his land, thrusting his big nose into your pockets for sugar cubes—a good, easy horse to ride before we finally put him out to permanent pasture. Plus he could eat thistles as if they were caviar. By the time he died he'd cleared both our main fields. Unfortunately, he could also suck the lower leaves right off a plum tree, so I had to keep the orchard double-locked. Whenever he managed to pop a gate he'd seek the sweetest clover within a square mile, and his Houdini tricks soon taught me where the best pasture was in our neighbourhood. He was a terrible beggar and would always come up to the narrow front deck and practically stick his head into the house if the door was open. His favourite trick, when we were foolish enough to let him into the front yard, was to upend the bird feeders and vacuum up the seeds.

Sometimes on a sunny morning I'd bring out a few carrots to the deck, along with my breakfast, and we'd eat together, until the day I dropped a carrot and it rolled under the table. I put my dish down to fetch the carrot, and before I was back on my feet he had licked the eggs, bacon, toast, and hash browns off my plate with one big slurp. I guess he was going for the toast but decided to hoover it all up. It didn't seem to bother him any, eating my bacon, though it sure irritated me.

During the years we rode him he could still perform his show-ring moves, and it was a delight to pretend I knew what I was doing. Sharon loved sitting on his back, letting him take her for relaxing tours through the tastiest grasses in the ditch beside the road, grazing his way home. Jackson kept his independent mind and private life until the end. Some nights I would see him out there galloping alone in the field, scaring the sheep and the ducks, prancing like a teenager. A friend, the poet Lorna Crozier, once told me the story of a white horse on the prairie, a show horse, that under the full moon, alone, would practise its fancy show-ring routines. Jackson wasn't that glorious, but he had some good moves.

After Jackson died we didn't want any more horses, but a few years later we ended up with both a horse and a tractor when our kindly neighbours moved away. La-Barisha, a glamorous Arabian grey, reminds me of a fading beauty queen. She thinks she's God's gift to horses, and the smug expression on her face when she's having her hooves trimmed is so arrogant I tease her about "having her nails done" and promise to paint them red one day.

THE COW'S TONGUE IS just as amazing as the tongue of the horse or the sheep, meatier yet equally sensitive. Cow tongue is also one of my favourite meats. A boiled tongue, peeled and thinly sliced onto a hunk of homemade rye bread with good mustard, is a disappearing delicacy. Fifty years ago it was a common lunch meat, but times have changed. Betty, our sole cow, had a tongue that looked a yard long, and she could lap a bucket clean, along with your hands and anything else that tasted good, and she could savour a pasture the way a gourmet can savour a good sauce or a bottle of wine.

With its near-supernatural tasting skills, a cow can lick the air and analyze the protein content of a pasture, the acidity and the alkalinity of grasses and clovers, and what part of the field is in its prime. Cattle, like horses and sheep, change their diet depending upon the time of day and the season because the protein content in grass changes according to sunlight, moisture, and heat through the year. The cow's olfactory world is so complex it's difficult to understand for simple-minded creatures like ourselves, but some organic farmers are learning to be grass farmers, as farmers once were—smelling the grass in the morning and the evening, looking for colour gradation and the shapes of the stem. It's easy to tell when a fence is broken but a lot more difficult to know when a pasture is broken and how to fix it. These New Age farmers might not be as smart about grass as a cow, but they are attempting to learn from their cattle—as well as reinventing traditional practices of cross-fencing and tending to the health of mixed grass, only with more scientific finesse. This way their cattle will inevitably become cheaper to raise and certainly healthier than the abused prisoners of the modern feedlot.

During the twentieth century agriculture shifted away from traditional practice and adopted the production efficiencies of the factory—raising cattle on minimum pasture and feeding them hay, grain, and silage. The cattle are then "finished" in feedlots where, as most people know by now, up to a hundred thousand cattle are imprisoned in obscenely filthy enclosures—sometimes knee deep in excrement—and are given corn-based feed, which acidifies their stomachs and provides a perfect host environment for the toxic bacterium *E. coli* O157:H7, the poisonous, deadly child of the feedlots.

Once the cattle are fat enough, their muscles slackening from disuse, they are shipped to slaughterhouses that resemble medieval torture chambers, where they are sliced open and cleaned, usually by immigrant labourers in the

United States, people with the courage and desperation to work in these horror houses. The unrelenting assembly lines force the workers to clean and gut up to a steer a minute. Anyone who has ever gutted a steer knows how insane that is. It often leads to accidental piercing of the stomach and the spraying of shit and intestines and their bacteria all over the meat. By the time we see that steer it's washed and wrapped in plastic. The bacteria aren't necessarily eliminated. Then we eat it.

CONSIDER LIVESTOCK FEED. ORIGINALLY it was pasture. As grain grew more common the farm industrialized. Then mixed-grain feeds came along. They were soon manufactured with animal by-products and mineral supplements and hormones. Unnaturally elevating the protein, fat, and starch levels can create larger livestock faster. It didn't matter that many of the ingredients—such as bones, feathers, blood, fish, canola oil, enzymes, soy meal, antibiotics, and alfalfa—were not part of the livestock's original diet, which is why BSE suddenly broke out. Feeding beef and other livestock by-products to beef is now banned. Yet when the outbreak first occurred in Britain, there were so many millions of tons of feed in circulation that the feed mills cleverly recalled and reprocessed the contaminated feed into chicken and pork feed, because chickens and pigs have yet to show symptoms of BSE. A dangerous economic decision that worked in that case, but do we want to trust these companies?

Antibiotics in feed constitute up to 70 percent of North America's consumption of these drugs. Owing to the growing wave of revulsion, the use of animal by-products and antibiotics is diminishing, but animal feed remains dangerous. While these feeds reduce the time needed to bring enhanced livestock to market, they are a progress trap—a term coined by Ronald Wright. Simplistically put, it means that what appear to be good ideas often backfire—they become evolutionary dead ends. Some of these feeds make livestock less healthy and too fat, and their use produces environmental damage and disease. That's not disputable. The big question is, Where do you draw the line on what is good feed? This is difficult because the line is an ethical, environmental, and health issue—not merely an economic one. How can you legislate that? Or common sense? Besides, nutritional knowledge is constantly changing, and the laws are difficult to enforce—unknown material is often introduced to rendering factories despite the current legislation.

I feed our livestock good pasture, supplemented with the appropriate grain, ground or whole. Unfortunately, industrial feed production has led to increasing shortages of regular grain, since the feed companies, like the manufacturers of modern breakfast cereals, make more profits from processed feeds. Relatively few farmers now use traditional feed.

Progress traps that arise out of modern feed and production structures can lead to strange results. The reasons for the foot-and-mouth panic in Great Britain were economic. They had little to do with the health of humans or animals. Foot-and-mouth is a nasty disease—a livestock version of measles. But it goes away in a few weeks, and then the animal is safe to slaughter. Nor will its immune system be susceptible to same variant of the disease (there are several strains) again. However, if you are holding fifty thousand feeder pigs in a factory, calculating daily the digestible protein and fat ratio pouring into the rotors that distribute feed to the troughs, time is essential to the financial equation. Slaughterhouse delivery is calibrated to the exact hour. A twenty-four-hour delay would make tens of thousands of animals unprofitable. A longer delay would mean economic collapse for the factories. That's why the British agriculture bureaucrats ordered the slaughter of everyone's livestock in the affected regions, not just those produced by the factory farms. The enormous carnage and the great heaps of burning corpses, including endangered varieties of livestock, were a symbol of profit protection, not safety.

BETTY WAS A JERSEY-HEREFORD cross—Hereford for the meat and Jersey for the bountiful milk to nurse a calf. She was a cow bred to raise a hefty dinner. She even came with a good calf, and the plan was to raise her calves for meat— one a year. Alas, Betty had a different plan. It consisted of eating everything in sight. Cattle, understandably, don't like being tied up. Mike used to tie his Jersey cow to his truck bumper and milk her. Then he sold the cow to a good friend, a knowledgeable farmer, and when Mike told him he just tied the cow to the bumper, his friend did the same, ensuring she was double-tight by tying her hind leg to the back bumper. He had a new, expensive pickup and didn't want to take chances. Maybe that was the fatal mistake. The cow decided she didn't like the arrangement, or the new truck—whatever—and started bucking. She flipped off the back hobble and kicked the shine right out of his truck,

112

ornamenting it with her personal hoofprint design from bumper to bumper.

Betty had similar feelings about the split-rail fencing between her and the orchard and soon was ginger-stepping between the rails and reaching for the lower branches of the fruit trees. Once she'd wrecked our cross-fencing to her satisfaction, she settled into eating everything she could reach. Thankfully, she didn't crack the higher fencing that kept her in the field.

Betty was a cranky cow, according to her next owner, but I got along with her fine once I rebuilt the fences stronger. I milked her every morning in the field where I'd dug a deep hole and stuck a post in it. When the early light fell on the land I'd bring her a bucket of feed, and she'd mosey up to the feed and start eating while I clipped her to the post, pulled up a chunk of firewood for a stool, and began milking her. She'd munch contentedly until I had our pail of milk. Sometimes, I'd hand-whip the milk of summer into a rich, golden butter that has forever given me contempt for that dyed, silver-foil-wrapped trash in the dairy section of the supermarkets. You can practically get stoned on real Jersey milk, especially in early summer (real milk and butter change flavour according to the season), when it's so rich and real, but, of course, it's illegal to sell anymore.

A friend, an Anglican priest on Pender Island, has in his possession a hundred-year-old letter from his great-grandfather in Scotland. The man was writing to a relative about his eighteen dead children, how he walked miles across the hills to a meadow and hand-scythed hay to provide a good supply for the family cow during winter, so it could deliver enough milk to feed and strengthen the young bairns who kept dying on him and his wife. It never occurred to him that the cow had tuberculosis and he was slaving to feed the tubercular milk to his children. Tuberculosis can be a dangerous business—though it's now nearly extinct in cattle. Despite the tragedy of that Scottish farmer a century ago, enthusiasts claim today's well-handled "wild milk" is far more healthful and less dangerous than a drive to the corner store.

HISTORICALLY, THE MIXTURE OF animals and humans on small farms provided opportunities for immune systems to interact on modest levels—with a few virulent exceptions (almost all caused by the unhygienic conditions provided by war, famine, or overpopulation). Unfortunately, in a bizarre way, the domesticated animals used by Native Americans—llamas, dogs, guinea pigs, turkeys—didn't have immune systems that allowed bacteria and viruses to leap into the human species as easily as the more agreeable immune systems of Eurasian livestock like sheep, goats, cattle, chickens, horses, and especially pigs—whose digestive infrastructure is so similar to the human gut. As a result, Native Americans were overwhelmed by diseases introduced by the European invaders.

Edward Jenner has been rightly praised for noting that milkmaids who'd encountered cowpox never caught the much nastier smallpox. However, it's been claimed that while inoculating people with the pustules from cowpox in cattle, he also, unknowingly, transferred tuberculosis, as well as the syphilis virus, which moved from maids to cattle when the cuts on their hands met up with cuts or

114

wounds on the udders of cows. Although the smallpox vaccine saved millions of lives, the rate of syphilis infections in children skyrocketed, along with tuberculosis, which killed Jenner's wife, son, and two sisters. As so often happens when the scientific method arrives at the small farm, a beautiful monster had likely emerged, combining immunity and infection in its early days.

With Betty long gone, I have to search out raw milk—a secretive endeavour for most old-style islanders, who love the real world and accept its dangers. Raw and unprocessed milk becomes more difficult to find each year as small farms disappear. Also, the milk police are becoming shiftier, and they masquerade as friends of friends and go around to farmers and tell them a neighbour sent them over for some milk. If a farmer relents and gives them raw milk, she will be busted for her generosity. Underground milk has become like the drug world, a kingdom of whispers, politics, and draconian policing.

Pasteurization, although it doesn't totally sterilize milk, eliminates potentially bad bacteria, protozoa, moulds, and yeasts as well as good bacteria. There's a growing revolt against it for just that reason, with enthusiasts declaring that the rise of autoimmune diseases parallels the elimination of real milk. This interesting argument, it should be noted, is also used against several other food processes that appeared during the past century. The worst legacy of pasteurization is that, like most initially plausible farming schemes, it's been captured by industrial production economies whose main purpose is to increase profit and reduce perishability (milk can last up to three or four months after some processes) at the expense of quality. This is why milk products no longer go deliciously sour; today's commercial milk rots. Homogenization, which somehow snuck into the pasteurization process, destroys the cream's structure, allowing it to be watered down. All pasteurized and homogenized commercial milk is watered. Manufacturers blithely claim the water is added "accidentally" during processing.

Even more strangely, people want their milk watery and defatted these days because they eat too much fat at the fast-food restaurant down the street, and thus they'd rather sacrifice the healthy qualities of real milk and its thick, sweet cream rising to the top of the glass bottles that we all used to keep floating in our cool streams and wells before the days of refrigeration.

When I was twenty-two I lived on Texada Island a few miles from an enormous woman who sold wild milk. I'd saunter along in the heat of summer down to her farm and buy a jar of cold milk from her cellar. The top third would be cream. I never had the heart to shake the milk and distribute the cream evenly. I would suck it up off the top, delirious from its rich fat, and then cleanse my palate with the thinner milk at the bottom. My favourite time for buying her milk was when the wild strawberries were out, and the neighbours would encounter me, moustached with cream, sitting on the roadside, picking at the tiny strawberries, which were more addictive than the milk. The neighbours would laugh and wave as they drove by, and I would smile a big, milky, strawberry smile while the dragonflies partitioned the air and the crickets clacked in the meadows.

9

MORE STOCK

· · · · ·

*E*VERY FARM HAS its specialty, but a truly mixed farm like ours needs various creatures, made of leaf or flesh, to become an organic whole, not only for my lunch today but for sales and healthy cultivation. Like the few surviving mixed farms on Salt Spring we raise sheep. Salt Spring lamb is world renowned, and though the taste difference is obvious, I always wondered what accounted for that difference, so I asked the Byrons. Mike told me it was the diet of Gulf Islands vegetation. The majority of factory-style lamb operations run their lambs on big, grass pastures, especially in New Zealand. Salt Spring lambs historically have been raised on small farms of mixed shrub land, orchards, mahonia, ferns, and pasture—bush lambs. Apart from a few big farms, the local farms usually raised between a half-dozen and twenty almost hilariously babied ewes until the government regulated island sheep into near-oblivion in order to make them better. The bureaucrats told local farmers they'd help us improve our traditional butchering. We soon recognized this meant we were doomed. At Trauma Farm we kept ten ewes, and produced about fifteen lambs a year, until the new slaughtering legislation ensured we'd lose more money than we could afford. We had to shrink our flock to a half-dozen ewes to manage the pasture. Many farms gave up altogether.

FARMERS HAVE MADE A few mistakes with sheep bloodlines, breeding stupidity into a once-brilliant animal, along with docility. I often say sheep have to be smart to be that dumb, and a sadness invades me when a young ram stupidly butts at the food bucket. Still, sheep are impressively intelligent in certain ways. Like horses and cows, they're artists when it comes to the qualities of grass. They might crap indiscriminately, but they also avoid grazing near potentially parasite-laden excrement. In late winter they will suddenly attack tree bark and branches and foliage they scorned all year, because they can sense their own mineral or enzyme deficiencies. A British study proved that sheep can recognize over fifty friends among their flock, a striking number when I consider my own hopeless ineptitude at recalling a casual friend's name. They know their society. The same study tentatively showed that rams prefer to mate with ewes that resemble their mother, but I won't go there. In another study, only of people, the extended family typically comprised around twenty of us. That's the closeness zone of our species. The village, a hundred or so people, is about the most we are capable of becoming acquainted with socially. Everyone else is a stranger, and our species has a long history of disliking strangers, the aliens who live in the next valley. What's really scary about this cultural behaviour is that it has many parallels with the social structure of the sheep in our field.

DOMESTICATED LIVESTOCK CAN PROVIDE their share of comedy. Our favourite ewe was Butterball, a Hampshire cross with unlimited patience and a benevolent, really dumb expression. One day, at feeding time, she got her head stuck in the bucket while I was distracted by the dogs. We happened to have our camera handy, so we now possess a photograph of a bucket-headed Butterball. She's standing, bucket upright, surrounded by the other ewes staring at her as if she were an alien. She started walking around blindly, so the rest of the flock fled in horror. She followed their fleeing footsteps, crashing often as we dived and skidded after her, until we caught up and yanked the bucket off her head.

119

Shortly after we arrived we'd bought a classic island herd, all mixed and scrambled, and we have been mixing them more ever since. Cheviots and Suffolks and Dorsets and Romneys and Jacobs. Our first ram was a gentle Romney and we named him Romeo. When the ewes went into heat he'd stand behind them and kiss the air, making cheesy pornographic gestures with his lips. Over the years we bought a few black sheep and bred them into our gang. Since we weren't going to make any money on sheep, we decided we might as well have the amusement of a flock of black sheep.

The problem with a small flock is keeping a viable ram. You want to avoid inbreeding, so island farmers naturally developed an irregular system of ram exchanges. If someone has a good ram, it might become community property. After the ram has finished with all the ewes on the original farm, you take it, feed it, maintain it, and then pass it on. This process can involve a skewed breeding season, but in our temperate climate that doesn't matter. Moving the ram becomes a social event. Dinners and wine are often involved. It can also get dicey.

When I mentioned that our last ram had gone infertile, Mike Byron showed up the next day with a honking big ram in the back of his truck. This behaviour was unusual for Mike, who often operates months behind schedule, being of the class of farmers who always have far more tasks than any normal person could handle. I was suspicious immediately, but we sorted out ewes, lambs, dogs, and pastures and unloaded the ram, who pranced off the truck like a superhero, took one look at the ewes, and made himself at home. This is good, I thought, forgetting my initial suspicions.

The ram was a real gentleman and went about his business mating with the ewes. He also figured out feeding time soon enough. A week later he took his first run at me. I thwacked him with the bucket and that backed him off. I didn't quite turn my back as I walked away, and that was smart. He charged again. I rotated quickly, kicking him in the chest, and deflected the charge. This wasn't looking good. Within a week I didn't have to turn my back before he attacked. A 250-pound charging ram is no fun. I slapped his face, but he charged again, and I slapped him again. I abhor hitting animals, yet he had no qualms about hitting humans. This was not fair. Worse, he regarded every slap as an incentive. He chased me around our small stand of birches. That day ended in a standoff, and I thought I'd calmed him down. He didn't make another charge. But one week later, after Sharon fed the sheep, she declared she wasn't doing that again. No story, no explanations. The decision was final. I didn't dare ask what had happened.

As can often occur on a farm, that incident incited opposing forces. The encounter with Sharon was the final straw for Sam, the border collie, who had enough good breeding to recognize a ram gone rogue. The next afternoon, as the ram pawed the earth and I stood ready, like a goaltender, bucket in hand, waiting for the charge, Sam leaped at his hind end and yanked off a mouthful of wool. This is totally illegal behaviour for a sheepdog, but considering the circumstances, I raised no objection, and watched events unfold. The ram whipped around. Sam was long gone. Lying in the grass, her jaws tufted with wool, she gave him the "evil eye" of a master collie. Though no competition-trained herd dog, Sam had inherited this "eye" and knew how to use it. She rushed him again and veered off at the last moment.

After less than twenty minutes of this intimidation dance the ram was cowed. I never said anything to Sam. She knew. She never hurt him, outside of yanking that first tuft of wool. By the time I closed the gate the vicious ram was trembling behind the ewes, and Sam proudly sashayed down the road at my side, spitting out bits of wool.

Living with sheep is a kind of collapsed life lesson. You learn and feel so much within a few years. They are born and they leap with joy, kicking up their heels—a sight that brings you rushing to the fence to watch. They grow fat and stupid. They get their heads stuck in the hay bin. They fold up in the corner of the shed with a great sadness, and then they die, and you are left with the dust of complex, confusing memories.

Sheep usually prefer living with sheep, although we did have a bottle-fed lamb who was convinced she was a dog and who sometimes joined the dogs on the deck, hoping to be let inside. Pigs, in contrast, love to intermingle with people. They can be more domestic than goats or chickens or horses. During the Korean pot-bellied pig craze I met a few house-trained television-watching pet pigs. The pot-bellied pig is notoriously personable, but so are most pigs. We stuck to more regular breeds. Our first lot arrived one morning in the back of my closed van. I drove them behind the barn and lifted them down inside their page-wire enclosure. It was well fortified—the wire dug into the earth. I mixed them up a batch of feed, and they set to it as if they were born here.

Pigs are often used to clear new land. It's easy to see why. Give a pig enough time and it will dig out and overturn a four-foot tree stump. I watched them do that in our pen over a period of several weeks.

We named our threesome Bacon, Eggs, and Toast—not distinguishing who was who. Never name an animal you are going to eat. This gang scarfed their feed trough clean and set about destroying every living thing in their enclosure and a few nonliving objects as well. I watched them for almost an hour. They seemed so happy. Satisfied that they were comfortable, I returned to my chores.

A few hours later I decided to check them. They were

gone. They'd burrowed under the buried page wire. I panicked and immediately phoned old Howard Byron, Mike's brother and the animal control officer. Howard was out, so I left a message. I spent all afternoon searching for those pigs. Long gone. Howard didn't phone back, which was unusual for him. And Mike wasn't home either. We didn't have a herd dog then, so they'd be tough to corral without help. My imagination went wild with visions of the pigs destroying some neighbour's expensive, exotic flower garden. I finally reached Mike on the phone. He didn't seem worried in the least.

"You fed them this morning before they broke out?"

"Yes, sure."

"Just leave the gate open. They'll be back by dinnertime."

I spent the afternoon turning the pen into a barbed-wire, buried-post concentration camp, which was no easy task, as it was a large yard. Exhausted, I returned to the house and was having a mug of tea by the pond when I heard a great barking on the road and Tara, the Labrador, returned to the house as if she were being chased by the devil. Side by side, three happy piglets trotted cavalierly past the barn and down the back road to their pen.

What most impressed me was their unerring sense of direction. Although they had been brought into the farm in a closed, windowless van, they'd escaped through the forest behind the farm. I'd tracked them with Tara for close to a mile in the opposite direction before she lost their scent. Yet they knew exactly where the road, our driveway, and their pen were. They barely noticed me as they trotted down to their trough, where they stopped and looked up expectantly. It was dinnertime.

Pigs are perhaps the only domestic livestock that haven't lost their natural intelligence despite our breeding strategies over the centuries. They are such clever creatures—they use toys and tools—with an unerring sense of what's going on around them, if they haven't been raised in the psychotic-sadistic environment of today's factories. A university professor with a sense of humour once taught pigs how to use their snouts to manipulate joysticks to play a simple video game. Generally good-natured, they also have a fearlessness that cracks only under the worst circumstances. A pig with its back to the wall will put up a hell of a fight, and the pig's only real predator in North America is the bear, though a cougar might take a run at a young one. On Vancouver Island, the black bears were once notorious for night raids on pigpens.

One of the most chilling moments I've had with farm animals was when I had to help a friend castrate the young males. They barely weigh fifty pounds, but it usually takes three men to hold them down and tie off the testicle cords. The unearthly squealing while the piglet undergoes this indignity is enough to chill your bones and make a man swear off raising pigs forever, yet you can't have two ungelded boars together in a small flock without catastrophic consequences.

SLAUGHTERING PIGS IS ALSO a gruesome experience. On a small farm, we don't usually confine them in scary chutes and use the hammer gun; instead we lure them to a green patch of pasture, shoot them between the eyes, and cut their throats. Their mates can be extremely callous about this. I have seen one lick the blood out of the bleeding throat of its brother, just before I shot it as well. The horse, who adores pigs, mourned the loss more than that piglet mourned its own brethren. Jackson ran around the pasture and then stood beside their fence and called for them. When they were alive he used to hang his head over that · fence, and they would stare nose to nose at each other for hours, having some secret interchange.

As soon as possible after they are killed you have to winch them up and dip them into a vat of 150-degree water, lift them out, and, with special scrapers, scrape the hair off their hides so you can keep your crackling. As grisly as it can be, one can only prefer the traditional raising of swine to the modern factory farms. Over the last fifty years our culture has progressively distanced itself from animals (except for pampered household pets). The animal kingdom is now a kind of Disneyland, in which the shit, the blood, and the brute madness are reduced to cuteness and sentimentality. In Vancouver the residents react in horror at the thought of culling the invasive and aggressive Canada goose population contaminating the lagoons and driving rare ducks away. I've actually sat with a woman weeping over the fate of those pretty birds while slicing up her pork chops that came delivered in plastic out of pig factories as large as cities. Cruelty is apparently acceptable if it's invisible to the general population. Which is why it's becoming increasingly difficult to smuggle photographs and videos out of these factories. They do their best to prevent people from witnessing how the pigs are treated.

In the biggest factories sows spend almost their entire adult lives clamped in a four-foot-by-two-foot pen. Which is why the meat is so tasteless and fat, despite being injected with polyphosphate to give it "flavour." It's also injected with water to enhance weight. People who have been in swine factories say the hideous screams of the pigs can be devastating emotionally.

The possibilities of bacterial contamination grow exponentially when you're dealing with a slaughterhouse that kills six thousand pigs in a day. These slaughterhouses and their feeder factories have to be treated as biosecure platforms. Even the once-rich offal of skin, bones, guts, and feathers buried, composted, and then dug up years later to enhance soil is now considered toxic waste, and the remains of pigs or sheep or chickens are sealed into steel cans and shipped thousands of miles to incinerators. This new processing is regarded as healthful and environmentally correct. What was once a small-scale and locally composted product that returned nutrients to the land has been converted into a immense, wasteful health hazard that diminishes the ecosysem on a scale that a normal person could hardly imagine... and doesn't.

When I was slaughtering I used as much of the animal as possible. I'm fond of pickled pig's feet, and I've also saved their tripe, and their intestines for chitterlings (delicious pan-fried) or sausage making; but with pigs, because they are susceptible to parasites that can infect humans, you have to wash everything meticulously and practise good hygiene, and also compost the offal for at least two years if you are going to use it in the garden. After singeing the hide, I will use a razor to trim off the hard-to-get hairs. Then we gut the animal. Once, in a hot midsummer slaughter at the height of wasp season, we were gradually covered with wasps as we worked, moving carefully to avoid being stung. We had to get out of there fast. Because I was feeling rushed,

I set the heart down on the butcher table behind me, forgetting to cover it. In the dozen minutes it took us to ready the carcass for the cooler, the wasps ate a hole through the heart. Mistakes are not always forgiven when you work in the natural world.

IN ENGA PROVINCE IN Papua New Guinea, there is an entire culture based on swine keeping and exchange—a culture as complex as the cattle cultures in Africa. It's said the men have more affectionate relationships with their pigs than with their wives. Pigs have a freebooting and generally unherdlike nature, which is why they coexist well only with stable, stationary cultures, running free in villages or in large enclosures, and this is why transporting a small-farm pig can be thrilling.

Trying to drag a three-hundred-pound young pig backwards by its hind legs is no easy trick—pigs deliver a powerful kick and have sharp hooves—but transporting a full-grown, heavyweight boar for stud duties can be a life-changing experience. Mike Byron has a knack for turning simple tasks into thrilling encounters. This is mostly because he thinks outside the box, and innovative ideas can backfire. For moving his much-prized boar he used the old-fashioned method of "gates"—four-by-eight-foot, lightweight, movable fences that can be manipulated to guide livestock. Moving swine this way should be an easy four-man job.

Unfortunately, this time, there were only two of us, using our gates to direct the red boar to the truck ramp. The boar understood the routine but wasn't interested

127

today. Before I knew it I was on my back, under the gate, the boar staring down at me.

"Geezus," Mike moaned. "Don't let him get away!"

"Don't let him get away?" I gasped beneath the eight-hundred-pound boar. "He's killing me!" Luckily, he had a kind disposition and wandered off my crushed ribs, searching for a few flowers to uproot. It took us hours to get him into the truck, and somehow this was all regarded as my fault.

FARMING IS COMPLICATED ENOUGH when dealing with the major livestock, but rural people are prone to innovation, and farmers have more dreams than common sense, which is why so many exotic livestock have come and gone through the centuries of domestication on small farms. Only a few notorious herbivores were resistant, like the zebra and the moose, but dozens of others also eventually proved more hassle than they were worth.

"Breeders," an old farmer contemptuously snorts at exotic livestock, whose only real market is in supplying expensive breeding pairs to other farmers. These are livestock pyramid schemes. When I was a child there was the chinchilla rage. Everyone was going to raise chinchillas in their basements and make millions. As with chain letters the only ones who make money in these affairs are those who start the fad. In the years since we purchased Trauma Farm, I've seen Korean pot-bellied pigs, llamas, alpacas, ostriches, yaks, and emus. The original purchase price can range up to $50,000. I know farmers who paid $15,000 for a llama and sold it for $300. They considered themselves

128

lucky to be able to sell it. Ostrich meat is great, and a single egg can feed a family, but the public wasn't ready to buy ostrich meat and the eggshells ended up as ornaments on shelves. I love ostrich meat and I keep an ostrich femur on a shelf behind my desk, but I'd never raise those birds. They have a kick that can drive a farmer through a barn wall. Collecting an egg might get your back broken. Despite all this I can't help but admire the intrepid farmers willing to take on the weird and the wild. One day, another "breeder" might yet become a success, as has happened in the past.

Aside from the peafowl—who have given us more than enough grief—and some exotic chickens, we've stuck to the standard livestock, knowing we couldn't learn all their ways in twenty lifetimes. Every animal that has set hoof or paw or claw on Trauma Farm has been a teacher.

10

FRUIT OF THE WOOD

. . . . .

*H*OWARD, MIKE'S BROTHER, lounged in the old chair beneath the Byrons' carport while I hauled on the handle, squeezing the juice out of the apple mash. "Pull harder!" He laughed like a mad galley-master on a slave ship as I threw a last heave into the press, sweating in the cool October air. This was a decade ago and Howard was in his mid-seventies, wiry and full of laughter, wearing his favourite, frazzled fedora. His ancient giant of a border collie, Big Mac, slept at his feet.

One of the Byron clan that settled the island in the Depression years, he not only worked his own farm but leased several others, running his Jacob sheep—the four-horned bicoloured black-and-white breed whose bizarre face was often used as the face of the devil in Christian iconography—on their fields. He also tended orchards. The

Brown orchard was the biggest, about 150 acres with at least two hundred apple trees.

The domestic apple arrived on Salt Spring around 1860, and our orchards peaked at the turn of that century as land was cleared and fruit planted for the gold rush of '98. A crate of winter apples in a cabin was a miner's source of vitamin C back then. Today Salt Spring is rich with ecologists who have been rebuilding these legacy orchards and planting more heritage fruit. The island is rapidly becoming one of the larger fruit tree resources in North America. There are over 350 varieties of apple on the island.

Snow apples. Spartan, Spy, Winter Banana, Gravenstein, Wolf River, Belle de Boskoop, Ben Davis... The Ben Davis is a legendary hard, winter apple that suddenly sweetens and softens in January. During the Depression boys used them for baseballs until Christmas arrived. Like many winter apples, the Ben Davis travelled well in barrels, but all these apples are increasingly endangered as they are replaced by the sweeter, showier apples designed to match globalization's evolving transportation and cold storage systems. Few farmers like Howard remain. You only had to show him an apple and he could tell you its name, its storage characteristics, and whether it was best for juice, baking, drying, storage, or eating straight up, and he could probably name the girl he gave one to when he was a teenager, after polishing it up on his blue jeans.

We'd picked close to five hundred feed bags full of apples earlier in the week and were only half finished our pressing, sugar-stoned on the juice. Howard could dip his glass into our barrel, taste the juice, and know what variety to mix in. "More Grimes, more Grimes," he'd say, waving his glass about. Then he wanted Wolf River because the flavour was too strong and we needed to thin it with a juicier apple. He was an apple gourmand, and it was a thrill watching him blend our juice while I grunted at the press. "Bring ten more bags of the kings and a couple of Cox's orange pippin. We need to sweeten this batch up." His commands made me recall Thoreau's ageless "Wild Apples" essay: "Almost all wild apples are handsome. They cannot be too gnarly and crabbed and rusty to look at. The gnarliest will have some redeeming traits even to the eye."

We squeezed many hundreds of gallons of juice, more than enough to drink and sell for the winter. So we decided to brew ten gallons of hard cider with the remainder. In one of those unfortunate "inspired" moments I also used the leftover mash to make apple wine. It was the most awful wine I've ever fermented—bittered by the seeds and stems that weren't winnowed out of the mash. Since I'm stubborn, I banged together an improvised still I could perk on the wood stove, and somehow distilled the lousy wine into a great Calvados. It was an apple brandy to die for, literally. I refined fifteen gallons down to six beer bottles of brew that was better than some of the $100 bottles of French Calvados I've tangled with, but the proof level was through the roof, and even watered down it could nearly make you go blind. My liver still quivers at the memory of it. The Calvados was so scarily successful I decided to end my moonshining career after the one batch, and the still went to the dump.

THE TRICK ABOUT GATHERING apples for juice is never to take windfalls, no matter how good they look, because deer graze the orchards, and they can excrete salmonella onto the grass and infect the crop. You won't have trouble if you are clean and careful and keep away from the windfalls. Islanders have been happily drinking unpasteurized apple juice for 150 years, but that's because we're local and small scale. The chances for contamination of big batches of apple juice grow exponentially with the size of the corporation making it, so it's hard to sympathize with our ministries, which are regulating small orchardists out of existence by demanding that we pasteurize our juice, which can't be done economically on such a small scale. Now the good juice is going the way of real milk, underground and through the back door. I buy any extra I need if I can find it. Sudden guerrilla forays of juicers will appear at Fulford Harbour, the word spreads, and everyone rushes down and purchases the juice, usually as a benefit for a local institution. Then everyone disappears before the apple police show up.

When we raised pigs we'd throw the windfalls into their yard, and they'd kick up their heels in delight. Even though their stomachs are similar to ours, they never have trouble eating windfalls. The ancient tradition was to run the pigs in orchards at fall. This is a perfect way of "finishing" the pig and sweetening its flesh, along with cleaning up the orchard. Diet has a terrific effect on meat. "Tell me what you eat, and I'll tell you what you are," the gastronomist Brillat-Savarin said. He knew what he was talking about. A neighbour who had a fish farm once tried raising pigs on his "morts," the dead fish from the aquafarm—killed by seals or otters or whatever—accomplishing two tasks simultaneously, raising the pigs and disposing of the fish waste. Personally, I would have made fish fertilizer. Even though he finished the pigs on a grain and apple diet for their last

133

two months, their meat still tasted so fishy it was inedible. The nature of small farming almost demands brilliant ideas that don't always work, but every once in a while the Dutch hoe or the Leghorn chicken gets invented.

HOWARD DIED THE YEAR after that autumn of many apples. Besides being a great farmer, he was also the island dog catcher. He could be harsh and accurate with the gun, and he was one of the most tender men with animals I ever met. He raised a blind deer and a crippled crow as pets. At Howard's funeral half the community showed up, farmers, loggers, the gay crowd, bikers, sculptors, poets, and developers. It was perhaps the most spectacular assortment of islanders from different worlds I've seen assembled. His beat-up cap was placed on his coffin and when they lowered the coffin into the ground, Mac, his collie, devoted to the end, tried to leap into the grave. There wasn't a dry eye in the crowd.

When they covered him with dirt they were burying an enormous knowledge of apples, sheepdogs, gardening skills, and livestock behaviour—a great raft of pages out of the book of local history. Another library gone to the ground.

134

"WHEN'S THE BEST TIME to prune your fruit trees?" a man asked Mike Byron, an orchardist equal to his brother in knowledge.

"When you have the time," he replied.

The orchard needs to live through four seasons and is both stronger and more tender than we expect. In our temperate climate there's only a couple of months of true dormancy. Pruning is like doing crossword puzzles. It's an art, a drudgery, and a test of decision-making skills. The reasons why some people can't prune are simple—they're either afraid of making decisions or incapable of making them.

Pruning is an easy and meditative art if you have a set of good, sharp tools—a pole pruner with a tip saw, loppers, and a set of bypass hand pruners. A bucket of water mixed with bleach is also good for sterilizing your tools between trees. First, you eliminate the water shoots, those vertical suckers that want to set a new crown; then you remove all your cross-branches and those that rub against each other. On an established tree, this is most of your pruning. If you remove more than a third of the branches, you will inflict excess work on yourself in the following year, since a healthy tree rejects too much pruning and will rebel by shooting up thousands of unruly suckers.

The only time harsh pruning can be justified is if you are dealing with sickness and neglect, such as canker-struck trees or split-limbed, near-fatal damage. Before our apple pressing adventures, I watched Howard Byron spend a couple of years reviving the century-old Brown orchard, which meant, in some cases, chainsawing the trees down to their trunks. I called this the Texas Chainsaw school of tree pruning, which he found amusing. These trees suckered like porcupines and were weak for lack of leaves to feed the roots, but within a few years he recreated the classic fruit tree bowl shape, pruning less each year as the trees renewed.

Well-tended orchards can date back many years. One orchard in England is known to be four centuries old. Most fruit trees will last less than fifty years these days. Modern apples are grafted onto weak, dwarfing rootstock. They fruit sooner and can be planted in less space, and the apples are easy to pick in the industrialized orchards. But they're cultivated with the knowledge that they'll lose their vigour in ten to twenty years. Grafting onto this inferior rootstock is the equivalent of putting a permanent tourniquet on a tree trunk. Fruit farming is no longer a tradition passed on to our children.

A few pruning decisions can backfire, as Sharon discovered once in a battle with tent caterpillars. These caterpillars have a seven-year cycle. If you live with them, they will die out naturally. On about the fifth year of the cycle you will begin to see a dot on the foreheads of the caterpillars. That's the egg of a wasp that lives in a symbiotic relationship with them. As the tent caterpillar population explodes, so does the wasp population—until the wasps kill off almost all the caterpillars and their populations collapse together. This ebb and flood of caterpillars in the orchard is best left alone, though I do tie a propane torch to a stick and burn off the worst masses so they won't set back the trees too hard, yet healthy trees will survive even a complete defoliation. The caterpillar/wasp dance is a circle, and interfering with it by spraying orchards with toxic pesticides will inevitably cause the pest population to mushroom while killing off its control predator.

There was a peak year in the caterpillar cycle that arrived when I was too busy to deal with the critters and they were massacring the orchard. Sharon, worried about the damage, went through the orchard with the loppers, whacking off the limbs bearing the worst of the webbed nests, piling them up, and burning them. A healthy, well-built young pippin had all of its caterpillar nests on one side, so she amputated those branches. The next year the tree suckered excessively on the unpruned side. I spent years attempting to rebalance the lopsided tree—but then the winter snows and windstorms got into the act, breaking the roots on the over-pruned, short side, and it began leaning. I stuck a forked branch under a limb to prop it up, and that's how it remains to this day, ten years later. While the pruning saved the tree from the infestation, it eventually mutilated it. Sharon just frowns during our orchard tours if I dare to compliment her pruning technique on that tree. However, since I've also had a few pruning mishaps I can't tease her too much.

We have several varieties of heritage apples. My favourite is the king apple—a big, sweet fruit. It used to be supreme among market apples before the Macintosh, the Delicious, and the Granny Smith appeared, but since it's susceptible to a condition called water core—its sugar reaches a level that makes the flesh translucent—it has been dropped by the orchard industry.

People are such faddish creatures. The evidence is in the thousands of heirloom fruit trees discarded during the last hundred years. Apples thrived at first in the new colonies of the eastern seaboard, cider apples especially, because the fruit was not eaten so much then. They quickly spread across North America, and the crops reached their peak in the west, where each orchard region planted the currently popular varieties. After Salt Spring's flurry of orchards following colonization, new orchards appeared in Saanich, on Vancouver Island, and they too enjoyed a brief monopoly. As each region and its varieties took over the market, great numbers of the older orchards were uprooted and lost,

137

the varieties made endangered or extinct. When Saanich faded and the subdivisions arrived, the famous orchards of the Canadian Okanagan greened the desert valleys before being overwhelmed by vineyards and more subdivisions. Then Yakima Valley and the surrounding region of Washington State became the apple capital of North America. This is where dwarf fruit trees and enormous orchards first appeared on a scale almost beyond comprehension. Storage and artificial ripening facilities became monopolistic corporations, and the massive chemical spraying of fruit trees began in earnest, wiping out millions of beneficial insects along with pests. These new, industrial-scale orchards also damaged songbird migrations.

Not too long ago you could walk the paved lanes of a Washington cherry orchard and view large cages filled with beautiful birds trapped during their migrations. Every so often a truck would come by, gas them all, collect the dead birds, and carry on. This carnage was merely "good management" for the industry. When the public outcry grew too loud the orchardists converted to the ubiquitous, irritating bird cannons, which randomly explode from dawn to dusk. Now the great orchards of Washington are fighting for their lives as China overwhelms the fruit market with a cheap labour force and few, seldom enforced environmental regulations. In twenty years China has become the world's largest supplier of apples and many other fruits. At present, it enjoys 40 percent of world sales.

THE APPLE GROWS WILD, but because our species considers the natural world too inefficient, we insist on breeding it better, curing its flaws. Generally this works—expert breeders have created impressive hybrids—though great varieties have also been found in "sports"—natural deviations that appear often in the ditches alongside orchards. We once had a Gravenstein cross surface among the thick branches of a *Magnolia grandiflora*. It's delicious.

While the industrial orchardists are lining up their super-sweet dwarf varieties, a few rural people retain the old ways—the science of tradition—which can be breathtakingly intelligent and, alas, sometimes superstitious and goofy. You always take your chances when you walk in the waters of tradition, but they are usually warm waters, and that's why they are tradition.

Harry Burton and his wife, Debbie, are south islanders who grow apples in an orchard that's neither traditional nor rigorously scientific, yet their orchard makes a marvellous, intuitive sense, so maybe that means they're traditionalists. I'm a big admirer of Harry and Debbie's technique. Since Harry is the more public figure of the couple I'll describe "his" approach.

First he plants his trees. Then he lets whatever weed or shrub naturally appears there grow around them. This includes thistles, which attract aphids, and nettles. These attract beneficial ladybugs that eat the aphids. There are salmonberries and mostly blackberries. He keeps manure tea barrels for irrigation and scatters oyster shells for calcium and phosphorus and other minerals. West Coast farmers spend their lives failing to eradicate the pernicious Himalayan blackberries that invaded the region after they were introduced in 1885. Harry lets them do his work for him. They shade the ground, their winter droppings of

139

leaves feed the soil, and they retain moisture. This is a cultivation methodology that comes out of long experience. The richest earth I ever encountered was the soil under a blackberry bramble.

Add some manure and seaweed and the trees are fat with apples. He mows once a year, and occasionally clears a space around the trees and pathways with his machete. Otherwise, he lets the ecosystem manage his orchard. He's rewarded with healthy, semi-unpruned trees, leaning and propped up in all directions, and an awesome blackberry harvest. He is also trying out different varieties, as he studies what apples thrive best in our environment. Lately, a winery in the valley has discovered that blackberries make an impressive port. So now this invasive berry is in high demand. A farmer's world is always full of surprises.

A century ago there was 180,000 acres of orchard in England. Today, there's less than 47,000. Preservationists estimate eight hundred varieties have gone extinct since the days of America's Johnny Appleseed, who planted apple seeds rather than grafting proven tree scions onto rootstock, because of his Swedenborgian religious belief that grafting was a form of wounding a natural creation. He knew the apple doesn't seed true, and planting seeds created greater diversity in nature. Legend claims that he planted the seed that became the Grimes golden, discovered by Thomas Grimes in 1832 in West Virginia. The Grimes golden went on to become the parent of the Golden Delicious.

The wild apple, *Malus sylvestris*, lives yet in the Caucasus. And I like to remember that an apple orchard was first mentioned in Homer. Despite the escalating loss of heirloom apples, I've read there could still be as many as ten thousand varieties remaining, a quarter of them in England alone. The great era of the English apple was the eighteenth century, during the cider craze. Over ten thousand hogsheads—about a million gallons—of cider was brewed every year in just the small county of Worcestershire.

THOUGH WE FAVOUR APPLE trees, we also grow a mixed orchard of cherries, pears, almonds, hazelnuts, and plums. The ravens, crows, and starlings are quick to clean out the cherries, even when we net the trees, so we are lucky to salvage more than a handful. I keep planting more trees, operating on the time-honoured farm tradition that I can "outplant the bastards." The theory is that eventually there will be more fruit than they can eat. The birds appreciate this deranged delusion. They also will take the pears if we don't harvest quickly enough. These birds might not realize it, but they're fortunate we aren't a modern, industrial orchard.

TWO YEARS AGO SHARON and I motored up to the Okanagan. It was the height of cherry season, and we bought a box of big, glistening Lamberts. Sharon dived into the unwashed fruit as we returned to our lodgings. They were too pretty to resist. Later in the evening her throat and upper chest turned a bright pink. That night her throat started to swell as the allergic reaction spread. A dose of antihistamine rescued her.

Canadian government regulations now specify that each orchard carry a record of its spraying programs posted visibly around its perimeter. The next day, on our way back to the George Ryga House (an artists' retreat named after the fine writer who once lived there), where we were staying, I noticed an orchard of dwarf Lambert cherry trees. The berries were full and sweet looking. I would have picked them if they had been my trees. But there was something artificial about these glowing trees in the blue dusk. I got out of the car and read the long list of spraying applications on the post. It was daunting: pesticides, fungicides, herbicides, including things like cholinesterase inhibitors, which could shut down the liver. These neurotoxins are components of biochemical weapons (such as sarin gas) and snake venom. Despite the apparent ripeness of the fruit, the instructions for final spraying specified that no one was to enter the orchard for a further eight days without wearing a full anti-contamination suit. I guess on the ninth day they sell the cherries to foolish victims like us.

A young friend who has just done a stint of cherry picking in the Okanagan told me that after only a few days the skin sloughed off his hands, so he quit. These could have been the same cherries that attacked Sharon's throat. The spraying regimes for other fruit are equally scary.

"Don't eat the apple!" For the first time in history that phrase has more than mythological meaning. The tree of knowledge that Adam and Eve ate from has proved dangerous indeed. When I think of our fresh, sweet fruit at Trauma Farm, I realize how privileged we have become in a society so immersed in poisons that supermarkets are now selling chemicals to detoxify the chemicals on fruit and vegetables.

Since many fruit varieties need to be cross-pollinated by another variety, we planted trees whose blossoming periods matched. This also allows us to enjoy extended colour

during the long, slow spring of our climate: the first ornamental plums of the garden crack pink early in March,
along with the stunning almond trees, followed by the
fruiting plums, pears, cherries, ornamental chestnuts, pear-
apples, and apples. It would be a pleasure for the flowers
alone. The fruit is a bonus. On sunny days the orchard is
alive with our honeybees and the more efficient solitary
orchard mason bees, each of which can pollinate thirty
times as many blossoms as a European honeybee.

I love the river of fruit and nuts that begins in July, when
we collect our few cherries and the golden egg plums adorn
the green leaves, reminding me of a Christmas tree with
only one colour of bulb. And the red blush on the yellow
Canors! The late, great crop of Italian prune plums. They
all come in their time, and it remains one of the joys of life
on this planet to stroll through an orchard over several
months and to finally reach up and pull down a ripe fruit.

We have close to a dozen fig trees in two varieties, Turkish brown and what might be a variant of desert king. My
late Italian uncle, Giuseppe, gave me a half-dozen cuttings
of the latter—about six inches long—which I merely stuck in
the ground, according to his instructions. They all sprouted
and thrived in the spring. He told me they came from the
old country—one of the many varieties brought over in the
pockets of impoverished immigrants. Most failed, but this
variety flourished and was passed through the community.
Now it dominates the Italian backyards of Vancouver, and I
pass along the vigorous cuttings in spring to islanders.

The fig is a sensual fruit. It's the oldest living tree whose
planting date is known. The Sri Maha Bodhi of Sri Lanka
was planted by King Tissa in 288 BC. Technically, the fig
isn't a fruit but a flower, and it is one of the kinkier plants

in the kingdom of flora. If you want to get very technical, it's not even a flower but a false fruit, a mass of flowers and seeds merging together; and, even stranger, it's part insect, since it contains minuscule wasps that crawl inside and pollinate and die in its ecstatic embrace, every tiny thread pollinated by a wasp. It's a meaty fruit indeed. And different varieties are pollinated by specific wasps, so I would suspect my uncles somehow brought the wasp eggs with them, accidentally, or a variety of wasp that already existed on the North American continent got along just fine with this green fruit from the mountain regions of Basilicata in southern Italy.

One of the encounters of autumn is the battle with the chattering Steller's jays. Brilliant blue bandits, their obnoxious cries signal that the hazelnuts are ripe, and the race is on. As soon as Sharon hears them she sends me up the tree with the ladder, grabbing nuts while the jays scream at me, often from the same branch, and the dogs scurry below, happily collecting whatever falls in the fracas, then go running off to crack and devour the nuts themselves. Despite this melee we usually manage to save enough for winter. In a few years, as more hazelnut trees come to prime, we will have many nuts, and sell them. Even the strong beaks of jays can't crack our almonds, so those trees give us both almonds and their fragrant pink blossoms. We lost one of my walnut pollinators to drought and thoughtlessness and had to replant it last year. It will take ten years to bear nuts, but I'm hoping it will pollinate its large partner sooner.

OCCASIONALLY PEOPLE ASK ME why, as I approach sixty, I'm still planting fruit and nut trees, some of which won't bear for ten to fifteen years, if then. So I tell them an old Arab story I heard decades ago.

While the sultan was travelling he noticed an old man in a field, planting olive tree seedlings. This aroused the sultan's curiosity, and he stopped to talk to him. "Old man, why are you planting olive trees when you won't live long enough to see them bear fruit?"

The old man said, "Sire, I am planting for my children as my father planted for me."

This made the sultan happy and he said, "Sir, if your fortune allows you to live long enough for these trees to bear fruit, bring the first bushel to me." Then he travelled on and forgot about the incident until many years later an ancient man arrived at his palace, declaring the sultan had instructed him to bring a bushel of olives. The sultan remembered him, and when he saw that the farmer had actually lived to see the fruit of his labour he was so pleased he had the olives in the bushel replaced with gold. The old man left enormously grateful that his labour had earned him and his children wealth beyond their dreams.

The next day a young courtier purchased a bushel of olives in the market and brought it to the sultan. "What is this?" asked the sultan.

"When I saw you reward that old man with gold for his olives, I thought I would bring a bushel also," the clueless young courtier replied. He was promptly stripped and whipped and tossed out in the street.

I have always understood that the continuum of time planted this garden for us to celebrate, and it would be shoddy not to enrich it for those who will arrive after I'm gone. During our years on Trauma Farm we have already created a living, growing wealth on this land. When the future arrives I would like its children to find themselves rich with grapes, persimmons, olives, walnuts, king apples, golden egg plums, dark wine and honey, cherries, sweet figs....

11

WHO'S FOR LUNCH?

· · · · ·

*O*VER THE HILLS and into the trees we ran. I was clutching an enormous sun-warmed watermelon. The farmer's tractor grumbled across the field, its dust rising like a nuclear doom-cloud. Did he see me? I loved the taste of fear in my mouth when I ducked down the ravine, tripped on a root, and fell with a sternum-numbing thud beside the creek, my hands outstretched, as if offering the watermelon to the god of garden raiders, or at least my two friends, whose eyes widened as they watched me sail through the air with our stolen treasure. The backs of my hands slapped the earth—the watermelon cracked in half.

I was trying to laugh and breathe simultaneously. My aching chest! I loved the panic on my friends' faces before they shifted to delight, snatching the halves and scooping out fistfuls of the red flesh while I tried to suck back the wind whacked out of me. Soon I joined them, and we passed the shells, biting into our juicy, sticky chunks. It was so sweet I felt stoned on the sugar, or maybe it was the thrill of the run and the clearness of the air and the pale armour of a crayfish haunting the stones in the creek bed. Our elders always told us forbidden fruit is the best. We are hard-wired to the taste of the taboo.

I was a prince of garden thieves in my childhood. Plums were a great prize. We'd wait for a tree down the lane to ripen, and then one day, like raccoons that can sense you're ready to harvest your fruit, we'd swarm the tree. For a few moments it would shiver with children, branches breaking, plums falling everywhere. Then we'd flee, screaming, our T-shirts bellied with plums. Strawberries, sweet tomatoes, raw corn—we'd raid them all. Carrots were another favourite. I'd just wipe the dirt off on my jeans. People grew real carrots then—fresh and young, they tasted nothing like those woody orange sticks in today's supermarket. I look back upon those thieving years with a mixture of horror and bemusement at the greedy insouciance of a troubled child—and the lost tastes of an era when the tongue commanded and the food was uncontaminated.

Today, almost fifty years later, I will have a simple lunch again, though more civilized—bread and soup and greens and a handful of fresh everbearing strawberries. It seems so basic, almost boring, though the infrastructure behind this lunch is complex, prehistoric, and world-striding.

I make a notorious "bitter salad" that I seldom inflict on my friends, yet it thrills me. Its simplicity is its joy. Shallots, a serrated-leaf variety of endive—Tosca or frisée —though their seeds are also difficult to find in today's shrinking seed catalogues. Perhaps some *mizuna* and a little radicchio. I slice the shallots thinly. We grow three varieties, each with its own taste, size, colour. Then I toss them among the ripped greens, add a vinaigrette, and sprinkle it with "raked" salt and fresh-ground pepper. It takes minutes to prepare, yet describing this salad makes it sound like a dish that would cost you a fortune in a pretentious restaurant. That's because it actually is an exotic creation—the ingredients gathered from the fringes of the world. The salt from a Portuguese beach, the endive and radicchio descendants of the chicory of Rome. *Mizuna* is a Japanese variant of *Brassica rapa*. The shallots, like most alliums, are from the steppes of Asia. It's a bunching onion, more tender, sweeter, and less hot than your average onion, which is why it entered my salad. The olive oil is from Italy, and the wine vinegar was made by a friend in Toronto who keeps a perpetual small keg in his kitchen and doles out bottles to his friends when they grow desperate.

We've already eaten all our Belgian endives, which we dig up every fall and behead and then plant with their crowns a foot underground. They sprout, pale beneath the earth, like bright bones, in the spring. Earth-blanched endives are outrageously tender, with only a suggestion of bitterness, and I eat them like candy, often scooping them out of the mud, wiping them off on my jeans, and devouring them raw in the garden, a child again.

But how difficult it is to be a child today. Deceptively beautiful yet potentially toxic fields and orchards can lure unsuspecting children with their poisoned fruit. Our orchard borders a relatively untravelled gravel road, though we've still had a couple of minor orchard raids. I'm grateful

149

the neighbourhood children know us well enough to trust that our fruit won't be sprayed, and I enjoyed scaring the piss out of them the one time I caught them. That's part of the social role of a good farmer.

Even twenty years ago in Third World countries you'd encounter honest, tasty produce like ours, but because of globalization the food supply is rapidly becoming scary worldwide. Eating in countries like China or Mexico has become a form of Russian roulette. Too many Third World nations are short on environmental regulations and enforcement, and toxins are slopped around indiscriminately; uneducated workers operate on the principle that if a little poison works well, a lot of poison will really do the job. Oddly, in impoverished regions, if the farmers are too poor to buy pesticides and fertilizers, their produce is clean.

The red earth of Cuba, where the American embargo has restricted oil-based fertilizers and pesticides, vibrates with life. It reminded me of mescaline trips in the sixties. I've never seen such verdant gardens so laden with giant vegetables, hand cultivated and healthy. Using real ingredients, the cooking in Cuba is plain yet wholesome. Only as income and trade routes improve do farm recipes grow as complex as ours.

Mike Byron says his family moved to this island during the Depression with eleven chickens. They were so poor they couldn't eat the eggs but sold them for money for essentials. They made a deal with a neighbouring farmer to dig his potatoes, and for their labour they got enough potatoes to eat. They also milked the farmer's cow while he took his crops to market off-island, and were paid with the milk. So they survived their first year on potatoes and occasional bounties of milk, along with whatever produce and fruit and venison they could scrabble up. When considering farm food and the multiple paths of human history it's so easy to generalize, and idealize, assuming that American and Old World local farmers or Chinese peasants or corn-eating Navajos lived healthier lives than we do today.

I look at my aesthetic salad again and start to feel embarrassed, so Sharon takes over. We don't often lunch together except during family events but she's here today, sweetening my bitter creation with tomatoes and herbs, a salad we can both enjoy, and I'm being pushed aside like an old and frail ewe being edged out of the feed trough.

Though we have conflicting tastes on a very few occasions, at least we haven't joined the tracksuit-wearing porkers trolling today's supermarkets, loading their carts with cardboard vegetables, tasteless meat, colourful boxes, and cans of processed junk cranked up with preservatives and additives—and the terrible triad of salt, sugar, and fat. We live in an era when people are so confused about nutrition that British mothers were recently caught concealing chocolate bars in their children's clothes after the schools banned junk food. The ignorant mothers feared their children "wouldn't get enough to eat." The era when children actually stole vegetables has gone with the dinosaurs.

Not only are hybrid vegetables in the stores relatively tasteless, they are also diminishing nutritionally along with their soil, as a result of single-cropping (the large-scale farming of only one crop rather than growing mixed and rotated plantings), which depends on oil-based chemicals and treats the soil as an engineered growing medium. Several recent studies demonstrate that some vegetables in Britain have lost one-quarter of their magnesium and iron and almost half of their calcium. Distance between the grower and the eater also depletes flavour and nutrition in produce after it's harvested—except for a few rare plants or fruits, such as winter apples, that need storage to reach their prime. Today's food is being shipped bizarrely around the world. West Coast hothouse tomatoes are sold in New York, and the salad greens of temperate Vancouver are imported from China or Mexico. Retailers prefer pretty vegetables and fruits that can be stored and shipped. It's cost-effective, even if they taste like cardboard. During the last fifty years we bought with our eyes, not our stomachs, until the local-food movement and the recent gourmet revolution in America combined forces.

SEVERAL YEARS AGO SHARON and I served a meal in honour of a visiting Italian poetry professor. Another guest complimented our cooking and asked the professor what he thought of the food. The professor snorted extravagantly: "It's easy to cook a meal like this." Our friend was aghast at his cavalier remark, but I laughed because I knew exactly what he meant. He was a true epicure. "How can they go wrong?" he blustered on, realizing his words had been misinterpreted. "Our hosts have real food, vegetables and fruits straight from the garden, meat from their land. These are the ingredients of the best meals. Only a bad cook could ruin them." He was right, and so very Italian.

I try not to gather our produce until we eat. We are fortunate to live in a climate where we can grow crops year-round, though we have to cloche the more delicate winter greens. This good fortune allows me to go out on a cold, dark evening and gather the precious leaves of *mizuna, gai lin, mei king choi,* and carrots under their mulch of seedless canary grass. We also grow and store good winter root vegetables.

My favourite vegetable is cob corn in September. I eat it raw in the garden, a leftover childhood habit. The traditional varieties are now known as "cow corn" because they're used to fatten up the unfortunate cattle in feedlots. We still grow old-fashioned cobs, though they're becoming extinct because the seed industries are eliminating most varieties from the market. The new, small-kernelled supersweets are too much like mushy candy for my taste. They don't have enough texture and density; Sharon is addicted to them, however, and we have to plant multiple varieties to satisfy us both. Corn is also determinate, which means each variety ripens in a certain number of days, so we grow early, mid-season, and late corn, ensuring a continuous supply and a few torchy discussions as we trade off favourites during seed ordering.

The sugar in corn begins turning to starch as soon as it's picked. That's why the hybrid super-sweets are grown for the public, because these can store for several days and still taste sweet, but a good cow corn, which has texture and density, is their equal when fresh off the stalk. Though I'm not fanatic enough to set up a corn pot on a propane burner in the garden next to the plant, shuck the cob on the stalk, and dip it into the boiling water, I've considered it.

153

IN TODAY'S ESCALATING FOOD debate, the slow-food and environmental movements have begun to spread a false mythology about traditional food in the same way that pan-nativism has occasionally created false impressions about ecological Natives and "recalled" traditional practices. There was a time when people lived as the land gave. Before farming, hunter-gatherer societies around the world spent the greater part of their days gathering food, since preservation was difficult. It took hundreds of thousands of years to learn how salt could preserve flesh and produce, in tandem with drying or smoking. Salt turned the abattoir into a strange kind of commercial temple, and in some cultures the abattoirs actually became temples. *Salaam,* the Arabic term for peace, derived from a word for negotiations over salt.

Wheat and barley in the Mideast, beans and corn and squash in America, rice in Asia—each began whittling away the permaculture that was the original history of our species. All of these are annual farm crops. They demanded the breaking of soil, the retaining of seed, and storage of the crop, which eventually required an infrastructure.

Thus began the transition from hunter-gatherer societies toward stable villages and small farms. Agriculture allowed human populations to grow beyond what wild land could sustain. It also created a need for crop storage as a survival tool against natural disasters like droughts and harsh winters. Once you begin storing produce and supplies, you need record keeping, and thus writing came into its own. The ability to keep records and communicate over long distances as well as record history allowed the unecological, exponential growth of our species, creating additional farms, villages; then cities arrived—filling up the planet while we contrived the impossible dream of endless growth, our tools and technology evolving faster than our social structures and brains. This is a mightily generalized history of 3 million years, and like most generalized histories it is dangerous. But sometimes we get so wrapped up in the details we forget the whole. If we consider the time our species has spent on earth as a single day, twenty-three hours were expended in hunting and gathering, about fifty-nine minutes on small farming, and one minute on industrial agribusiness.

THE SOUP FOR OUR lunch? Well, that's a history which needs telling. I look at it steaming on the wood stove. Is a soup just a watery stew? Did it originate, like tea, when the first leaf fell into a earthenware pot of steaming water? Did someone throw too much water into the first gruels, and was he too hungry to wait for them to boil down? Or maybe gruel came out of a broth of grains boiled down. Or did the soup arrive even earlier, a cave mother scooping up the last of the cold greasy boar and brilliantly deciding to melt the fat off in a gourd full of hot water in the warm ashes? Human history is the history of soup, among many other histories, and the variations are beyond cataloguing.

When I first met Sharon she was an uneven cook with a tendency to torture a beef bone and some noodles into a gelatinous soup. What can I say? She was from Thunder Bay. After I introduced her to the idea of terroir, food grown naturally in its region, and to the ethnic cuisines that enthralled me, her natural intelligence caught on quickly, and she soon became the master of our dinners, though she still has dangerous tendencies to invent recipes before she looks at a cookbook—a practice that leads to delicious new combinations, although it can also give me crossed eyes and much hamming of a death by poisoning. One of the pleasures of our relationship, for me, has been the opportunity to introduce her to fine cooking, and then watch her surpass me.

Born of this new generation spoiled by global trade and travel, we make Thai *tom yum* soup, Mexican chicken broths with chickpeas, and creamed European soups, vegetarian or with meat. We often cook together, and this can lead to differences of opinion, sometimes amiable, sometimes not. I tell her cooking is a contact sport, a statement that usually gets me the evil eye.

But I continue in my ways. I keep the corpses of scrawny old hens in the freezer, beside the bones of game or pork or beef. Chicken feet make the ultimate broth. When we feast on crabs I've captured on the beach at low tide, we boil the shells and detritus after dinner with garlic and herbs and then freeze the broth for a good bisque. Generally, we make our soup bases in winter and freeze them. The wood cookstove in the kitchen not only simmers our broths but heats both the house and our hot water via a complex series of pipes recycling the water through a preheater that leads to our hot-water tank. A good soup simmering on the stove is an ancient cultural pleasure.

The chicken broth can be difficult because our old, tough hens—pot chickens—are too delicious and tender upon finally hauling them out to cool and debone. A little salt, and we start picking at the carcass—an addictive behaviour—and before we know it there's no meat to add back to the soup.

The trick about a traditional broth is never to boil it, which clouds the broth. Then we add every old vegetable within reach, clearing out the fridge or the reedy remnants from the garden, along with chopped garlic and tomatoes that we sun-dry or dehydrate in the summer and use all year long, and leaves from our bay tree and fresh herbs. (If it's for our vegetarian grandchildren, we omit the meat base.) After we cool this concoction in the greenhouse overnight, we skim the fat and strain out the cooked-down vegetables. If we want a minestrone, then we'll add fresh, finely chopped vegetables and boil semolina noodles in another pot (I can't abide overcooked noodles in a minestrone; they add a wheaty taste to the broth).

There's nothing like a traditional broth and fresh vegetables and noodles. I rip off a hunk of bread and slather it with butter or dry-dip it and eat two-handed—bread crust in one and soup spoon in the other. Soup and bread are only a variation on each other, the soup a watery gruel and the bread a baked gruel. Thousands of years of cookery have merely refined the recipes.

An eccentric way to imagine the invention of bread is via a grain soup that was left out too long and then fermented. Afterwards it was dried and baked. More likely it was a slurp of old soupy gruel splashed on a hot rock on a fire. Flatbread! Bread, soup or gruel, and beer all apparently arrived around 10,000 BC. The fungi that fell out of the air into the batter and made sourdough have taken bread making through some exotic changes around the world. Bread has even driven people to madness and convulsions in what's known as St. Vitus's dance—if they ate rye bread infected with the ergot mould, which is related to LSD. At least our modern breads have revived since the sliced Wonder Bread hysteria that began in the 1930s and sped as fast as a yeast strain across North America and England.

Bread is alive like clay. Just as potters will tell you that a pot never stops firing, a great bread never ceases its transformations. The yeast fungi are one of our earliest domesticated organisms. Let them loose in wet or sprouted grain, and they develop a kaleidoscope of tastes.

In the seventies I possessed a sourdough from the California gold rush of 1848, or so I was told when it was passed on to me almost like a hallowed relic—a finger bone of the bread Buddha. You can imagine my guilt after I murdered it with neglect in my refrigerator. My latest sourdough is merely a baby. I began it with potato water and a few ironic prayers less than a decade ago, but it has some life and is slowly building up a range of tastes. I make a complex ciabatta bread with it. My focaccia I inherited from my mother. It resembles a modern two-thirds whole-wheat flatbread, pounded flat and basted in olive oil, sprinkled with garlic, salt, oregano, and basil. The good news about this bread is that if it's left out to dry it still tastes good, chewy and filling, and perfect for soup dipping—the chewier the better.

When we are in a frenzy of cooking, especially if the grandchildren are about, we all get together for focaccia nights, where everyone sprinkles the flatbread with a topping of his or her choice. During my childhood this was how my mother made pizza, layering the focaccia with ground hamburger and tomato sauce, cheese, and spices. I favour mine with sliced tomatoes and the original ingredients, though truthfully, I like the simple herb base best, without the tomatoes. But I've been tempted by black olives and pickled artichoke hearts and feta sprinklings, smoked salmon and onion slices. The choice is endless, depending on what's in the refrigerator, and I thrill to watch the grandchildren invent a new topping when they arrive at the farm. We bake flatbreads on a round pizza stone given to us by a good friend, and if we need more bread I gather kiln shelves from my pottery studio and use them. A stone is always better than a pan.

Bread is the stuff of civilization and family. It's a communal dish that's gone through a million mythologies and rituals. Turn around and someone will stick a biscuit in your mouth and call it the body of a god. It's also the base rate by which most civilizations judge themselves. When the bread ran out the cities died. The Egyptians made their bread in such vast quantities that illustrations show bakers kneading vats of dough with hoes. Our granddaughter Jenna, mucking sauces onto the dough, or the astonished expression on the face of our grandson, Aubrey, as he bites into an olive and anchovy pizza topping—they are just a continuation of the great tradition.

SHARON HAS GONE BACK to the garden. I am alone savouring my bean soup, salad, and focaccia. I feel like a thief because I know that this is a rich feast for a man in debt, and that I am lucky enough to live in a time when even a low-income farmer can eat like the wealthy if he has his wits about him. Maybe this is why we farm. I also recognize this simple meal is a form of gluttony. Despite my futile attempts at ecological living, I am still looting the planet— the sources of my "basic" lunch circling the world, like my breakfast. How complex the simple lunch has become.

Now I've spilled soup down my shirt front. I'm an enthusiastic eater and accidents happen. I'm so full I'm starting to think about a nap. This tendency is known medically as "dumping." The word scares me. I better get outside and working before I fall victim to the hazards of a fat lunch, which is why many farmers I know will only stop for an apple or a handful of plums and a cup of tea. They are smarter than I am. And instead of contemplating the work that needs to be done, I'm thinking about the food in my belly and on the table, its provenance and its structure— these variations on the vast palate of my species. We are grazers of enormous range and tastes. But I will save the meat that surrounds the good bones for dinner.

12

SEEDS OF THE DAY

. . . . . .

$\mathcal{I}$ WAS STANDING WITH my arm around Sharon's shoulder on the front deck on a romantic summer afternoon, the year after we arrived at the farm, watching the sky turn white as gusts of thistledown blew across the pasture like snow out of season. Since then, every year, skies of seeds and pollen have whirled around us, whether it's the whirligigs of maple seeds, the fluff of dandelions, or the rich yellow pollen of Douglas fir. Within the richness of summer the land is always planning for winter and, more importantly, the next spring. Now that the horses are gone in this eighteen-year-long day at the farm, the thistles are returning, and we have to remember the ancient farmer's charm, which only works with back-breaking labour. And one missed year forces you to start all over again:

> *Cut thistles in May, they'll be back in a day.*
> (They resprout.)

Cut thistles in June, they'll be back soon.
(They resprout, though weaker.)

Cut thistles in July, then they'll die.
(They don't resprout and they don't seed.)

SEEDS WILL DISPERSE IN many ways. They fall to the ground and scatter their genetics a few inches. They drift high in the air and float across oceans or hook onto fur or skin or clothes or hair. They explode in every direction. They are eaten by birds and deer and civets and shat in a distant valley after, travelling with their hosts. They rot in their fruit and rise into giant trees born of decay. Seeds are patient. Some survive a century until they decide conditions are right. I've encountered domesticated plants that must have come from miles away sprouting among our vegetables. No wonder the Mayans declared seeds the "spiral of life."

Aside from lichens, fungi, algae, rusts, ferns, and their ilk, all the plants around us are born of seed—the germ. The germ was once a beautiful creature, until 140 years ago, when the word was first used to label a disease rather than a source of life. My *Oxford* tells me that a germ is capable of developing into a new organism, as well as being an elementary principle or an original idea. *Germ* derived from the Latin word for "sprouting." Out of a tiny germ is born the giant sequoia.

There's no knowing when the first astute neolithic hunter-gatherer recognized that those little things falling off a plant would become another plant next spring. It was probably a woman, as women were almost universally the

162

gatherers in pre-agrarian societies. We do know that plants were found in a sixty-thousand-year-old grave in Shanidar, Iraq, and some had medicinal uses, so they were probably collected. Wild wheat has been found in paleolithic sites. Emmer and Einkorn wheat are the most ancient grains. Black Einkorn is still grown in Ethiopia, and we regularly seed a row in our garden because it is a lovely ornamental with feathery bracts and kinked stems.

Another archaeological discovery was a man christened Otzi—his 5,300-year-old tattooed corpse was found frozen in a glacier in the Otzal Alps. It's believed he fled into the mountain heights after a violent encounter, tried to build a new bow, and then set all his gear down and quietly bled to death. An analysis of his stomach contents shows his last meal was venison and an unleavened bread made out of Einkorn grain. That strikes me as a fair last meal.

We got our Einkorn seeds from Dan Jason's renowned Salt Spring Seeds. Dan is a tall, likeable man operating his worldwide network out of a small island residence and, with the help of growers across North America, building a web of gardens that provide heirloom seeds to North America, Europe, China, India, Africa, and Australia. He specializes in beans and seed garlic, though he now stocks more than seven hundred varieties of vegetables and flowers. An avid gardener, he was one of the earliest of my generation to recognize the looming extinction of seeds and to do something about it.

Despite their beauty and variety, seeds are being intentionally eliminated by agribusinesses. Their variety alone is the bane of the factory farm. There's even a seed potato that's illegal to sell in Canada because its tough, ropy leafage tangles up large machines. Canada's Department of

Agriculture and Agri-Food, in its eagerness to support industrial farming, has been attempting to drive this potato into extinction for at least twenty-five years, but the Caribou potato has proved remarkably government-resistant. Developed a century ago by a hermit living in a wilderness cabin, it's a delicious, crisp-fleshed, winter-keeping potato. Although you can be arrested for selling it, farmers have discovered it's not illegal to give someone four potatoes for "experimental cultivation purposes." The more the potato police try to enforce the law, the more the potato spreads. The Caribou potato has become a matter of principle among guerrilla gardeners and a protest against our government's agricultural policies.

SOMETIMES AT NIGHT, AFTER I shut my eyes, I dream of the dark earth, its texture—life, marauding earthworms, mycelium spreading, microbes, bacteria. This is the home of our major crop at present, garlic—*Allium sativum*—the "stinking rose." A different kind of seed, resembling an elongated pearl, the garlic clove grows and divides and builds a bulb filled with what could be the greatest assortment of medicinal compounds ever in a single living organism. It's a food, a spice, a cure.

Garlic, like corn, wants a friend—to dig up the bulb, separate the cloves, and transplant it. Forgotten in the ground for a second year, each clove will attempt a bulb in confined circumstances, some rotting, some sprouting simultaneously. Without us it would undoubtedly devolve into a few survivors with tiny bulbs struggling on an unknown steppe, as the wild form, *Allium longicuspis,* did for centuries. I would love to have known that first brave individual who stuffed a whole roasted chicken with garlic bulbs. Originally garlic released seeds, but we tried to breed evolution out of garlic, creating seedless bulbs in the hills. A lot of good that did. Over the years the seedless clones evolved in our gardens, using gardeners as tools to help diversify.

There are two major subspecies of cultivated garlic and an impossible number of varieties. Despite, or maybe because of, thousands of years of cultivation, garlic nomenclature is a confusing mess—imagine a seed catalogue that lists tomatoes by their colours or by the countries where they're grown. Sharon and I grow nine kinds at present. Observant people can easily tell the difference between the soft-necks and the rocamboles. The hard-necked rocamboles form miniature bulbil stalks like twisting serpents; after that, identifying a garlic becomes a dicey business.

Earlier I mentioned the complexity of farming. It's a surrealistic house in the world, doors leading to rooms with other doors, stairs going up and down, rooms inside rooms, all lateral or converse to our demands. Seeds are such an endeavour, and garlic is a great seed, maybe because the clove is not even a real seed, though we call it that. It has many rooms within the haunted house of stories where we were born. According to Herodotus, garlic was fed to the slaves who erected the great pyramid of Cheops, and the first recorded strike in history occurred when the workers were deprived of their daily ration of this energy-giving herb and staged a wildcat walkout. It's commonly believed that garlic originated in the Eurasian steppe and was cultivated as long as ten thousand years ago. A fine storing bulb, it followed nomadic hunter-gatherers, invaded with Genghis Khan and Alexander the Great, and returned with Marco Polo. Mention has been discovered in Sanskrit writings, on clay tablets and papyrus, and in ancient versions of China's reputedly 4,500-year-old Hsia agricultural/astrological calendar. The price of an Egyptian slave was fifteen pounds of garlic.

Garlic's healing powers have been extolled since history began. My diminutive Italian uncle, even in his sixties, was a terror on his dancing feet. But after suffering a heart attack and recovering slowly, he could hardly walk, was depressed, and decided his dancing days were over. Then I saw him months later. He was a ball of fire. Entering the room he immediately challenged me to a boxing match. I was shocked by this resurrection. After much cajoling I learned what had put the Italian back in the Italian. Garlic! He'd encountered an old family healing legend about finely slicing a raw clove of garlic into a cup of warm milk each morning.

There are thousands of folkloric claims for garlic's curative powers. Its ingredients and the ways they break down are so complex they're difficult to analyze. Garlic's major power lies in a compound called allicin, which is also responsible for the notorious odour. This highly unstable substance can dissolve into a maze of pharmacological activities, trace elements, and healthful supplements. Garlic's antioxidants slow the deterioration of the brain in rats with a syndrome that resembles Alzheimer's. And to top everything, it appears to help the brain's serotonin system in controlling depression. That's right; its enthusiasts claim garlic can even make you happy.

GARLIC IS PLANTED IN the fall—when the ground is cooling and the leaves are turning. Since we have wet winters, we trench around our raised beds to drain the water away during rainstorms—after we've mixed in our rock phosphate, ashes, kelp, composts, and manure. First we break the bulbs apart, discarding the diseased; then we dibble the ground and plant the cloves two or three inches into the earth, where they will send out their roots, sucking up nutrition. You should plant your clove base-down and pointing at the sky above, though legend has it that a wrongly planted clove can do a backflip underground during a good winter.

A couple dozen cloves of garlic grow easily, promising wealth for new farmers. However, garlic is a sensitive, labour-intensive crop, as you soon learn while breaking thousands of bulbs into cloves for planting. Sharon gets tendinitis every autumn. A single bulb dries beautifully. Five thousand bulbs need a barn, drying racks, fans, and an absence of rain in the two weeks before harvest. Like a good, maturing wine, the bulbs demand proper storage. They also need workers to trim the roots, peel the dirty outer skins, sort according to size, and discard the sick bulbs that might infect the drying shed with bacteria. For a plant with so many medicinal properties, garlic is surprisingly prone to disease. White smut can infect a field for at least seven years. That fungus blew through our islands like a storm ten years back. Good luck and good drainage saved us, but a few friends still cannot grow garlic without having it rot into guck in the ground.

WE ALSO GROW PEPPER and tomato seeds for Salt Spring Seeds. I love my peppers many ways: fresh in a salad, baked, stuffed, preserved in olive oil, or stir-fried in a black-bean or Szechuan sauce. We grow heritage varieties to eat as well as sell their seeds. I once abhorred hot foods because I'd grown up living in a macho culture where burning your tongue with chili sauce was considered a culinary high. Ugh! Then I went to China. Tasting real Szechuan sauce, I instantly understood how a hot sauce can make flavours explode and unfold into complex variations.

Tomatoes are another of our favourite seeds. Today Sharon cultivates and collects about eight varieties. Along with the pepper, the tomato originated in the Americas—probably on the west coast of South America, where ten varieties still grow wild in the Andes. Once called the love apple, the tomato was first regarded as poisonous by North American colonists. As late as the beginning of the twentieth century North Americans kept it at arm's length. Yet in continental Europe, where it arrived courtesy of either Columbus or Cortés and was first documented in the mid-sixteenth century, it moved from ornamental fruit to food within a century. Today Italians assume the tomato has always been common to their country's diet, along with the bean, which illustrates that "traditional memory," as accurate as it often is, can also exaggerate.

Now the tomato is ubiquitous, one of the most common fruits we find in our produce. Mandatory at salad bars, it's also essential to many sauces. I eat tomatoes sauced, fried, dried, roasted, and fresh in any variety of recipes. One of the lovely qualities of the tomato is that the fruit has evolved to match recipes that use it. We grow Romas for their thick pastes and sauces, and big slicers for just that. Sharon's brother passed on to us an unnamed heirloom he'd encountered, so we called it Graham's Goodkeeper. It lives up to its name and sells well in the seed catalogue.

An indeterminate variety, it continues ripening and fruiting until frost, and the tomatoes are long-lasting. Another of my favourites is the Principe Borghese, a drying tomato. Its centre is juice and seed, without any divisions. You can scoop it out with a spoon and then dry the shell, which we do in our food dehydrater. It's also determinate, like corn, meaning these tomatoes generally ripen around the same time, so you can preserve them in volume. It's great for soups in winter. Our decorative tomatoes, yellow cherry, tiger stripe, and green apple (which ripens without turning red and tastes like a green apple), give style to a salad. Some tomatoes have a higher acid content, so they are grown for canning, because they are not as susceptible to botulism.

Sharon gathers our tomatoes and runs them through an Italian hand grinder, a clever heritage machine that crushes tomatoes and squeezes the juice out for us to freeze while separating the seeds and skin, which she puts in a bucket of water and ferments in the greenhouse. Tomato seeds need to ferment for viability, as the fruit does in the wild, dropping to the ground and rotting. After the bucket develops a thick layer of mould, she stirs the mess, releasing the seeds, 169 which sink to the bottom; she pours off the top gunk into the compost and rinses the bucket until the seeds are clean. Then she sieves them and scatters them onto a plate or a piece of glass to dry. Afterwards they can be stored for the following year. Meanwhile, we pour the paste-juice into containers and freeze it for later in the winter, when we are less busy and can cook large batches of barbecue or tomato sauce, or salsa on the wood stove. We put aside our own seed and sell the remainder to Salt Spring Seeds, since they are all heirlooms and breed true.

UNLIKE PRE-AGRARIAN SOCIETIES, WHICH thrived more on perennials and fruits—what we now call permaculture—farmers have shifted increasingly toward the annual crops of today. Along with fruit and nuts, these crops dominate our produce. Thus we have become dependent on seeds. However, as the transnationals systematically buy up seed companies, they are reducing their stock through attrition.

A real seed catalogue should be a winter fantasy. We settle back with it by the fire, drinking hot chocolate, dreaming the summer and fall cornucopia into existence—every plant perfect and in far greater abundance than we will ever grow in reality. A gardener needs those fantasies to accept the reality of what summer produces, because gardens are always what they are, not what we imagine.

Seed catalogues of the past were filled with dreams, dreams that are disappearing like the people who live the rural life. The scantiness of today's catalogues compared with the enormous volumes of fifty years ago depresses anyone who has gardened for years. What was once a joy is now a litany of loss. Just picking up these thin booklets is heart-rending. What's gone this year? The crops that used to be anticipated are now the first disappointments, as you scan through the pages and learn that another favourite endive or corn or lettuce has disappeared.

It also used to be, in the mists of history, that the local farmer grew tasty varieties that might not ship well or weren't perfectly shaped or coloured, or were incapable of cultivation on an industrial scale. These varieties are vanishing quickly from the corporate catalogues, which are designed more for the industrial grower than for the home garden. Sometimes I wonder if the corporations don't want us to grow tasty fruit and vegetables to compare with the colourful cardboard sold in the produce departments of today. In addition, the majority of commercial seeds are now hybrids that won't grow true in a second generation. That way you can't keep your seed but must buy it again every year. The companies will tell you they have nothing against heritage seeds; it's just good business to stream their customers into consuming what is more profitable.

Several of these multinationals produce pesticides and herbicides and fertilizers, as well as farm machinery. The business plan is to remove the seeds from the farmer's control and retain a limited number in the hands of the corporation, seeds that are designed to work best with that corporation's chemicals and machinery. They now sell such "packages" to farmers: herbicide, plow, seed, fertilizer, pesticide, harvester. The culmination of this philosophy is the notorious "terminator" seed that was being developed by the U.S. Department of Agriculture and a subsidiary of Monsanto until the United Nations Convention on Biological Diversity requested a moratorium on its development in 2000. So far, that moratorium has been successful.

Combine the loss of seed diversity with the invention of GM (genetically modified) seeds, which are infecting the basic crops of corn, soy, cotton, and canola, and the history of human cultivation is facing its worst crisis since our neolithic ancestors discovered seed saving. Of 350,000 of the world's known plant species, 60,000 are threatened with extinction today. Domesticated plants are disappearing faster than wild varieties. Seeds handed down in families and villages for centuries have been eliminated in this continuing botanical holocaust. Since the nineteenth century 95 percent of cabbages and 81 percent of tomatoes are no longer grown commercially, retained in seed banks, or listed in seed catalogues—gone!

Even more dangerous is our tinkering with GM seeds, which is radically different from the simple breeding humanity has performed since we began cultivating plants and domestic animals. Although traditional farming has ultimately created an enormous diversity of plants and animals, it never crossed the species line. You can't interbreed different species naturally, though there's a couple of plant species that experts are debating about, but that's likely a classification issue and not a species cross. Diseases can cross from species to species, but that involves mutation, as with avian flu. That's why the inability to interbreed is generally referred to as the "species barrier." The closer you get to it, the more difficult interbreeding becomes. Thus hybrids will not breed true to their parents, nor will their offspring resemble them. To create a hybrid plant you have to breed two extremely different parent genera and produce one generation of seeds. Next year you must breed those two parent genera again. The same with animals, only they seem to hit the infertility barrier more often. If you breed a donkey with a horse you get a mule. Sterile. End of the line. GM crosses that line by creating mutations, injecting genes from one species into another, and, as its proponents say, opens up the universe. GM can create butterfly-killing corn, tomatoes with frog genes, and potatoes that are pesticides.

GM seeds also have the potential of creating a rogue plant. Imagine a terminator gene leaping from plant to plant: The end of flowers. The end of fruit. The end of vegetables. This

scenario is far-fetched, but some of the accidents in the production of GM seeds suggest it might not be as far-fetched
as transgenetic enthusiasts would have us believe. The
numbers are shifting too rapidly to say how many North
American crops are GM, but it is well over 50 percent in the
varieties of crops released so far, and these crops are now
cross-pollinating with natural, organic crops.

Equally scary is the potential of a gene containing a pesticide like Bt (*Bacillus thuringiensis*) spreading from plant to
plant, endangering pollinators. Albert Einstein is rumoured
to have said, "If the bee disappeared off the surface of the
globe then man would only have four years of life left. No
more bees, no more pollination, no more plants, no more
animals, no more man." This statement isn't entirely accurate, like most great quips. There are many pollinators
besides the European honeybee. But releasing insect-killing
plants into the natural world is no way to farm wisely or
guarantee that life on our planet will survive this century.

Of the first ten efforts to inject a gene into a plant, all
went wrong. The initial commercially produced GM corn,
Starlink, engineered to enhance cattle growth, was not fit
for human consumption. (Imagine developing an allergenic
corn unfit for humans!) In its first year of commercial production this modified corn was accidentally funnelled into
food products worldwide, sparking recalls of trainloads of
corn, tacos, and breakfast cereals.

The reaction against GM seeds has been so intense that
the agribusiness enablers (political and bureaucratic) of
both the Canadian and American governments refused
to legislate mandatory labelling on the grounds that adult
human beings, though capable of voting in a democracy,

are incapable of deciding what they should eat and might be subject to food panics (such as not buying GM products). Government bodies insisted "voluntary labelling" was the solution. However, the first major supermarket chain in Canada that stocked food labelled "GM Free" was visited by representatives of agribusiness, and suddenly afterwards it refused to stock any food that was labelled "GM Free" because it would give uncontaminated food an unfair marketing advantage. This tactic of banning labelling happens all the time in the food industry. That's why it's illegal for an American dairy farm to advertise that it doesn't use the controversial bovine growth hormone, and thus the incentive to raise untreated cattle is removed from dairy farmers.

Without labels alerting us, we end up buying GM produce unknowingly. The industry can now claim that almost everyone is eating GM foods, so these Frankenfoods must be healthy and we should create more. That's why it's assumed the corporations contaminated corn and soy and canola with GM genes first—these grains are in almost every processed food in existence.

174

Inserting frog and fish genes in tomatoes is a creepy business, but it gets really scary when companies like Monsanto start creating herbicide-resistant plants. Not only have these genes already crossed over into organic produce, but they've also passed into wild plants, creating superweeds that are herbicide resistant. It's also feared they will make pests Bt (the best organic pest killer) resistant and kill too many beneficial insects. Between crashing pollinator populations and superweeds, the monster might already be unleashed.

The worst danger is the partnership between the transnationals and government regulatory bodies. Patent laws now make you liable if your fields are polluted with GM seeds in Canada. If I am growing organic canola and GM pollen drifts onto my field, I could lose my organic status. Worse, I'd be legally obligated to pay the seed company for the "theft" of its product and be forced to allow it to bomb my organic fields with poisons to destroy the "pirated" crop. According to the laws of Canada, GM businesses also have the legal right to herbicide-bomb grain fields they only suspect of stealing their genes. If not all of the crop dies, that means there are GM-patented genes contaminating the field, and the innocent farmer is liable for damages. This automatically destroys an organic farmer's legal status because the farm has been sprayed, even if the farmer is innocent.

The GM manufacturers are attempting the same strategy in the United States and Europe. Since it appears that GM genes are moving quickly into the natural environment, some environmentalists have claimed it's no longer possible to grow organic canola, soybean, and corn in North America. Contaminated corn has been discovered in the isolated mountains of Chiapas in Mexico, where traditional seed collecting has continued for centuries. The drift is big.

UNTIL ABOUT THREE DECADES ago the fate of North American seeds was in the hands of hundreds of tiny seed companies, a few large ones, a cluster of surviving sixties communes, a few old ladies from the Ukraine or fussy Italian tomato growers, and so on. When the transnationals began creating GM seeds and taking over seed companies and eliminating their stock or shutting them down, a growing storm of back-to-the-landers, old-time farmers, and ecologists recognized the danger, and the battle was on. Dozens of organizations like Seeds of Diversity, Seeds of Change, and Seed Savers have sprouted, along with rebel seed companies like Dan Jason's Salt Spring Seeds. It's a strange, sometimes hilarious guerrilla battle between transnationals armed with fat lobby funds and agricultural ministries tucked in their pockets, and a fluid underground of gardeners and farmers and ecologists attempting to preserve the seeds of history.

I volunteered at a recent Seedy Saturday on Salt Spring—these charity events for seed savers are a redoubt of local food—promoted by educated rebel growers and a host of vegans. I packaged the seeds while mothers and ancient hippies and retired professionals with gardening habits thumped their donated bags of seeds onto the counter. Local growers, cooks, alternative-energy promoters, bamboo lovers, relief organizations (Seeds for Malawi), and orchardists displayed their retail goods. The hall was packed. It was practically panic collecting as seeds were donated, then sold for a song, or just handed over, because a half-dozen of us couldn't package them as fast as they were donated. We raised thousands of dollars for all the good causes, and by late afternoon the place was cleaned out. There were mislabelled seeds, wet seeds, and dead seeds, but there were far more good than bad germs given back to the community. So despite all the obstacles thrown at the seeds of the world, wild and domesticated, I still can't help but smile when those gauzy summer winds of thistledown float like clouds across the field—declaring that the planet still intends to seed itself—for now.

13

STOP AND LOOK

· · · · ·

*T*HE SKY WAS a propane-fire blue. The old ghetto blaster was cranked up to abusive volume. Our pack of rap-playing nineteen-year-olds were splitting and stacking thirteen-foot cedar rails and digging ditches according to my erratic instructions. It was a moment when you stop, aware of something, although you have no idea what's different. We turned as one and saw the two giant birds swoop overhead and circle the ponds before they landed on the tall maple.

"What are they?" Joaquin asked—bare chested, head shaved, wearing big wraparound sunglasses, blocking the sun with a dirty hand while attempting to make out the birds against the shimmering light. And he thought the birds looked weird?

"They ain't eagles," I said, "and they sure aren't vultures—they're ospreys!" I'd never seen them on these islands. One dived off the big-budded maple and circled the ponds, gliding lower and lower. The ducks remained undisturbed, although an eagle would send them into hysterical formations. They knew a fish eater when they saw one.

The osprey plunged into the pond, enormous wings folded back, talons extended, head down, at what seemed around forty-five miles per hour; then it sank out of sight— a stunning assault. We could see its huge dark shadow swimming. It was flying underwater! It came up, beating its wings against the surface, thrusting itself into the air. Gaining altitude it approached the limb where its mate had supervised the performance. It landed, shook the water off, and leaped into cruising mode again, before diving and failing to find prey once more.

That was it for work. Seb brought out the beer, and we all took seats on the deck, cheering this useless hunter while his mate (judging from the sour look she gave him after his first failure, our male crowd automatically assumed she was the female), who refused to hunt, became more peeved. Within an hour she was shrieking and he was foxtrotting mechanically, one talon up, one talon down, a psycho on his branch, while she denounced his incompetence. By then several empty beer bottles were rolling around the deck and we were guffawing mercilessly at every failed dive. "That bird is too useless to catch my goldfish!" We wondered if he was fresh off the nest and if they'd just become an item.

Finally, the female left in a huff, while the male danced himself into a frenzy on his branch. Then he launched again and hit the pond with a crack you could hear a half mile away. By now, I figured the goldfish were hiding two feet under the mud at the pond bottom, but suddenly the osprey surfaced like a god out of black water, a golden fish between his talons. As he gained altitude he effortlessly flipped my ten-inch goldfish face forward so that the fish resembled an orange torpedo hanging from a bomber's fuselage, in an undignified yet streamlined formation. The triumphant osprey performed a victory flight ten feet over our heads, displaying his trophy, and we couldn't help cheering, though I had some regrets about my goldfish. Then he landed in a tree across the field.

I took out my binoculars and watched him lunch. He held the goldfish the way a kid would hold an ice cream cone, only it was still twitching and slapping about. He calmly began chewing its face, holding it up and looking back at us, while the fish spasmed between his talons. It was the cruellest lunch I've ever seen, as he decapitated that living fish, working his way down to the meat, taking his time. Predators don't have our sentimental morality. The boys took turns with the glasses, and the excitement faded. Watching this gory lunch wasn't anybody's idea of fun. They gradually straggled to work, and I followed, thinking about more than diving ospreys.

We all live in the world, but what world do we live in? This was perhaps the only opportunity in their lives for these young, healthy men to witness an osprey hunt and its aftermath. They are modern kids. They didn't enjoy watching a victim being eaten alive. They returned to lifting rails onto the fence and hollowing out their drainage trenches. And I recognized that's why these young, rambunctious idealists had come to Trauma Farm—because it was an opportunity to witness what was disappearing: the natural world of simultaneous beauty and laughter and terror.

179

NOT TOO LONG AGO I encountered a knowledge test. Do you know ten local birds, ten local trees, ten local flowers? Shut your eyes. Now, point to the north, point to the west. What phase is the moon tonight? Where will it rise, and when was the last time you watched it rise? What kind of ground is beneath you, and when was it created? Who were the first people who lived where you lived? Do you know how an internal combustion engine works? What is the second law of thermodynamics? Can you find the North Star at night? Can you recite more than three lines of a great poem aloud? Of course it's not a real knowledge test, but it asks wonderful questions about our quality of life. The poet Patrick Lane used a similar test for his students and was shocked to learn how many would-be poets couldn't name more than three local birds or trees. Then he asked them how they expected to be writers if they didn't know what was going on in the environment. That got a sea of blank faces. They thought writing meant expressing themselves—not recognizing the world celebrating its diverse expressions all around them.

It's said we live in the age of information. Modernists make stunning pronouncements like: "The average person today knows fifty thousand more facts than the average peasant from the sixteenth century." I smile when I hear this. We live in the age of trivia, not information. Real information has become subverted by sound bites and statistics flung about in defence of far-fetched arguments. That's why I keep in mind Mark Twain's sassy quip: "There are three kinds of lies—lies, damned lies, and statistics." Despite my distrust of numbers I still find I also have to use them.

But we are paying too much attention to the wrong information. Certainly, there's little harm in zoning out with a well-designed piece of gaming technology. Urban living has many glories. But if we consider how we surround ourselves with repetitive trivial information and celebrity gossip it's apparent we have become sleepwalkers who've forgotten the grandeur of the planet—the osprey and its hunt.

When I consider the sixteenth-century peasant who supposedly knew so little, I think of someone who could smell hay and recognize its food value, identify hundreds of medicinal flowers, berries, and vegetables, and tell you when to plant or harvest and how to preserve; someone who could milk a cow and create or fix almost any tool in the house; someone who lived for the most part in grace with a natural environment (when not being a victim of the feudal politics of the era). Comparing "old knowledge" with the knowledge of how to operate a remote control or play a new video game, it's clear that an important range of experience has been lost. What can we say to a world where a child on a bus in Vancouver looks out the window and asks his mother, "Is that a crow?"

ALMOST EVERY FARMER I know, female or male, has the ability to stand still, gazing—at things or events most urban dwellers wouldn't even notice—often with the wry, laconic expression of the experienced: "Well, would you look at that?" Yet we're a diminishing crowd of gawkers standing in our pastures or walking through the frozen wheat fields of the winter prairie, the Brazil nut forests of South

America, the Southwestern mesa valleys with their peach trees, or the bamboo jungles of Thailand. "Being there" has become a tourist experience, not a way of life. Now that the human community is urban and cocooned we find ourselves without natural miracles, addicted to the fast-edited images of media that can give people vertigo when the images are flashed at epileptic-fit-inducing frequencies. The world has become a jumpy, twitchy place. Though riding a roller coaster can be fun, we also need the capacity to walk slowly. Like farmers, people from aboriginal cultures also have a tendency to move and talk slowly, until the moment calls for an explosion of action. This leads to a dry humour. If you've lived long with the landscape you learn to smile because you never know how the world will come at you.

Other creatures also stand still, pause, look, listen, smell—gaze meditatively on a meadow. Yeats, the peacock, will sit for hours on the split-rail fence or the second-floor deck outside our bedroom and stare endlessly at nothing—or everything. His meditative skills are extreme. All animals have great reservoirs of patience when they watch their world.

One hot afternoon Sharon and I walked up the hill to admire the moss and wildflowers in bloom. The last ewe had yet to lamb, late in the season. As we passed the corral by the driveway, we noticed she was down, panting, in the middle of a large circle of stumps, almost ready. Upon returning a half-hour later she was lambing. Since all was going well, we stood in the driveway and watched.

We suddenly became aware that the whole gang had moved up to where the ewe was lambing, and they were also watching. It was a scene out of a nativity painted by a naive artist. The ram, the other ewes, and their lambs surrounded her. The black horse, Jackson, stood sentinel among the sheep, and the peafowl perched on the stumps, the cock fanning his tail. Our Araucana rooster stood erect and alert on another stump, while the cluster of hens clucked softly, pecked at the grass, and watched. Even the dogs had entered the corral and sat patiently among the chickens. It was as if the creatures of the farm had drawn a holy circle around this birth, blessing it. Grace lives in the land and awaits the moment when it can surprise us with its tenderness.

NOT LONG AGO A young Steller's jay fell out of its nest and miraculously survived cats, dogs, and raptors as it ran around our yard, unable to fly, while its parents screamed useless instructions. We heard the ruckus and saw the jay— and the cat closing in. I snatched up the baby jay, and that really sent him and his parents screeching. In one of my few moments of brilliance, I sized up our species quince, which offered little by contemporary standards—a thicket with a scattering of pale, applelike blossoms and a few tiny fruits— unlike the orchard quince, which bore giant, heavy golden fruits, or the decorative quince with its bright red flowers. We'd kept the shrub because its near-impenetrable tangle shelters migrating songbirds from cats. A covey of California quail lived underneath and would spend the day darting out to the fig tree where the bird feeders hung, dining off the scattered seed from sloppy eaters.

I thrust my arm into this thicket without decapitating the chick and sat him on a branch, safe, while his parents

183

berated me. As I peered at him on his branch—his jay-spike not yet grown so that he reminded me of a mohawked punk standing on a skateboard—he abused me even more.

For the next few days his parents dutifully brought food to him in the quince while he cursed the world, his parents, and the quail. We were grateful when he finally gained the strength to fly off, though I miss him in the way you miss an irritating yet interesting relative.

DELIGHT IS MULTITUDINOUS. IT is everywhere you stop and become aware, when letting it flow through your veins, and perhaps that's why I often recall that story of the Zen monk and his reaction to the dinner gong, which like a clock striking midnight brought him to perfect attention. Moments. The world is a constant astonishment. Rain in a storm—each drop pounding so hard against the pond surface that the water reaches back up like a fist threatening the sky. An opium poppy suddenly sprouting unseeded and rebelliously wild in our vegetable garden. "Where did that come from?"

184

Japanese horticulturalists bred the camellia so that its blossoms begin dying even as they unfold. The idea was to create a pristine, complex blossom that also illustrated the transitory quality of life. Glory and death simultaneously— like discovering a rat-child on the road. It was near dark, the hour after sunset; the birds were shutting down, except for the ravens putting order to the last dregs of the evening. I had shut up the coop and was walking back around the barn. Suddenly I noticed a tiny creature squirming among the weeds and gravel. It was a baby rat. Rats! My nemesis. I had been fighting them for so long in the feed shed that I'd taken to midnight forays with the new pellet shells, which have a range of about ten feet—shooting the rats out of the rafters until I discovered that the minuscule pellets, at close range, could just puncture the tin roof. Now I have two leaks and am even more annoyed at the rats.

However, this was a blind baby, slow and lost, as if it had accidentally crawled out of the nest too early or someone, cat or dog or raccoon or mink, had murdered its mother and it was on a last, slow, desperate crawl for life. I knew I should kill it, but I didn't have the heart. I was reminded of Mike once shooting starlings in his cherry trees while simultaneously raising baby starlings that had fallen out of a nest. He hated those starlings for their thievery and the damage they were doing to endangered songbird populations. Yet babies are different. Every creature deserves the chance to reach its prime. However, an adult pest is another story, and then it's every bird or man for himself. I knew I'd bring this rat baby into the house, feed it, warm it by the fire, and then release it far away in the bush. Sharon would be annoyed at first, superficially, before she helped with great tenderness.

185

Sam, the border collie, came up behind me. She saw the baby rat and, before I could move, snatched it, killing it instantly. Then she tossed it up in the air as if it were a toy, caught it, and swallowed it whole, happily trotting off down the road again, while I stood alone in the bluing darkness, overwhelmed once more by the arbitrary casualness of death.

WHEN YOU CAN'T STOP moving, then you have stopped living. We exist in a strange era whose landscape remains

as slow as ever, yet our lives keep speeding up. Trauma
Farm provides us and our guests the opportunity to stop
moving—to regard the world. A string of hummingbirds
following their mother like beads on an invisible chain
floating through the air. A fairy slipper orchid at the edge
of the clearing hit by a streak of low yellow light as the
sun sets, or the haunted flower of the ghost orchid beside a
stump in deep forest....

Summer afternoons I often sneak away to a local swimming hole. Every year a truck mysteriously appears and
dumps sand on this patch of road allowance fronting the
lake. The docks anchored offshore are anonymously main-
tained and replaced by unknown farmers and citizens. All is
unspoken because of today's liability laws and wacky insurance claims. Rumour has it there's even a mysterious bank
account where locals can donate $50 to cover general main-
tenance, but like everyone else I have no idea who runs it.
Another farmer donates a portable outdoor toilet to stand
on his neighbour's property just next to the beach. All this
allows the glory of summer to unfold for the many island
children who luxuriate at the beach daily.

Salt Spring is fortunate to have a swimming hole for
every social group, or maybe islanders worked it out
through the mysteries of community osmosis. There is the
howling mass of children at Stowel Lake, swimming and
banging about among the trout, water lilies, leeches, and
docks, while once in a while a turtle with a six-inch shell
swims blithely among them. I've watched it several times,
its sage's head on a snaky neck high above the water. Yet
somehow, magically, the children seldom notice these gentle, wise old creatures usually sunning on a nearby log.

Blackburn Lake has a nudist dock surrounded by mud and lilies. This is where the young island workers with their beer and joints stop by for a dip after a hot day roofing or house framing. It also is frequented by a squad of young tattooed women with face metal dangling from their piercings, as well as hippie elders, everyone enjoying the luxury of a swim and an opportunity to dry naked in the sun. This dock can be hilarious around five in the afternoon when it gets crowded and sinks to water level under the weight of too many sunbathers. Thousands of daddy-long-legs live on its floats and are forced to surface onto the decking as the floats sink, which causes eruptions of panicked sunbathers fleeing the harmless spiders. Lately, this dock has been overrun by what the locals call "skids and vandals," who insist on bringing their dogs.

Then there's the dock anchored in the middle of Weston Lake, usually occupied by our wealthier elders, also without clothes—quiet and meditative. You have to enter the lake via a narrow trail and swim out to the dock. It's calm and relaxing. Cushion Lake has a wharf and seems to be fancied more by teenagers and local families, but this dock is looked down upon by a few waterfront residents who would prefer the lake for themselves and fret about liability and pollution of their drinking water by the swimmers.

Despite the many children screaming and kicking sand, my favourite swimming hole remains the tiny community beach at Stowel Lake, where dozens of babies, kids, teenagers, parents, and grandparents all gather in a mutual chaos that works out just fine. And I'm hoping we can eventually rescue the nudist Blackburn Lake from the dog owners who make it miserable.

THE SWIMMING HOLE

I'm sorry,
   my darling
but the chores are undone,
   the lambs unfed,
   the wood unchopped,
   the beans not weeded.

It was hot
   and the sun lives
in a strange sky.

It made me think of many things.

   I found myself at the lake,
   floating past the dock,
where girls with enormous breasts
sun naked on the cedar planks
while the skinny boys pretend
they are only dancing in water,

but I was not watching.

The sky unnaturally blue,
   the bullfrogs humming among the lily pads,
   I was drifting in a black lake,
   stunned by a single scudding cloud.

It's the swimming hole.
What can I say?
There are so few of them left.

I floated away
on my back, defenceless
in a changing world,
the limpid water
very soft,
and very sweet.

Working with earth and animals draws us into the
world, nourishing our ability to be surprised—empathy—
the ability to pull up our lawn chairs and blankets and wine
and hot chocolates with good friends and their children on
the grass of a meadow on a summer night under the stars.
The Perseids in full fiery glory, the avalanche of shooting
stars catching our attention in the clear August evenings.
Embers of white light shooting across the sky while we
exclaim and laugh and love the night. Thomas Mann said:
"Hold every moment sacred. Give each clarity and meaning, each the weight of thine awareness, each its true and
due fulfilment." He knew the world, like that crazy monk
throwing down his hoe.

The ground is changing beneath my feet. It always has. 189
Living with the land is living within the river of life. By the
time this story becomes a book there will be many more
victories and defeats. Lives and legislation will change.
Change is everything, always was. I write these words as a
mirror to a moment—what I know and what I've seen—so
that the children who follow will learn what was lost, what
was won, and what still lives.

This afternoon the air is warm and yet there's a rest-
lessness in it, and I see the swallows are flying low over
the pond, which means the barometric pressure is driving
the mosquitoes down, and there's a composty taste to the

air. The weather will shift tomorrow, maybe even tonight, although only a few cirrus clouds are parked on the horizon. As if the same thoughts have just occurred to her, Chloe the goose raises her snakelike head and utters a long, plaintive honk, the sound wave dimpling the dark slate of the pond.

14

ONE MORE FOR THE BIRDS
(AND THEIR FRIENDS)

* * * * *

*T*HE PLAINTIVE CRY of Chloe on a humid afternoon is like a gong flooding my mind year after year through our timeless story pool at Trauma Farm. And she will always be here every afternoon that I am alive on this land. She was the oldest survivor of our original flock of Toulouse geese—the most ancient domesticated variety of goose I know—descended from the wild Graylag.

There's the usual confusion about how long ago the goose was domesticated. Even Darwin could only remark that it "is of very ancient date." We know ducks lived with the Chinese at least four thousand years in the past, but the goose slipped more seamlessly into our culture, likely around then. Ducks and geese were the earliest poultry because they were large and gregarious and self-sufficient. The ancient Egyptians were fond of their geese, and according to Pliny, the temple geese of Rome were given the most "tender food." This was because the sacred geese of Juno were credited with saving Rome in 390 BC when a raiding party of barbarians, sneaking in to sack the city, accidentally awoke the temple geese, which alerted the guards, and in the ensuing cacophony the whole city woke up and thrashed the unlucky pillagers. Geese are better than dogs as alarms, and they can create a spectacular racket if disturbed. This is why Dumbarton Distillery kept its beloved "Scotch Watch" of a hundred Chinese geese, enough to discourage the most ardent whisky thief.

At Trauma Farm visitors seldom catch us by surprise. Our earliest warning is the parrot, who has a view of the driveway from his window, and makes raucous, sometimes mortifying invitations. Outside, the geese start up (especially when we had the full flock), alerting Raj the peacock, and then the dogs rush down the road, barking. Although no neighbour is within sight of the farm, everyone hears that we have guests.

UPON BUYING THE FARM, we were informed there was a tradition of maintaining the three resident geese—Lucy, Maude, and Chloe—and we thought it a good tradition. The interim caretakers (who had no interest in farming) told me they'd named them after a film about lesbian lovers. These geese were my first chance to study free-range animal behaviour for an extended period of years. That's one of the delights of farming—living with the politics of animals.

During the first months there was a ruckus every day, with much squawking and honking, so we decided these geese needed a gander to sort them out. We were told to visit the elderly but still spry Howard Byron. There was nothing Howard didn't know about animals, and what he didn't know, his brother, Mike, did. After we negotiated a price for a gander in its prime, Howard ordered his collie, Big Mac, to fetch it.

Howard stood imperiously in his field, leaning on a long-handled fishnet, while the dog herded a goose through the maze of chickens, sheep, cattle, goats, and his blind pet deer. Mac, unerring and unrelenting, edged the gander up to Howard, who casually dropped the net on it. He was showing off, yet it was such a hammy display I fell for it. Mac got a biscuit and a pat on the head. We promptly named the gander Toulouse the Goose because that was the breed of our flock.

But life on a farm is never that straight a line. The ruckus continued for a few days. And then finally, in one of those majestic awakening moments, I realized that Lucy was a he, and Maude too, and both ganders were fighting over Chloe. I was horrified that we'd introduced a third gander— Toulouse. Luckily, wise old farmers and magic dogs aren't perfect either. Sexing a goose is not a sure thing. Toulouse turned out to be no gander, and suddenly everybody paired up. Domestic bliss settled upon the farm.

Lucy is the king, old and monstrous, and we soon decided his name was the short form for Lucifer. My neighbour remembers him from her childhood, and her memories weren't always pleasant. He lived up to the name. I've had to hold him off with a board more than a couple of times. His legs are bent and arthritic from wrestling raccoons after midnight, one of his many aggressive hobbies. He is also fond of chasing the horse. His favourite trick is to surprise Jack when he is eating and latch onto a hind leg, then hold fast, wings out, gliding behind the fleeing horse. A great stunt, which fed Lucy's ego, though it embarrassed the horse. After letting go, Lucy would waddle around the field honking proudly, informing all that he was Lucy the mighty horse tamer. This he practised with regularity until Jack ran through the grape arbour with Lucy attached. Lucy's wingspan was about two feet wider than the narrow arbour. He hit the posts with a thunk you could hear a block away. Once the feathers finally settled, Lucy staggered off like a drunk, his horse-wrangling days ended.

STANDING IN THE HOT afternoon by the pond, remembering Lucy's adventures with the horse returns me to a morning several years ago. I'm half asleep, still undressed, drinking my coffee. Sharon has gone to work, a twelve-hour shift at the emergency ward, and I'm looking forward to a sunny summer day on the land—the garlic needs pulling, and this good weather is perfect for drying the thousands of bulbs. Lucy and Chloe had hatched a flock of ten goslings. Lucy protected the eggs all spring, and his proud chest jutted out so far he was tripping over himself. Now he kept a careful eye out for eagles and walked a tight flock of goslings, with Chloe on rear guard. But today I noticed one of the goslings caught in the page-wire fence, its neck and wing through the wire square as it strangled itself. I put my cup down, slipped my gumboots on, and dashed out to the fence. It was only as I began extricating the thrashing little creature that I realized the gate was open and Lucy was approaching in full honk, aimed directly for a man's most tender point.

The only thing I could do was turn aggressor, and since I already had one hand occupied, trying to release the nippy young goose, I grabbed Lucy by the throat and lifted him off the ground—an indignity he didn't appreciate. He flapped his powerful wings at me, just out of range, squawking hoarsely as I tried to save his gosling. Then, *hell*, there was Chloe, and she went directly for the same delicate feature, and I found myself doing a bizarre calisthenic version of a samba dance, holding Lucy in the air, swooshing my ass to avoid the thrusts of Chloe, while still trying to release the gosling. Finally, I got it out of the wire and dumped Lucy on top of Chloe. It took a second for them to untangle themselves, and by then I was on my way to the house, where I slammed the deck gate shut.

Inside, I kicked off my gumboots and sat down with a graceless thud in my chair at the sunroom table. My coffee was still warm.

SEVERAL YEARS LATER, MAUDE, the small gander, died of old age, which upset the balance again. There was obvious discomfort in the flock, but we tried to live with it. This puzzled me because I always assumed a gander would gather as many geese as he could service, but not with this gang. Toulouse and Chloe were competing. Finally, we brought in a new gander, whom we named Murphy because he was kind of stunned—brainless and full of himself. Chloe and Toulouse had the same opinion, and the mighty Lucy, although now ancient, brutalized him. Murphy got the cold shoulder from everyone and was forced to follow twenty yards behind the flock. Sometimes he managed discreet trysts with Toulouse if Lucifer the Terrible wasn't looking. Those geese gave me more lessons in power politics than I had ever dreamed possible. One day something happened by the pond. Murphy got fed up with the bullying and swagger of Lucy, and the big fight was on. This time, Murphy won. Filled with the ego of the young stud in all his glory, he drove the ancient Lucy away.

The old giant sat lonely on the fringe, plaintively honking for his love of many years (geese are supposed to mate for life), Chloe, but the old tart defied tradition and switched her allegiance to the new hero. Once again I learned how time and history take us, though it broke my heart to watch Lucifer—so crushed by his defeat he even let the chickens drive him from the feed trough.

A week after he lost the battle with Murphy he had a stroke and could no longer walk much. He went blind, and since he couldn't see Murphy, the young gander tormented him at will. This is the way it works in the natural world, but it also works other ways. I grabbed Murphy and cut off his head. Then I plucked and gutted him and we smoke-cooked him with a cranberry sauce on the side, proving once again to myself that not all the decisions we make while living with the natural world are smart or environmental—such as bringing a young gander into an old flock. But he was delicious.

A LITTLE OVER A year later Toulouse died, probably from egg binding, a condition where a bird can't lay an egg and goes toxic. This left only Chloe and Lucy. Lucy would swim blindly in circles for hours, honking, yet I didn't have the strength to put him down. According to local estimates he was a fabulous thirty-seven years old. Every night I brought grain to the pond and poured it into the shallows so the sheep couldn't eat it. Chloe, in an old-age display of tenderness, would honk, and he'd follow her voice to the grain and then step all over it, blindly feeding, while she stared in disgust at the mess he was making of their dinner. But every night she would call him in until he died, and we buried him under the willow tree.

If I consider the intelligence and politics of geese I can't help but admire them—and regard with horror the gruesome practice of foie gras. When it comes toward me on a biscuit these days, I turn it away. I prefer our own version, with the livers of animals naturally raised that we've slaughtered. It's not the same quality, yet it has some virtue—the animal wasn't tortured. Because geese and ducks have no gag reflex, they are perfect vehicles for being tightly caged—in the old days with their feet nailed to the floor—and force-fed through tubes. *Foie gras* is merely the term for a diseased "fat liver."

Chloe stood guard for years after we arrived at the farm. Her call in the night would rouse me, and I'd listen in the moonlight until I was sure she was not alerting us to a predator or a dog pack. She had the best ears on the farm, and when I cracked the feed bin in the late afternoon she'd bellow her dinner honk, which roused the sheep and brought them up from the lower fields to the troughs by the gate—until the day, only two years after I began telling this eighteen-year-long day, Sharon went out to feed the sheep and saw Chloe floating asleep in the pond with her neck tucked under her wing. It took Sharon a few minutes to realize that Chloe was dead. She returned to the house teary-eyed, and told me she thought Chloe had tucked up for the night, ancient and regal—then died in her sleep. That bird always had class.

WE NEVER RAISED MANY ducks, especially after a flock of Muscovys escaped from our neighbours, packing their young up to our ponds, and became a great feast for the eagles, which picked them off, one at a time. Even the ravens got into the act. They would fly at the young in waves, one bird returning over and over again as the ducklings got used to the cycle of diving and surfacing, diving and surfacing, until the second raven came in as the duckling surfaced....

Duck eggs are a delight. I separate the white and mix it with minced, spiced pork and green onions and then put it in a dish surrounding the yolk and steam it. It's a Chinese tradition I picked up somewhere. It also works with the even stronger-flavoured goose egg. These days a friend keeps Indian Runners and provides me with the occasional duck egg I need. This will change soon. The avian flu hysteria has suppressed public sales of ducks in North America, and only a few varieties are raised for food in distant factories. Duck eggs are difficult to find in stores, and a multitude of varieties are endangered.

AS THE GOOSE AND duck declined in our diet over the past century, the ascendancy of the chicken and the turkey began.

The wild turkey is a canny bird, as any turkey hunter will attest. The best place to surprise the clever, skittish turkey is from a hunting chair in a tree, which the birds don't notice because the adult turkey has no real airborne predator. Amateur hunters are notoriously inept at attaching their tree chairs and have a tendency to get drunk or nod off—so they tumble out of the trees at an impressive rate. Thirty-six percent of hunter injuries in Georgia in 1990 were caused by plummeting from trees.

The wild turkey—our table variety is a pathetic descendant—is an intelligent, beautiful creature that can fly fifty-five miles per hour and run at eighteen to twenty-five miles per hour. It has a lifespan of about fifteen years. The wild turkey is so smart that Benjamin Franklin volunteered it would make a better national symbol for the USA than the bald eagle, a carrion eater that is pretty but cowardly— qualities that some unsympathetic American political commentators consider apt. In America, it's traditional for the president to pardon a turkey every year. That turkey gets to live out its days on a "sanctuary" farm. President George W. Bush pardoned more than twice as many turkeys as prisoners on death row. The first turkey pardoned was a pet of Abraham Lincoln's son Tad, who became hysterical at the thought of eating it for Thanksgiving, and thus the tradition began.

Not much is known about the early days of the domesticated turkeys because the colonialists destroyed almost all the Native American records they encountered. Surviving fossil evidence shows the birds are at least 10 million years old and that they were raised confined by Natives in Mexico two millenniums ago. Both Columbus and Cortés took such a liking to these birds and advocated their use so enthusiastically that by 1530 domestic flocks were appearing around Spain. The Pilgrims were well acquainted with them before that legendary first Thanksgiving dinner of Native American crops and game.

At Trauma Farm we've raised standard bronze turkeys, a variety that resembles the wild turkey and remains capable of surviving without human intervention. Many of our friends raise other varieties. Bev and Mike Byron tend to grow the white broad-breasted—the commercial bird. However, Mike runs them free-range and feeds them grain, so they are delicious even if he loses birds because they aren't bred to thrive in the natural world anymore. Like all free-range birds, these cook faster than the fatty, confined birds fed high-protein pellets because they're active, making their meat denser and more heat conductive. Other friends are part of a desperate continent-wide community attempting to save the last, endangered remnants of the great breeds.

The inbred domestic turkey, debeaked and declawed, is raised in darkened, ammonia-stinking sheds housing up to fifty thousand birds. More than 300 million turkeys a year are produced this way. The white broad-breasted is preferred by the factories. Fed their own recycled excrement, rendered animal offal, and reject grain formulated into chemically fortified pellets, factory birds are often diseased by the time they reach your Thanksgiving or Christmas table. If the turkeys are not confined to individual cages, which they almost never are, and if a door is opened to an outside pen, which shed-raised birds would seldom dare to explore, they can legally be called "free-range" and sold at an increased price. Ninety percent of all factory birds are tainted with bacteria, including the nasty campylobacter. The last U.S. Department of Agriculture estimate I could find stated that 35 percent of the birds have salmonella. The number is greater today, which explains the pressure to irradiate meat with gamma rays. Salmonella and *E. coli* and other bacteria die when they're nuked, so irradiation will allow the slaughterhouses to become even dirtier and spray more meat with excrement during slaughter.

That's why I want to know my turkey before I eat him. I check out the farm, its range, the feed. When that's no longer possible, I'll probably join the growing millions who prefer their birds in a tree, not in the oven, and sit down to the dreaded tofu turkey. According to the National Turkey Federation, 97 percent of Americans ate turkey on Thanksgiving in 2007, consuming 45 million birds on a single day. This is another of those statistics I suspect; nevertheless, these numbers make me wonder who actually has the strongest flocking mentality.

PEOPLE ASSUME CHICKEN HAS been central to our diet since time immemorial—that the bucolic fantasy of the small farm and a flock of chickens in the yard goes back to Babylon. This is not true. Though the chicken was domesticated early as a fighting bird rather than for meat or egg production, wild birds fed the lower classes around the world more than chickens did. Aside from domesticated geese, ducks, turkeys, and the occasional chicken, local diets of fowl included pheasants, pigeons, quail, peafowl, and whatever other bird could be trapped or killed. Peafowl were generally reserved for the aristocracy, but poaching is an ancient tradition. They have a reputation as a tough-fleshed bird if not hung properly. Yet it can be delicious—one of my best meals ever was a broiled, curried peahen.

The poet P.K. Page visits our farm occasionally and, like most guests, is enamoured of our peafowl. She once told a story of a king who grew so angry with a peacock he had it sewn up in a leather bag and left to die. She couldn't comprehend that kind of cruelty, but she's never been at the farm during breeding season—from April to July. The scream of a peacock can be bloodcurdling at close range (as scary as a cougar's wail). It sounds like a woman's high-pitched scream for help. At a distance, oddly, the pitch changes so that the cry becomes haunting and romantic. However, hearing the mighty Ajax scream at two in the morning while perched on a balcony rail outside our bedroom window is enough to lift us right off the mattress. Repeat that sound every hour and every night for a couple of months, and sewing him up in a leather bag starts to sound like a good idea if you're an uncontrollable king.

Peafowl, originally from Indochina, have been domesticated for millenniums. Brought to Europe via Egypt, they became the favourite bird of kings and monasteries. I sell the cock's moulted feathers to pay the flock's annual grain bill. As a child I was enthralled with the peacocks at Stanley Park in Vancouver, and their cries haunted my dreams. I promised myself if I ever owned acreage I would have peafowl. (Because of the noise factor, they need a minimum ten acres—otherwise the neighbours will be holding public meetings about you.) So I told Sharon they were one of my musts when we moved to the farm. She's never quite forgiven me.

We ended up with four peafowl running free on the farm. They became our friends, even as they demanded hand-fed grapes or raisins and raised havoc in the garden, dust bathing in freshly seeded beds or devouring the broccoli and cauliflower. We survive the screaming, though it leads to near-divorce every May. The male is merely standing guard, acting as both a lure and a warning system for predators, real or imaginary. Fifty feet off the ground on a narrow branch, and ready to fight, he's a formidable foe, unlike the peahens, who are vulnerable on the nest. Being good mothers, they're reluctant to leave their eggs, even under attack. Our survivors have grown wise and usually nest close to the house where the dogs can protect them.

Peafowl are inquisitive birds, and they often peer in our bedroom window in the morning, as if wondering why we aren't up yet. It's been dawn for twenty minutes! In the summer months they consider any open door an invitation. When our backs are turned they scoot in and rush along the low windowsills, snapping up the dead flies. This makes for impressive housecleaning, but the reward is usually a big plop of skanky peafowl shit on the spruce floor in the front room.

Sharon's father, Andy, visited the farm during the last years of his life. Almost blind, in his eighties, suffering from Parkinson's disease, he'd drift in and out of delirium because of the combination of strong medicines he'd been prescribed. After a while we got used to his rambling and didn't pay attention if he announced there was a ferry boat parked in the pasture or those CIA agents were in the closet again.

Preparing dinner late one afternoon, Sharon and I were in the kitchen, with her father nattering away in the front room. We couldn't see him behind the adobe divider, but his occasional bizarre announcements made us laugh, softly, despite ourselves. He was a dear, sweet man. After a while he began talking about how all the birds loved him. He declared himself the king of birds. I decided to peek around the corner. He was in his armchair blindly basking in the warmth coming from the sunroom. On each side of his chair sat the peafowl like regal attendants, Ajax to his left, his long tail fanned out behind him on the spruce floor, and Juno on Andy's right. Both birds held their heads erect, staring proudly at me.

ON THE OTHER HAND, meat chickens are grotesque creatures these days, and a very different fowl than their ancestors. The only good thing to say about the avian flu hysteria is that much of the commercial stock was destroyed during the panic, at least in Canada, and so breeders had to go back a few generations to start rebuilding their flocks with real chickens.

The average North American has not tasted a real chicken for years. Earlier, I wrote about the egg layers, their feed, and the growing conditions. The world of meat chickens is equally harsh. Just as the choice of laying breeds is narrowing, the remaining hatcheries offer an increasingly more limited range of meat birds. The current commercial meat birds are almost entirely descended from the feisty Cornish cross. Their offspring, the Cornish giant, has a tendency to grow as fast as a cancer, and its heart can just explode as the bird waddles over to the feed trough. But the Cornish giant is merely the grandfather of the new standard hybrids—the sickly Hubbard and the misshapen Arbor Acres, which, like the turkey, was bred to have bigger breasts and smaller thighs because that's what the market demands. I couldn't raise Arbor Acres and sleep at night. They require a controlled environment and enhanced feed to survive. They'd die if kept in the open air and fed traditional grains. The Hubbards were bred to be raised indoors. Put them in a pasture and they'll catch cold. Up to 20 percent will die after a few rainy days. The Cornish giants can still survive on a lower-protein scratch diet, which slows their unhealthy growth speed. Unfortunately, too many "free-range" farmers raise them on the recommended pellets. Cranked on this stuff, these overbred birds get a heart disease called water chest and fall over or have spectacular heart attacks, suddenly somersaulting into the air and turning purple. They're dead when they hit the ground. They also grow faster than they can produce bone-building calcium. An unforgivable number of the poultry in "free-range" factories turn into Quasimodos, all bent up with twisted legs and inflamed and calcified joints. Yet North Americans have become so habituated to the Jell-O-like quality of meat in supermarkets that they recoil upon first facing the denser, darker meat of a real chicken. After a few bites of our old laying fowl, long simmered with sea salt, or one of our authentic free-range broilers barbecued on a grill, they understand what they have been missing.

We raise only a hundred meat birds twice a year, in spring and summer, fifty to a coop and field—one behind our bedroom and one alongside the entrance driveway. We're still legally allowed to do this because we raise fewer than two hundred chickens a year, the current limit before you must buy a quota and become a factory farm. That's also a good number for us to raise healthily.

205

WHEN I BEGAN WRITING this history, both domestic and wild birds were being called a worldwide threat during a viral panic ignited by the apperance of avian flu. Electronic communication has the ability to create these panics, mostly because modern corporate media thrives on fear and uneasiness. A potential international epidemic is hotter news than tales of feisty hens in the hen yard. Epidemics are natural to human populations, and they often arrive with the interaction of species in crowded, unhealthy conditions. Sometimes a virus or a bacterium makes a jump to a new host—such as us. This is the fear with avian flu. The difficulty is that transnational agribusinesses, utilizing their enormous lobbying powers and alliances with agricultural ministries, are pushing the world's governments toward eliminating all free-ranging domestic fowl and thus ending our long natural history of living with birds, while the factory system creates disease vectors.

As far as can be determined, according to Andrew Nikiforuk in *Pandemonium,* the avian flu originated in a cluster of filthy factory farms in Guangdong province in China, where chicken sheds intermingled with pig sheds. Pig biology is close to human biology. The enormous volume of manure created at these animal factories was sprayed over the ponds of fish farms, providing high-protein feed to the fish sold in restaurants and grocery stores in many countries. This practice made those ponds an infection point for migratory bird populations, which rapidly spread the disease around the world.

Rather than dealing with the underlying causes of this potential pandemic, governments are considering banning chickens from the open air. Already in Canada, the factory farms are complying with a "voluntary" policy of keeping poultry in biosecure, closed systems with filtered, screened air. The government is kind enough to supply the specifications for the appropriate "voluntary" bird factory. This fits in exactly with the agenda of the giant agribusinesses (whose inhumane chicken factories have been increasingly undermined by the growing success of the slow-food and organic movements). They would like to see traditional farms regulated out of existence.

Almost as dangerous as the diseases are the panics that follow them, and our subsequent overreactive behaviour. In British Columbia 19 million birds were slaughtered in the Fraser Valley in 2004, to stop the spread of a milder variation of avian flu that wasn't fatal to humans. I talked with bird lovers in the valley afterwards, and the carnage was disheartening. Hired amateurs gassed chickens badly. Lost truckloads of dead birds were abandoned to rot. Chicken factories were flooded with firefighting foam, suffocating the birds. This was so successful that many of the killers are advocating that all chickens be foamed to death. They also invaded yards and butchered family pets. There were reports of guys in white suits chasing ostriches with machetes. Rare and endangered varieties of birds being nurtured for their contribution to the gene pool were indiscriminately slaughtered, even those known to be not susceptible to the virus.

At the height of the hysteria there was foolish talk of killing all waterfowl in England in the name of biosecurity. The authorities in Ho Chi Minh City, Vietnam, began poisoning their pigeons and wild birds. Holland

207

banned all domestic chickens from the open air, and Germany did the same, though that order was later rescinded after the uproar from organic poultry enthusiasts.

While agribusiness and governments conspire to eliminate real free-range poultry around the world, they are ignoring the fact that their systemic inbreeding of domestic fowl has damaged the birds' immune systems. Combine this with overcrowding, stress, and processed diets, and they've created exquisite breeding conditions for disease. That's why, although droves of wild birds have died, their percentage of fatalities is less than for birds in factory farms, where up to 80 percent of flocks of sixty thousand birds can die in a few days. The health authorities should be banning the raising of *more* than two hundred chickens in one location, rather than punishing those who grow two hundred poultry or fewer in a traditional manner. But since corporate agriculture has the greater influence, that alternative is unthinkable. More crucially, it is uneconomic in today's world, and would lead to chaos and famines if done abruptly. Our sole choice today is to develop a hybrid system of factory farms and revived traditional farming, and then move gradually back to the future of traditional farming.

MEAT CHICKENS ARE REGARDED as dumb creatures. I'm nervous about considering any animal dumb. One year we had a variant flock of Cornish crosses—intrepid, smart, strong-boned. They weren't the usual slow, fat, and stupid meat birds. They were as lively as layers, and they took to roosting on the perches, which most modern broilers can't

208

do because they're too fat and weak. Everything looked good, except they kept shaking their automatic watering dish loose. It would fall onto the floor and flood the coop, so I quick-fixed it with a football-sized rock on top of the pipe to steady it and prevent the chickens from roosting on the board holding the pipe, and then I forgot to properly repair it. One day I went out in the early morning after Sharon had gone to work and checked the coop's feed and water. They'd gummed up the water dish again, somehow unscrewing it.

With farm tasks you can go beautifully blank as you perform them, intent only on the task—the moment farming you. Fiddling with the dish, I was suddenly struck on the head, and I blacked out. I awoke lying on my back in the shit and the shavings, stunned. The chickens were gathered around me like ghouls at a funeral, or were they sizing up my eyeballs? I couldn't move. I was paralyzed, and the pain was excruciating. I'd been struck just above the forehead, and blood was running down my face and the back of my skull. I couldn't organize my thoughts until I saw the big rock lying beside me. Oh no! They'd still managed to roost on the pipe and had loosened it so that when I fiddled with the water bowl, the rock came down on my head. I heaved myself up to a sitting position, scaring the chickens back for a moment. I don't doubt that if I'd lain there unconscious for longer, they would have been at me. I was reminded of the story my dad told me when I was a child—about a farmer who fell into his cement pigpen, and all they found was his boots.

I crept to my feet, my head throbbing, blood pouring down. As I staggered out I realized that even raising chickens can be a fatal operation for the stupid, especially if your chickens are trying to kill you.

⸻⸻

LIKE MOST FARMS, WE keep dogs for flock protection and herding, and cats to check the rodent population, though the cats sometimes develop a taste for songbirds, which causes us anguish. Still, every farm needs a barn cat, although they can be more trouble than they're worth. Blame it on the Egyptians. Four thousand years ago a smart farmer by the Nile noticed that mice disappeared when *Felis silvestris libyca* showed up. Otherwise known as the Libyan wildcat, this sharp-witted and needle-clawed feline soon had the farmers offering plates of milk and fish. It's been like that ever since. Cats became regarded as manifestations of the god Bastet, which caused one wit to remark: "In ancient times cats were worshipped as gods. They have never forgotten this."

We named our latest tom the Emperor Wu. As imperial in manner as his name, he's a dynamic, graceful predator. One night, when we had laying hens, I ventured out to lock up the coop. In the dark I started counting the heads on the roost because we'd been having raccoon trouble. There was one head too many. This is not common, as anyone with chickens will agree. I muttered and counted again. Then I realized the extra head belonged to a cat, Wu—or, as he soon came to be known, "He Who Sleeps with the Chickens." Chickens will huddle on their small, round branch perches, keeping warm and emotionally comforted by the touch of their neighbours. Wu had joined the crowd once he realized that rats had bored a hole into the coop and were sneaking in at night to raid the grain feeder. The last thing the rats saw was a "chicken" leaping into the air with its claws out.

GOOSE AND DUCK, TURKEY and chicken, and guardian cats and dogs. These are all stories on a mixed farm, the digressions and "teaching tales" we've been telling ourselves since that first seed was kept over winter and the first goat corralled—each story a part of another history—all intertwined and endless. Our minds can't encompass the multiplying intersections of a farm's diverse interactions: it's a mystic star map whose interconnections are larger than human imagination and certainly beyond the reductionist mind trap of the logic that led to the thrills of gobalization. You can live well among those mystic connections only by using equal parts of tradition, intuition, and science as guides, along with a good dose of common sense. But my chickens are shut up for the night and the dogs sprawled on the deck, keeping their nonlinear guard, and for now I can sleep with that story.

15

PEST CONTROL
SYNDROME

· · · · ·

WEEDS ARE EVERY gardener's nightmare. One way to avoid weeding is to eat the weeds. Your weed is often my salad—dandelions, miner's lettuce, purslane, chickweed. Then there's steamed pigweed: delicious. Nettles make a stunning pesto. Eat them if you can't beat them. Wilding—eating the native plants and fungi—has always been an important pleasure of rural life. After I talked Sharon into her first suspicious sampling, she turned into a real weed eater too.

Apart from never having enough time to weed, we long ago learned that the best pest control, apart from eating the weeds, is usually another pest, or providing the environment for every inhabitant to fulfill its natural inclinations. Weeds can also be homes for beneficial insects, such as lacewings or ladybugs. The greater part of farming is weighing the scales of harm and help. Too many weeds will suck up the life of a plant and leave it stunted—a target for predatory insects or disease. Besides, there's a reason why we say, "They're spreading like weeds." Weeds invariably reseed at alarming rates, so they'll drive you twice as mad next year. That's why I constantly remind myself of Voltaire's aphorism: cultivate your garden!

THE GARDEN IS RICH and vibrant today, the longest day of the year, lush and overgrown with weeds—pigweed, buttercups, Queen Anne's lace, thistles, nettles, chickweed, burdock, and others. This abundance is not due to any calculated effort on our part. There are so many it can be depressing if you let it get to you, but it's merely a symptom of traditional farming: "When's the best time to weed?"

"When you have the time," says Mike. He has the same advice for pruning, chopping firewood, seeding, and most any other farm task. Weeding is not a duty; it's a way of life—a practice, like meditation. If you have a goal in a garden, you're doomed.

213

I WAS HAULING SOME bags of apples into Mike and Bev's cooler one autumn evening when I noticed a humongous wasp nest in the rafters of his covered deck. "Whoa," I said, "look at that mother of a nest!"

"Don't go messing with them or you'll regret it," he said needlessly. This comment made me remember back to my university days. A friend had a massive wasp nest on his third-floor apartment balcony. Since I had a reputation for being hard to intimidate back then, he asked me if I could deal with it.

"Sure," I said. "Where's your hockey stick?" He handed it to me, and I told him to stand behind the sliding door and slam it shut as soon as I leaped back inside. Then I stepped onto the balcony and drove the nest with an overhead slapshot out to the lawn far below. I nimbly stepped inside while my friend slammed the door shut. Not a wasp followed me. We cockily observed a mass of them banging against the glass, and congratulated ourselves on that excellent solution. It was time to celebrate with a drink.

Then we heard a crash from the apartment below and a lot of screaming and thumping. With horror I realized that the occupants beneath us must have had their windows open. Since there was nothing we could do we just sat down and were very silent, pretending that nobody was home, while the crashing and banging carried on for several minutes until it finally died down. Since then I've never messed with wasps unless they messed with me first, though I have to kill them if they get in the house because Sharon is allergic. But I was surprised Mike would leave a nest in his carport through which his entire family, including his grandchildren, passed regularly. "Why don't you spray it?" I asked.

"You crazy?" he said in his usual blunt way. "That nest is cleaning out every aphid within a half-mile." Mike is old school. Rather than destroying the beneficial nest, he figured children soon learn to keep away from wasps.

Until then I'd never thought much about wasps feeding on aphids, but of course they do. Now I'm happy to watch the wasps hunting our garden like gunslingers, cleaning up insect pests better than any insecticide over the long term. We even plant nasturtiums every year, which aphids prefer, creating a permanent feeding ground that maintains the wasp population. There's much truth to the folklore of companion planting, where you grow different plants close together. Some companion plants attract beneficial insects, while others repel noxious insects. Nature is always creating checks and balances, feedback mechanisms, and if you follow its teachings, you will do well. We used to be religious about intermingling companion plants with our produce, but we've grown lazy and tend to merely stick them in where there's room. That often works, and when it doesn't we eat fewer cabbages or cucumbers. Acceptance is the hardest work of a gardener. The second-hardest work is learning to recognize that pest management is relatively simple: don't ask how to eliminate pests—ask why you are attracting them.

Healthy plants generally don't attract bugs. Unhealthy plants succumb to every kind of disease and bug passing by. If the plants are living in the mixed ecosystem of our garden, they have an excellent chance. But it's not a perfect world, and strange insects and diseases come flowing over the hills. They arrive on the winds of winter, and my lovely pecan tree will suddenly wilt and die in the spring. That's life in the garden of the world. Raging against disease can lead to raging against health, and if you cultivate a garden you can't treat one illness in a way that causes other illnesses. You must learn to accept some losses rather than damaging the whole system. Our species has turned to chemical farming because we prefer impeccable fields and high yields rather than doing our best and appreciating the results. The compulsion to achieve perfect gardens is the real disease. I call it pest control syndrome.

Since Salt Spring Island is in the vanguard of the organic and local-food movement, almost all the gardens are organic—only a few chemical-using dinosaurs lurk among us. This means the wild flora and its fauna are stable, including the beneficial insects that regularly rescue us from plagues of harmful insects. We helped the process at Trauma Farm by planting bird-and-insect-attracting plants as soon as we arrived, so our ecosystem has many checks and balances. For instance, during the winter we often encounter woolly aphids in our houseplants introduced from florists, but once we put the plants out on the first of June, the young wasps and ladybugs soon clean up the aphids.

Knowing the tricks of the garden is what makes older farmers and gardeners important. They've been through the wars and have developed innovative strategies for survival. Just as the pen is eventually stronger than the gun, garden gossip with knowledgeable neighbours is stronger than herbicides and pesticides. For instance, we live in a region that suffers from carrot maggot. Because of our temperate climate overeager and uneducated gardeners plant their carrots early, during the rainy season, which washes the seeds away more times than not. If the rain doesn't get the carrots, they begin maturing as the fly hatches. But we plant late, in May, and harvest before September, missing the two hatches of the flies, and our carrots are untouched by their maggots. If we want winter carrots, we mulch them heavily and don't pick any from that crop until late October, when the flies are dead. Every time you pick a carrot you break hair roots. The fibres left behind release a scent that attracts the flies. If the ground is undisturbed, they don't know the carrot is there. And as a last resort, if we're greedy for carrots every week, we cover the row with remay cloth, a gauzy, tight-knit cloth that the flies can't penetrate. But we have to bury the edges, as the sneaky little devils will crawl under the cloth.

The only sprays we use are lime-sulphur, mineral oil, and fixed copper, and maybe soap-water or diatomaceous earth for thrips on the gladioli and onions. In past extreme situations I've used "organic" pesticides—rotenone or pyrethrum—but I haven't used them or copper spray for a decade. I'd rather the produce meet its fate; I know that by not interfering I am creating the environment for a healthier crop next year. We are also safe because we don't plant too much of any crop, though we are growing dangerously close to having too much garlic. But then how can you ever have too much garlic?

In the 1990s, another blight appeared—a cross between the Mexican and Irish blights that was able to survive our mild winters. In our era of invasive diseases and species, these misfortunes occur more often than in the past. Tomatoes were once a fine Salt Spring crop, but this new blight ruined both tomatoes and potatoes. One of its parents, the infamous Irish potato blight, was responsible for the starvation of a million people in the mid-1800s—because the Irish poor single-cropped one variety of spud too extensively, and the loss of an entire crop in a year meant doom. This blight will flow down the vine and rot potatoes in the ground. When you dig them up, they will be mush. The first year of the blight was disastrous on our island—almost everyone's tomatoes and potatoes were destroyed. The problem was magnified because casual gardeners let their tomatoes sprawl susceptibly on damp ground rather than staking them.

We were spared major damage because we grow our staked-and-trimmed tomatoes through holes pierced into black plastic covers. Not only does the plastic afford protection and heat for garter snakes, which are another living insecticide, it provides extra heat in the soil for the tomatoes during our damp springs. We reuse the plastic over the years until it becomes so shredded we finally have to recycle it. With the plastic the blight can't bounce up from the soil during rains or when we turn on the big farm sprinklers. But I'm still trying to figure out a way of eliminating the plastic ground cover altogether.

Once a potato vine ripens and withers, it won't transmit the blight, so if you plant potatoes early the tubers can store nicely underground until the cold, wet weather of late fall. Other islanders cloched their tomatoes and shifted to drip irrigation. Not a grower that I know took up expensive fungicides. Organic gardening is a delight and an adventure. It makes us think in original directions, as ecology itself does—and it's smarter than the eventually ineffective, toxic chemical weapons that agribusiness puts its faith in.

In the late afternoon the garden is alive with bumblebees and birds and moths, and the wasps hunting among the colourful nasturtiums. If we are lucky, we will see the majestic sphinx moth in the larkspurs. The big bucket I use to soak my bonsais has mosquito larvae in it, and I'll have to dump it. Usually I don't worry about mosquitoes because my ponds contain fish and the larvae provide feed for them, but the West Nile panic is upon us. We work at keeping the local mosquito population down, not just for us but to avoid providing habitat for dangerous public health managers like the one from Victoria who, during the initial West Nile panic, insisted on spraying all the mosquitoes in southwestern British Columbia, because "they're not good for anything, anyway."

Not good for anything? My local bat, dragonfly, nighthawk, trout, and swallow populations would disagree equally with his pronouncement. Mosquitoes feed a myriad of wildlife—entire ecosystems, in fact, are based upon them—but we still have a colonialist, kill-them-all attitude toward pests. While it's true that extreme health emergencies might need limited and intelligent reactions in special cases, the nature of the chemical approach inevitably leads to excess.

On Salt Spring we've also been battling attempts to aerial-spray for gypsy moths—instead, we use volunteer trap setters and inspectors. Since our island hasn't been sprayed for decades, we have a vibrant, healthy, diverse moth and butterfly population, including a number of rare and endangered varieties. The government wants to aerial-spray with Bt, which it blithely tells us doesn't harm humans—only a few "dangerous" moths—neglecting to mention that it will kill rare butterflies and moths on some of the best organic farmland on the island to eradicate a small population that can be better controlled by spot-spraying from the ground, hand collecting, and pheromone traps. When I survey the hosts of caterpillars and the moths fluttering gorgeously around our garden, I consider the damage that ripping them out of the ecosystem would do not only to them but to the entire community of insects that thrive on their carcasses, including the parasitoid wasps. Yet if we don't extensively and expensively hunt the gypsy moth, this invasive species could undergo a dangerous population explosion—it's all a question of common sense.

In 1958, when Mao initiated China's Great Leap Forward, part of it was the Four Pests Campaign—the elimination of mosquitoes, flies, rats, sparrows. He decided to include house sparrows because he'd learned a sparrow can eat ten pounds of grain a year. Six hundred million Chinese citizens were ordered to kill sparrows on a single day, tearing out their nests and running around banging pots and making noises, keeping the birds in the air until they fell from the sky with exhaustion—causing a catastrophic destruction of the sparrow population. What Mao wasn't told was that sparrows eat more insects than grain and feed locusts to their young. Within two years the crops were overwhelmed by noxious insects, especially locusts. This was one of several ignorant "scientific" decisions about farming that led to the famine in which 20 to 40 million people died.

If I see dragonflies haunting the water above the ponds, I know that they, along with the swallows, are feasting on any mosquitoes whose larvae survived the goldfish. Dragonflies aren't called mosquito hawks without reason. They can eat their own weight in half an hour. They also are captured and eaten by the swallows even as they are eating a mosquito in the air. A lucky dragonfly can survive as long as a summer. I love it when the great spring and autumn flights of carpenter ants and termites erupt into the sky, because then the dragonflies will hunt in packs, and it's an amazing sight. There are eighty-five varieties in my province, of which twenty-four are listed as endangered.

Their young nymphs eat underwater, devouring mosquito larvae, other water bugs, and tadpoles until they emerge and moult, leaving their clear nymph shells attached to our iris leaves. I've made arrangements out of the leaves, which can give a thrill to visitors who suddenly notice the clear casing with its legs, abdomen, and head on a leaf among the blossoms on the table.

The more I live on the farm, the less damage I want to inflict, except maybe on the nasty imported European slugs—not the giant Pacific slugs, those slow, liquid sages of the forest floor, harmless and beautiful. I love using nature to help us garden. When I rototill I'm usually followed by peafowl and robins snapping up the fat, pasty-fleshed cutworms as they're exposed. For the birds I am the gifting god of their summer garden, revealing the feast of pests.

THE EAGLE IS MERELY one of many predators and pests that haunt small farms, and with the peafowl on sentry duty, I don't worry about their attacks much, though they might snatch the occasional chicken. The inability to accept loss is the greatest weakness of farms both great and small. That said, an eagle will kill and pluck a full-grown chicken in front of the cowering flock and then fly away with the corpse, leaving only the gizzard behind on a pile of feathers. Roosters sometimes attempt to defend their hens, but they're puny and useless against an eagle—unless they raise enough of a ruckus to alert the peafowl. Then the feathers hit the fan, and the advantage shifts.

Our eagles are not sport killers, and they don't slaughter indiscriminately like cougars, mink, raccoons, or a rogue

221

raven. This might not be so true in other regions. Also, they can be startlingly brutal. Several years ago the vultures circled a thicket in the lower field. Trouble. I found the ewe huddled in the trees. Her lamb had stuck while being born. The ewe was still alive, but there was an eagle eating the head of her lamb even as it was being born. I chased the eagle away and got hold of the leg of the lamb and dragged the poor headless body out of the distraught mother.

Hawks will infrequently take a shot at a young chick. Hens might be small, but they can be valiant defending their young. At night the barred owl is a master killer of chickens roosting in trees. It will land on their branch and sidle up next to the chicken, tuck right against it, then lean over and—chomp! Their depredations are balanced out by the saw-whet owls, which specialize in mice and voles and are impressively brave as well as nosy little birds. More than once I've been startled while standing on someone's deck suddenly noticing this tiny owl sitting on a branch a few feet from my face, gazing curiously at me.

Our greatest aerial danger on these islands can be the ravens—intelligent and friendly birds, with a sense of humour, they are also territorial. I have a gentleman's agreement with our pair. They are large, well fed, and getting on in years. I ignore the occasional theft of a goose or chicken egg, and I always "accidentally" spill a little grain at the sheep trough. I've seen a raven soar right into the coop and fly back out with an egg in its beak. Luckily, my ravens don't make this a habit, so I assume they do it only when they're desperate. They will also feast on the corpse of any animal.

These ravens, fortunately, keep our territory tightly controlled, except for the occasional sneak attack by an outsider.

Our birds seem exceptionally smart and mischievous, and I enjoy watching them torment the dogs at dinner. Once they hear the goose honk, signifying feeding time, they fly up and park on the trough. As soon as I open the pasture gate the dogs give chase to these "enemy birds" at full speed. The ravens fly three feet above the ground, gliding just slowly enough to keep ahead, as they take an extended tour of the fields, until the dogs' tongues are hanging down to the ground at the end of the far pasture. Then the ravens return and perch in the birches near the trough while the dogs, exhausted, lurch back to the house, their duty done. When I lock the pasture gate on the way out, the ravens fly down and scurry amid the sheep, picking up grains of barley. Afterwards, in the summer months, they fly up and have a little dessert of cherries. I've tried netting. I've tried paper owls and spangled streamers. Nothing scares off the ravens for long. To add insult to injury, they start on the pears after they finish off the cherries. I'm forced to count my blessings. So far they aren't eating the plums and the apples.

Then there's the obnoxious and brilliant jays, who nest in the spring, disappear to torment other farmers and their crops in high summer, and return the week before our hazelnuts ripen. Their first chatter is like an alarm bell at the farm, and within days we are fighting them, branch by branch, for the hazelnuts.

Sometimes a farm can't win, and it's our stubborn spirit that makes us want to change nature, which seems easier than changing ourselves. Planting dwarf grafted cherry trees or hazelnuts in netted enclosures would be the most efficient method of discouraging bird robberies. Otherwise, you end up with the American fruit farms and those traps exterminating tens of thousands of ravens, crows, starlings, jays, and migrating songbirds. Crop growers, especially vineyard owners unwilling to net their vines, will employ radar systems to detect bird flocks and then send out shooters, disguising their gunfire with the propane bird-scare cannons that go off from dawn until dark and drive neighbours nuts. Scare-eye balloons, distress calls, biosonic devices, flares and other pyrotechnics, fake owls, hawks (with handler), shotguns that shoot firecrackers and streamers, and hilariously wonky inflatable clowns operated by motion detectors or radar—all work to a degree, but the birds eventually seize their share of the prizes if the fruit isn't netted.

Beyond insect and bird pests, North American farms are locked in a permanent duel with several mammal pests and predators. Trauma Farm's most consistent pests are mink and raccoons, which can wipe out a chicken coop in fifteen minutes. Afterwards the raccoons will wander off to one of those green-concrete hobby farms and be fed because they're so cute, though the owners don't recognize that the exploding raccoon population is destroying the low-nesting wild bird population of the island as well as our chickens. Brown eyes always beat harsh reality when it comes to our species, and that issue brings us face to face with the deer epidemic.

Our island's nature conservancy recently brought in a particularly impressive government biologist for a lecture on the exploding deer populations, which are extirpating the majority of our native flowers and shrubs, including the island's endangered orchids and the fabulous ecology of the wild Garry Oak orchards. When we first arrived the meadows were alive with flowers. The only fawn lilies and orchids that I see today are on cliffs where the deer can't reach them, including a spectacular fawn lily wall across from a lumberyard. Without cougars or coyotes, and with the rapid decrease in hunters, the deer infestation is spiralling out of control. In our early years two varieties of orchid flowered profusely along the forested margins of our pasture. Sharon and I would take enchanted afternoon walks among them. I haven't seen one in ten years.

Encouraging deer where there's a shortage of predators is the equivalent of feeding Norway rats, another beautiful creature that, once its ecology collapses, will spread disease and illness and reproduce in fantastic numbers. If you feed deer, it's illegal; but worse, it is as ecologically dangerous as pouring oil in a local creek. Fed by sentimentality and "brown-eyed environmentalism," the deer are not only remaking the ecosystems of the continent, they're being trained to regard farms and gardens across the continents as food banks. My neighbour is a deer feeder, and I have counted twenty-nine in her abandoned hayfield. According to the biologist not only are the deer altering the deciduous forests of eastern America, they will eventually make extinct the great cedar forests of Haida Gwaii as they prevent any seedlings from growing.

While there's an increasing number of ecologically sensitive small farms, farming history is uneven. Farmers, despite their pretensions to a romantic, bucolic lifestyle (as with my foolish deer-feeding neighbour), can also be a bloodthirsty lot. Wolves moving into a territory will hunt down competition if they can, as will farmers. This doesn't mean small farmers are responsible for the world's extinctions.

Population growth is the real enemy of the planet. Hunter-gatherer cultures have been no less ruthless than farmers, and the great mammalian extinctions of the Pleistocene era in North America were likely caused by a fatal combination of hunting and climate change, just as globalization and escalating populations and climate change are increasing the pace of today's extinctions in the ever-shrinking wilderness. Once farmers have reduced predators, they've historically tended to eliminate grazing animals that compete with their livestock for forage, as well as to supplement their own diet. Finally, the farmers are forced to confront the explosions of small-pest populations created by their meddling with the food chain. And then, if faced with plagues, wars, famines, and overpopulation, people in search of food will hunt the small and the strange and the sad, which is why you find food enthusiasts for stag beetles in Thailand, grub eaters in Africa, and sparrows on sticks in China.

If you're a poor peasant scrabbling out a hopeless living on the land, the need to protect it from predators is over-whelming, even when this leads to further environmental damage that will return to haunt you. Consider the live-stock farmers of the prairies. Wolves will sometimes take cattle or sheep. Packs that become habituated to dining on livestock have to be dealt with, but they generally stay away. The difficulty with exterminating wolves is that they are a check on the coyote population. They also stabilize moose populations. Once wolves were brought back to Yosem-ite, they immediately started hunting the coyotes. Within a few years the coyote population began shrinking and the moose left the sandy riverbeds because they no longer felt comfortable in the open. As a result, willows returned to those riverbeds and the ecosystem renewed its traditional balanced habitat.

Trapping and poisoning the wolves and coyotes in the nineteenth and twentieth centuries led to gopher population explosions. So rancher-farmers have turned gopher slaughter into a Sunday sport with Rodenators and other explosive devices, filming themselves laughing as burning gophers whiz past and then uploading these cruel videos onto YouTube. Yet the gophers still proliferate, injuring livestock with their dangerous holes and degrading the grazing land of the once-lush prairies.

THE REAL NIGHTMARE OF any farm is rats—not so much the local, native rats but the ubiquitous Norway rat. A pair can produce fifteen thousand descendants in a year. Rats are attracted to farms because there's so much feed and shelter. They love grain and compost and fallen fruit and almost everything else. Our island can be particularly rat infested at times, but you won't find that in the tourist brochures. We have an equally noxious feral cat population caused by eco-urbanites who consider it "natural" to release a house cat into the wild when they grow bored with it or move away. The feral cats are hell on the songbird population but oddly, not on the mice or rats.

I often eliminate our rats for several months. Then suddenly there's one, and then there's dozens, and the war begins again. Outside of Antarctica, a few uninfected islands, and Alberta, which insists rats don't exist (I'm deeply suspicious) within its boundaries, Norway rats are everywhere. No doubt they and their sometime

227

companions, the cockroaches, will outlast the human race. While we rapidly push the planet toward mass extinctions, they're waiting for the leftovers.

TRAUMA FARM HAS THE standard assortment of dogs and barn cats assigned to patrol for rats and field mice (another professional pest). We use metal containers for feed and follow the best procedures, but still they burrow up through the ground or chew holes in the walls. The rats and mice worked us over pretty good during our early years here—a few even got into the attic above our bedroom. I resorted to poison pellets. Once! Little blue pellets. I put them in the sealed attic where our cats couldn't enter. Despite my precautions, I soon found poison pellets stashed at the back of our medication drawer in the bathroom. Rodents are smart! Not only that, but they obviously weren't just in the attic. We got more cats and set up more traps and finally drove them out of the house.

Rats and farmers can beget far-fetched stories. A tender-hearted artist long ago witnessed a brutal farmer kicking his sheepdog. After that, for years, this gentle artist, with impish glee, would release his live-trapped rats at night in the farmer's barn.

In her young years Sam moved so fast she could snatch a leaping rat out of the air and break its back. I'm relentless when it comes to rats and mice, especially after someone I knew died from hantavirus—probably contracted from mouse droppings.

Traditionally, farmers deal with mice by filling a wooden-handled bucket half full of water. Then you tie a strip of bacon around the loose handle. The mouse will run up the metal handle and touch the wooden grip, which rotates, tossing the mouse into the water, where it drowns. I tried a variant for rats with a garbage can in the feed shed, filling the bottom third with water and floating a tiny dish of feed in it. The method worked too horrifyingly well. I found whole families of drowned rats. One would fall in, and the others would bravely, suicidally leap to its rescue. This was too cruel for me. But then I'd also seen rats that had mutilated themselves when caught in traps. The whole business turns my stomach, yet to surrender would have worse consequences.

ALTHOUGH I'M NOT A Christian, the traditional Christmas with its carolling, gaudy tree, goodwill, rum-and-eggnogs— all of it—is nearly enough to convert me every year. Despite the ugly shopping orgy it's also become, Christmas remains a warm tradition we celebrate with gusto. Every year on Christmas Day we declare a truce at Trauma Farm, disarm the traps, and throw feed and grain to every animal and predator in sight, pests included. The next day the wars begin again.

229

One year I couldn't kick myself into the mood. Sharon wanted me to find our Christmas tree, and our gift making and purchasing had fallen behind. I was too busy and too broke to worry about Christmas trees. Then we had an early morning power failure. Without the refrigerator running, we heard a squeaking. We searched everywhere but couldn't discover its source. After the power returned and I was cooking breakfast I heard it again and realized it was behind the stove. Crawling around on the floor, I noticed a little tail sticking up behind an electrical box attached to the adobe wall. A mouse! His tail wagged ferociously before he jumped out from behind the box and rubbed his face with his paws. He repeated these actions several times.

"He's hurt," I said to Sharon. "There's something wrong with him. Pass me the goldfish net from beside the pond." Sharon fetched the long-handled little net and handed it to me where I lay semi-trapped between the stove and the counter. I floundered after the mouse, while Sharon supervised over my shoulder, releasing the occasional squeal of support or fright—I couldn't tell which.

The mouse continued this obsessive behaviour while I struggled to reach him. Suddenly, an enormous furry, red-bellied wolf spider, at least half the size of the mouse, darted from behind the outlet, straight for my head. Both Sharon and I shouted as I whipped the net around and whacked the spider with the handle. Gimped up, it kept crawling aggressively toward me, so I beat it to death. It was him or me. I've encountered some large spiders in my life, including a tarantula on a Texas gravestone, but this was the biggest, scariest, most aggressive spider I've ever met in a house, let alone while wedged alongside a stove. It died three inches from my face. The attack was so scary I almost felt like moving back to the city.

The mouse stood beside the outlet, stunned. That's when I understood we'd been overhearing an epic battle between the mouse and the spider, and I'd just flattened the mouse's breakfast into hairy juice on the floor. Worse, the disappointed, spider-bit mouse wasn't going anywhere, so I said to Sharon, "Hand me a rubber glove, and I'll grab him."

230

Gloved, I dug in again behind the counter, stretching toward the mouse, then he lunged for me. This was one Schwarzenegger of a mouse! I scooted backwards, banging my head. Sharon was now standing on a chair, shrieking.

"He got away!" I exclaimed. "He made a run for it."

"He didn't get away!" Sharon screamed. "He ran up your sleeve."

"Oh posh! He didn't run up my sleeve." That's when I felt something wriggling around in my armpit between my shirt and the light flannel shirt-jacket I wear in cool weather. It was the first time in my life a mouse made me scream. "Arggh!" I ripped my flannel overshirt off faster than you could say "cheese."

I managed to trap him in the sleeve and ran for the door with the bundle. Sharon flung it open, and I bolted down the walkway to the road. The mouse was still squirming as I went out the gate. By now I was full of admiration for this valiant mouse. I didn't have the heart to kill him, so I decided to release him in the feed shed. If he was as smart as he was intrepid, he could survive the cats and me and never have to worry about dinner again. I shook out my overshirt. 231

No mouse. Nowhere. I was so terrified I started checking my pockets and my crotch. I didn't say anything to Sharon after I got back, but I left the shirt outside. Later, four of Sharon's girlfriends arrived for lunch. While the women wined and cheesed away I decide to haul in the week's firewood. Entering with the second wheelbarrow load I was greeted by five screaming women, and a dog circling the chesterfield. The mouse from hell had returned. Needless to say, after much sofa lifting and furniture rearranging, there was no mouse. The women went back to their wine.

I continued with my firewood. When I arrived with the next load all the women were screaming again, and both dogs were barking. Only this time one of the women had snatched the fishnet and in a remarkable feat of dexterity whanged it down on the mouse as he raced across the floor.

I lunged for the mouse as he attempted to squirm out from beneath the net. I caught it all up, net and mouse, and ran for the door, remarking to Sharon on my way past that maybe she'd have to drive me to Timbuktu this time, to make sure he didn't come back. Instead, I walked him into the bush so far I practically got lost, and then I held out the net. The mouse clambered up the netting and perched on the rim, staring at me with absolute aplomb. He noticed a stump nearby, and made a graceful leap to a pile of leaves beside the stump, where he busied himself digging and searching, occasionally glancing back.

Everyone knows that feeling you get when you think you're being watched. Well, I got it. I slowly lifted my head. Only no one was there—except the forest. I was ringed with trees. Christmas trees! They were perfect!

They were all around the stump, and while the indomitable mouse gazed up at me with curiosity, munching on a seed, I was finally infused with the spirit of the season.

16

GRACE AT WORK

. . . . . .

*T*HE FIRST TIME I showed the grandchildren how to bake our bread for dinner the kitchen looked like it had gone through a snowstorm, but it was a fine loaf that came out on the baking stone. I love kneading bread, because it is so much like kneading clay for pottery. I can knead the dough in the two common patterns that potters use, the more complex Japanese chrysanthemum and the simpler calf-face. The kids love it when I knead the dough into the calf-face because it looks just like a calf's face. Then, two years later, we were given a bread-making machine. It makes lousy bread; however, using it to knead the dough works remarkably well, so we use it just for that and then move on to normal baking on a stone, braiding loaves, and so on. It's a hell of a lot less messy. Sharon gratefully assumed I'd hurricaned my last kitchen with my

flour-tossing talents. Bread making almost grew boring, so
we began making homemade noodles, which really thrilled
the grandkids, and I became a happy frog in the flour bag
again. If there's a way to make a mess, I will find it.

Later, I initiated them into the mysteries of honey. They
were soon spinning the stainless steel gears of the extractor,
the honey oozing out of the combs. This made them feel
important, and after we had cleaned our sticky hands and
the machinery I treated them to honey toast and they each
got a little chunk of honeycomb to chew, and we were soon
all sticky-handed again, blessed with the magic of honey.

Traditions survive only if they are taught to children,
and we've done our best with our two sons, who both ended
up being landscape gardeners; so now we have the thrilling grandchildren to corrupt with my anti-authoritarian,
see-for-yourself attitude, despite the rolling eyes of their parents. We thought we'd start them in the kitchen and move
on to the gardening and firewood later. That's also why
Sharon taught them the gentle arts of the cookie and the pie
before I was allowed to lead them into my messier world

234 of bread.

I LIVE TO WORK and work to live. The blessing of a small
farm is that it's not a job—like food or poetry, it's a calling.
It's a thousand jobs, most of them intermingled, often cul-
minating in the afternoon when, like the average farmer,
you find yourself trying to complete everything simultaneously. Work inherited our suspicions only when it became
a commodity. True, in any endeavour there's inevitable
drudgery. Hand weeding five thousand bulbs of garlic can

translate into drudgery fast, yet I've learned to love the multitude of tasks on a small farm, though Sharon will testify she's seen her share of incidents where I've gone hysterical while repeating a mindless job for the thousandth time. On the farm everything is continuous, and few tasks are completed. Construction projects like barns and sheds are never-ending. Training to be a potter years ago is how I learned that a pot never finishes firing. Even porcelain glazes—and window glass, a glaze in another form—continue changing after leaving the kiln. Over the centuries the glass in the windows of Europe's ancient cathedrals has flowed down, displaying visible changes in thickness and colour. The miracle of ancient potters is that they used traditional knowledge to create for the future. The famed Chinese "crab claw" crackle glazes would barely begin to crackle during the lifetime of the potter. They were designed to achieve their finest form long after the potter was in his grave and had passed his secrets on to his apprentice. A well-maintained small farm has that kind of continuity, passing its traditional knowledge from generation to generation.

Whenever we take on a new farm helper, I remind myself it is the duty of the young to be thoughtless. I know this because in my younger years I stomped off my share of job sites in frenzies that, in retrospect, were undeserved, and I've also lazily inflicted too much bad craftsmanship on a number of employers. Since then our hired hands have exacted revenge on me for my own years of idiocy. Hired help definitely ain't what it used to be, though I'm betting farmers have been saying that since Babylon. Here, in the lotus land of the Gulf Islands, we get them all—the boys with bones through their noses and women with so much face metal they tinkle. Because of a lack of affordable housing there's a constant labour shortage on the islands, and farmers like me go begging for labourers in unlikely places, snatching whatever wandering but work-willing hippie goes by—a hiring practice that can lead to encounters with fabulously interesting people, along with the occasional scary or ludicrous consequence.

Butterfly, a Maori-painted spokesperson for the new "Freedom Camp" in Fulford Harbour, announced to our local paper that she and her fellow squatters were protesting an ugly subdivision many miles up-island and would only abandon the public beach they'd squatted if greedy islanders would donate a mere thousand acres of land so they could live in harmony with nature. One of this sharp-witted gang of ecologists had discovered a loophole in the law that allowed them to camp below the legal high-tide line, which is higher than the physical tide line—in a comfortably dry squatters' lawful limbo where they set up their tarps, tents, and driftwood structures, polluting the fragile eel-grass ecosystem of our bay. These are the kind of eco-urbanites who ruin the hard work of real ecologists.

Naturally, farming being what it is, I had to swallow my pride and offer work to the Freedom Campers, one at a time. Usually, they didn't show up before noon, and often they didn't show at all. Sometimes we wished they hadn't. Except for one stalwart flat-nosed, nipple-pierced fellow— who turned out to be remarkably nice, hard-working, and intelligent—the Freedom Campers were notably averse to work, and the camp soon turned into an awful mess, which they abandoned as winter came on.

Then we found a neighbour who was reliable and helpful, a real sweetheart who, when Sharon instructed him
to weed the garlic, did just that, snapping off several thousand garlic tops. Fortunately, he was such an inept weeder
that the garlic survived, though dwarfed and unsaleable for
the year. He was a smart, likeable fellow with a university
degree and, apart from this spectacular accident, became
a fine worker. Acceptance is an important part of farming.
Another helper lasted an hour mowing the lawn before he
announced it was too hot to work. That night he carved a
bloody cross in his forehead and took to ripping up the sap-
lings on the farm where he was staying. Fortunately, they
got him medical attention before he hurt himself further.

A surprisingly useful helper received instructions from
his television set, which made Sharon nervous. He worked
like a tornado but soon decided he knew what to do best
and when to do it. If you gave him the gas Weed Eater, a
tool that thrills all the boys, he'd do the whole farm and
the public roads if you didn't catch him in time and take it
away. And there's nothing like soothing old bones, naked in
the hot tub at dawn on a peaceful farm, alone in the woods,
and suddenly hearing your lawn mower start up around the
corner of the house. But he was a good-hearted fellow and
gradually drifted off-island, following his voices....

For several months a slender young woman, sun-
browned and as hard and skinny as an arbutus branch,
became an excellent helper. A farm has many duties that
tend to drive away female workers, but she had the strength
and the fortitude to toss the hay bales, shovel manure, and
wield a mean pickaxe, although her first day at work was
surprising. Sharon explained the garden tasks that needed

237

doing, and the young woman, surveying the jobs ahead of her, said, "Well, I better get to work, then." She promptly whipped off her top and started weeding.

"Uh, we have guests coming shortly," said Sharon, somewhat taken aback.

"That's all right," the bare-breasted woman replied. "I don't mind." I didn't either, though it was distracting. Sharon thought it was all rather amusing in the end.

Our all-time favourite helper was a willowy, big-bearded fellow who belonged to a society that advocated "marijuana milk." The members of this group thrive on the seeds of (legal) hemp, sprouted and blended into a drink which, apparently, like many other rare plants advocated by enthusiasts, is "the most nutritious food in the world." He looked so frail you feared he would blow away, and he moved so slowly it gave me a nervous breakdown just watching him. Yet this mellow, sluggish helper accomplished an astonishing amount of work and never lost his cool. He usually finished more than what we asked him to do by the end of the day. A perfect combination of natural laziness and high intelligence, he moved more slowly than honey across a piece of toast, and no gesture was wasted. It was like a miracle every day, watching the jobs efficiently eliminated one by one. We practically wept when he and his family were driven off the island because they couldn't find housing. We still hope to get him back.

Following his departure, our first interview was with a labourer who, upon arrival, announced he charged more to do construction work, couldn't do heavy lifting (including wheelbarrowing) because of a bad back, couldn't distinguish weeds from vegetables, wouldn't use motorized lawn mowers or tillers because they were detrimental to the environment (even though he arrived in a big pickup truck), and refused to help with the sheep or the chicken coops because he was a vegetarian and livestock were a blight on the planet. Then he was annoyed that I couldn't provide him any farm work.

I still have a fondness for our clutch of nineteen-year-olds who spent the first years with us—that hard-partying, sometimes feckless gang of anarchists who taught me a lot, though there were days I couldn't get them out of bed after a particularly enthusiastic night of partying. Once I grew so pissed I walked into their room and started up the chainsaw. The combination of sour gas fumes and noise soon had them jumping that morning.

They also caused their share of damage.

My belt sander wore out, and I bought a fancy, expensive replacement because we had a lot of work ahead, since we'd ripped off the roof of our large log house and were erecting a new, intricate, gabled roof. We admired the sander at lunch, after which Joaquin carried it out to the barn, placed it atop the two-by-twelve he was sanding for a windowsill, and plugged it in. Naturally, the trigger had been accidentally locked on during lunch. The belt sander took off at high speed down the board, launched into the air like a ski jumper, and crashed into pieces on the floor. This was so gruesomely hilarious that I threatened to have a T-shirt made up proclaiming Joaquin the world champion "belt-sander racer" as I returned to the store to replace it.

There were several legendary lunches like that—such as when Jason, a big and strong worker who'd returned from off-island, was delegated to dig the last of the drainage trenches in heavy clay we'd been pickaxing out all week. Once he was through we could finally lay drain rock and Big 'O' pipe to drain the soggy lawn. When his morning's work was done, Jason came in to lunch, collapsed in a chair at the table, covered in mud and dirt, exhausted and proud of himself, and declared, "Well, I got it done. Filled in every trench!" The entire crew looked up from their soup, horrified.

My favourite incident with this gang was a repeat performance. Once we had the gables framed for the roof, we left a beam hanging out as a handhold for returning because the roof had tricky angles and was dangerous. Unfortunately, the beam was also at perfect head-banging height when you climbed from the deck to the roof. Each day, after breakfast and lunch, every one of us would bonk our heads on that beam, curse our forgetfulness, and carry on. Crossing the tin roof inevitably made us forget the beam, which we needed to return. Within days all of us had bruised foreheads. To entertain lunch guests I would take them to the front lawn and say, "Watch this." As the crew walked out onto the high roof after lunch, my guests and I would double over, choked with laughter as each of the gang would crack his head, curse himself, and carry on—like a row of sheep stepping into the same hole, one by one, over and over again.

ONE DAY I WAS cleaning up the offcuts thrown onto the lawn from our framing when Seb charged down the first sheets of red tin laid on the roof and flew off the low eaves, right over the narrow front deck and onto the lawn, where he did a couple of rolls, rose to his feet, and calmly walked off. I was horrified. It was at least a twelve-foot leap. "DON'T JUMP OFF THE ROOF!" I roared between gritted teeth.

"Who jumped? I fell," Seb said casually as he crossed the lawn to the back deck to return to the roof. Danger lives with us everywhere.

I lost a finger to an accidental, self-inflicted shotgun blast in my twenties, and faced logs rolling off a hillside when I earned my living as a logger and saw enough to convert me into an environmentalist for life. In White Rock, shortly before we moved to the farm, I balanced my chainsaw overhead and sawed off a chunk of rotten deck until I hit a nail. The chainsaw kicked back, striking my face. I could feel the blood trickling down my cheek as I made the slow walk into the basement and its bathroom mirror, assuming I'd taken a chunk out of my face, afraid to touch it. In the mirror I saw only a tiny cut, bleeding profusely. The saw must have stalled on the kickback and struck my cheek during the brief moment when the chain stopped, because by the time it was back at arm's length it was fully revving again. How's that for luck? I still bear the tiny, near-invisible scar as a symbol of foolishness and survival. The hazards of the working life walk alongside the laughter, and only the wakeful among us survive, and sometimes not even them. The grace of work is beautiful, joyful, and dangerous.

Ever since we moved to the farm on that winter day and discovered the one lonely piece of punky alder in the woodshed, I've been obsessed with accumulating firewood and kindling. Luckily, within days we'd found a woodcutter with a load of firewood that was—unbelievably—dry. Unscrupulous woodcutters claim they have cured, dry wood, whether they do or don't. Once you've worked with firewood for a few years it's easy to tell from the grain, the checks, the weight, and the bark not only the type of wood (balsam fir, for instance, is useless compared with Douglas fir) but its dryness and age. Since the house is enormous, it consumed twelve cords a year for the first years until I developed alternative heat and reinsulated and sealed up the holes. I practically became a high priest of fire.

Woodcutting is a great unsung calling—these days a religion known only to rural communities. Loggers used to be mythic heroes in a dangerous profession, but because of the greed of the multinationals, their honest, dangerous labour has been tainted by the environmental degradation caused by bad logging practice. Also, surprisingly, burning well-cured wood in today's high-tech stoves is not environmentally dangerous, unless you live in a populated valley prone to air inversions, where some regulation might be necessary.

My favourite wood is arbutus—called ironwood by the locals, with good reason—but big-leaf maple and Douglas fir are fine, and alder is usable. How many people can recognize the difference between a standing fir and hemlock? Fewer can recognize these trees by their wood. How many chop their own wood today? Like farming, chopping wood is becoming a lost art. Will our grandchildren be living off algae and synthesized proteins, dwelling in homes heated by solar arrays or distant power-creation megaprojects? Will a thermostat be all they know about that human essential—warmth?

Once, a citified friend was cooking on our wood stove, and her stir-fry began turning into a stew. She gasped, panicking. "How do I turn this thing up!" There were no knobs, of course. My father used to say: "If you want a fire, you have to burn wood." And there's nothing like a bin of cedar kindling to set the stovetop glowing orange. Chinese stir-fry and coffee are natural allies of a wood stove. My favourite sound on a cold morning is the clanking of a kitchen stove being cleaned and fired up.

Those who live with wood spend hours, days, perhaps years in front of the chopping block. The art of the axe must be learned through long practice. Chopping wood only looks easy. In the old days, children learned to cut kindling and, if they kept all their fingers and toes, graduated to the axe. Mike, as a tyke, had to stand in a zinc washtub to protect his toes. Some woodchoppers prefer a single-bitted axe, others the classic double-bitted blade—a tool of beauty, but like household knives, it's impossible to keep sharp if helpful friends get hold of it. As much as I love a good axe, I shifted to mauls long ago because enthusiastic guests kept ruining my axe blades. Also, I have to take down our giant big-leaf maples when they go punky. Splitting a knotty, four-foot round with a double-bitted axe is no fun. Besides, you can reverse the maul and use it as a sledgehammer on your steel wedges.

Wedging is another art. For a start, like the axe or maul, the wedge requires finding the key spot at the rim of the round. Amateurs will whomp an axe into the centre of a wet green round and then spend an eternity wriggling it out. Learning the art of "seeing" the split point in a round is a lifelong quest. As with a karate punch or chop you aim for the bottom, not the top, of your round. The blow is achieved by seeing your way through to the other side.

243

It's been remarked of the lumberjack: "He makes all his love in the forest and chops all his wood in the whorehouse." The woodcutter walks in and out of history and mythology, whether it's *Gilgamesh,* humanity's first recorded work of literature, which takes its impetus from logging a sacred forest, or Paul Bunyan, or the heroes of fairy tales like "Little Red Riding Hood." The Japanese have long known the special quality of woodcutting, and it is a mighty woodcutter in *The Seven Samurai* who's one of the first to come to the aid of the stricken townspeople.

Finding yourself outside on a cool autumn day, shimmering with sweat in a red plaid shirt—the dogs lying behind you, the peafowl dancing suicidally in and out of the flying chunks of wood as they race for black ants and the fat, glistening bodies of termites—is as satisfying as pausing on the way into the house and admiring a full woodshed. Cutting wood means losing yourself—the way you do in meditation. That's why electric or gas-powered wood splitters are an abomination. "It is with their muscles that humans most easily obtain knowledge of the divine," according to Aldous Huxley. The Woodchopper is a famous yogic posture, a continuous-motion exercise, used to release tension and "to energize and stimulate the whole body."

Zen monks long ago learned the meaning behind woodcutting. "I pump water, I cut wood. How wonderful!" Their texts are full of such quotes: "When chopping wood, chop wood. When breathing, breathe." My favourite is attributed to a particularly venerated sage: "Before enlightenment, I chop wood and carry water. After enlightenment, I chop wood and carry water."

Perhaps we woodcutters are all students of the Catholic monk Saint Benedict of Nursia, who said, "To work is

244

to pray." Cutting firewood, moving fluidly yet living inside the cave of the body, is a kinesthetic meditation. Every log holds the possibility of enlightenment—the moment the blade drives through, following the grain, splitting its linear universe. It's the poetry of the everyday, the kind those monks preach; the ability to find the extraordinary in ordinary life—like a wolf on the hunt, at perfect attention to the world.

17

FENCE BUILDERS
AND TOOL USERS

· · · · · ·

*I*F I DON'T WALK our fences in the morning I walk them in the afternoon. A good farmer knows fences are a blessing and a curse, and demand regular scrutiny.

There was a careful man who raised emus and built his fence to the specifications of a government bulletin, complete with a strand of barbed wire on the top to discourage dogs from leaping over and attacking the emus. The fence seemed sturdy and sensible until the man realized the emus were entranced by cars and would race alongside the road, often with their heads over the fence as they tried to keep pace. It took only one mistake for an emu to slit its own throat and die, flopping beside the fence.

Animals have impressive techniques for killing themselves with fences, or wrecking them, mostly because fences are designed for our pleasure and not theirs. Our horse, LaBarisha, is a master at tangling herself in page wire or snake fences that she's knocked down trying to get at the neighbour's pasture. She's such a pro that she recognizes immediately when she is in trouble and will patiently stand there until we discover she's missing, search her out, and unsnarl whatever mess she's gotten herself into. This afternoon in our eighteen-year-long day is no different. Extricating a horse from a pile of crossed rails can be disheartening, yet she's so trusting she will allow me to lift her hind leg and back her foot up five inches, following it with the next leg. She taught me that snake fences look picturesque but they're near-worthless with large livestock.

Robert Frost's neighbour in "Mending Wall" said, "Good fences make good neighbours." I don't fully believe this. Fences are traps for stealing your time and crushing your fingers and have caused their share of feuds. In many early tribal cultures it was an insult to your community to fence a field. When we fenced our lower field across from where the new neighbours were building their house, we didn't realize they'd sited their house to enjoy the view of our "wild meadow" instead of the generally more preferred water view of the strait. Our sheep soon created a bucolic, grassy pasture, grazing down the invasive weeds, and our neighbours were hugely disappointed because it was no longer a knee-high flowering meadow.

AFTER MIGRATORY SOCIETIES SHIFTED beyond hunting and foraging but before they succumbed to property ownership, they gated not their world but only garden crops likely to be damaged by either wild beasts or wandering livestock. The livestock—fowl, pigs, goats, cattle—lived alongside, tethered or free, depending on the local conditions.

As villages and their livestock populations expanded, the surrounding area was usually treated as a commons for all. Once the grazing around villages grew deficient as populations swelled, the animals would be herded even farther away and brought to their corrals nightly for feed or defence, breeding or birthing—if at all. Since the fields were open, to fence a house garden was regarded as merely self-defence. With further growth, good grazing could be found only so far away that families began to "own" certain areas, and eventually they moved out to work and live near their livestock. Thus began the rural life we know today. Around the world, these various stages of farming still exist, though they're diminishing rapidly.

Grazing is an evolutionary characteristic inherited to protect herbivores from parasites and predictable actions that will attract predators. The grazing instinct also discourages overgrazing (as long as too many herbivores aren't confined in one area) because it makes the animal constantly seek new pasture. Actually, grazing is not restricted to herbivores. Everyone, at some point, wants to graze beyond their fences, whether it's for money or sex. With livestock, at least, grazing creates a balanced and healthy diet, especially if pasture land is not all in grass. That's why cross-fencing and rotational grazing work better than feedlots.

Fencing ranches and farms became a legendary subject of dispute in North America, horrifying the free-roaming Native tribes. Sitting Bull noted about the colonialist farmers: "They claim this mother of ours, the Earth, for their own, and fence their neighbours away." The fencing conflicts with the Native cultures culminated during the invasion of the American West by settlers and farmers; and then, shortly after, small herder-farmers also found themselves battling the big cattle ranches when they began fencing their land.

Barbed wire, "the devil's rope," is a monstrous creation. We picked up a couple of rolls of barbed wire in our early years, mostly to wrap around the base of the cages (animals go under, through, and over fences) built to protect our fruit trees from deer and livestock. My history with barbed wire consists of five years of putting it up and ten painful years of untangling it and taking it to the recycling yard—and I have the scars to prove it. Barbed wire will grow right into the ground, wrap around anything moving (including sheep or me or the horse), generally endangering lives, temperament, and skin. It can spring the fencing nails out of a rotten cedar post and attack you from thirty feet away. The dogs love watching me wrestle a length of old wire into a roll. Dogs are secret sadists, and they will leap barking around me as the wire slowly eats me alive.

UPON OUR ARRIVAL, Trauma Farm was an abandoned goat ranch with only one distant neighbour. As in the early days of settlement around the world, the goats freely roamed the fields cleared by the original owners. There were corrals for milking and separating the billy goats, and a deer fence around the garden and the house, but that was knocked down. Without goats the meadows were waist-high in places. I wandered through the grounds and discovered many exotic introductions: *Magnolia stellata* trees chewed to the ground, rare pines and roses, a few fruit trees. It doesn't take more than a couple of years in this climate for a garden to return to the forest. Sharon was thrilled (that changed later as the workload increased) because this was her opportunity to garden on a large scale.

I set our nineteen-year-olds to the firewood and fencing immediately. I'm still grateful for their energy and what they taught me about being young again, despite the near-constant head-banging rap music at full volume on the ghetto blaster, which Sharon once threatened to throw into the pond during a particularly misogynistic song. It's said rail splitting made Abraham Lincoln into the man he was. I believe that. It's hard work and an art. Those lads made more than 2,300 cedar rails for the snake fencing that we erected to cross-fence the acreage. Joaquin, wide and muscled, was a great rail splitter, but our boy Roben, smaller and wiry, had both the eye and the strength and could split thirteen-foot-long rails so fast it would make Lincoln spin in his grave. Roben often made as many seventy-five cedar rails in a day. I got chainsaw elbow from bucking up all the deadfalls and sick cedars I felled for fencing.

FENCING IS NECESSARY, BUT gates are the pathways through the world of the farm. Livestock soon learn to wait by the gate at dinnertime. I watch them amble up the field in the afternoon, moseying along, grazing as if the dinner bucket were the furthest thing from their mind, but they know where it all comes from, and they look upon the house as a temple and me as a capricious god who mysteriously appears with the grain they covet. This does not stop them from attempting to help themselves. Our first horse, Stonewall Jackson, was a master gate cracker with those rubbery lips like fingers. He'd draw back the bar on a gate before you could turn around and yell, and then he'd rip a bag of feed out of the pickup in the driveway. I finally had to put spring-loaded latches on the gates—as well as the pull bars.

Sometimes farmers get so carried away making gorgeous fences they forget their original reason for building them. Young Charlie Byron, a good man killed in a tree-falling accident several years ago, once bought a big prize bull, picked it up, and drove it home. Descending from the livestock trailer, it looked around, didn't like what it saw, and walked right through his elegant split-rail fence. Charlie shot it on the road as it was grinding its way into the hood of a terrified neighbour's car, and then he dragged its corpse onto the farm with his tractor and butchered it. So the unfortunate bull ended up spending its last day on the farm after all, and Charlie and his family ate tough, expensive beef for a winter.

Working rural land teaches you to look and then look again. It's an unending lesson in the competition between the human drive for a linear, mechanical world and the natural world demanding complexity. Startling moments flash past and snap you to attention, whether it's the heron suddenly flipping a goldfish as big as a plate out of the pond or a surprise guest at the gate.

251

THE FROG ON THE GATE LATCH

More brilliant than an emerald on wood,
the tree frog sat out the morning, taking its sun
the way some of us take our wages—
demanding only what we deserve and nothing more.

In the golden burn of the afternoon
it found the shade the latch provided.
Later in the evening, when I watered the orchard
and fed the sheep, I noticed it again,
still perched on that strap of cedar
which barred one world from another—
imperious, like a bright emperor, its hooded eye
studying me for false or dangerous moves.

There were none in my heart, not this night,
and I slid the latch home with a tenderness
the brittle wood hadn't known for some time—
    the gate an ancient victim
of the aimless battering of sheep, the escapes
a horse devises with its rubbery lips, or my despair
after a hard day making nothing out of stupid dirt.

This small green king offered grace and patience
while requesting only a perch for itself.
The gates might open and shut and we may
often find ourselves lost in our own homes,
    but there is always someone else,
    ready to embrace our crazy landscapes.

Gates are magical creations, and I try to construct interesting ones. I also make it a habit to have all our gates open
away from the house; this way helpers with their hands full
don't have to fiddle around figuring out which way a gate
opens, though one of the boys repaired a couple of gates
and made them open the wrong way, which drives me batty.
I dislike metal gates, but I can tolerate them. They are like

Walmart farming—functional and ugly. And they're hard
to fix after you back your truck over them. With wood you
can always jury-rig something. Though every fence must
be designed for its use, whether to protect a garden against
marauding rabbits and deer or to keep livestock in, there's
something about gates that makes us want to get ornamental in their construction. I've built a lovely moon gate out
of wood scrap, along with a few other eccentric gates. And
we had a friend weld us a small garden gate out of broken
garden tools in a radiating design. It's much photographed
by guests.

If you're a visitor, the rules for dealing with farm gates
are simple, because there is only one rule. You leave them
as you find them. If a gate is closed, then close it after you
go through. If a gate is open, make sure it stays open. Farms
have lost herds of cattle or sheep when a helpful duck hunter
closed the gate that led to the water hole. More often the
problem is leaving the gate open. Bev and Mike's farm
stretches to Stowel Lake and the swimming hole beside the
road. A few adventurous kids know there's a secret gate to
his bottom field, hidden among the blackberries—a shortcut
to the private wharf. The Byrons wouldn't dream of putting up a NO TRESPASSING sign, yet they're not keen about
strangers wandering around the rickety wharf that projects
their water intake valve into the lake, especially since so
many south islanders are already using the swimming hole
at the boundary of their land. It also makes Bev's little grandchildren nervous when they go fishing and encounter big,
shaggy strangers skinny-dipping off the dock.

I was returning from fishing on that dock one day when
I encountered three young boys. I could see they'd left the

gate open, despite the grazing sheep close by. After the usual farm-friendly hello, I got to the point with the head of the pack.

"You boys supposed to be in here?"

"Oh sure."

"Who gave you permission?"

"Mike Byron," he beamed. He was a cocky one. He'd have to be pretty dumb not to know this was the Byron place and that Mike gave permission to cross his property to everyone who asked. Only they were supposed to close the gates. The boy's cheekiness made it obvious they didn't ask, and the open gate showed they didn't care. I decided to give them something to think about.

"Oh that's fine, then. Have a good swim. By the way, did you see the bull?" There's more than one way to deal with an aspiring delinquent.

"Bull?" The boy's eyes widened suspiciously, and his voice rose. "He's got a bull in here?" He surveyed the mix of pasture and heavy brush they'd have to traverse to reach the lake.

"He picked it up a week ago. It's big—a touch mean if you piss it off." His eyes grew wider, and his friends looked fearfully around. One hacked up a cough when he noticed the old milk Jersey lurking behind a tree. "Naw, that's only the cow. The bull is big and black and all drooly-faced. If he takes a run at you, you have to grab the ring in his nose." Mike's gentle old bull had actually gone into the cooler a few days earlier, but they wouldn't know that. "Have a good swim, boys," I smiled and marched off toward the gate. By the time I had unassembled my fishing rod and put it in my truck I saw them leaving, carefully shutting the gate behind.

254

BEFORE WE THROW PARTIES where there are going to be city guests, I move our livestock to the bottom pasture and hang a sign on the gate: BEWARE OF RAM. To my knowledge, nobody has ever gone through that gate when the sign is up. Apart from our encounter with Mike's ram, the only ram we ever had that showed signs of being grumpy was a notorious Suffolk ram a few farmers shared for stud use. He was gentle as sin, yet when you turned your back he'd hammer you. After a couple of gimpy backs he ended up as mutton burger.

But no matter how good your gates and fences and signage, people will still find ways to ignore them, sometimes at great cost, and farmers have to resort to more innovative methods to keep people out of dangerous fields. I have two favourite farm signs that I once saw in a magazine:

DON'T CROSS THIS FIELD UNLESS YOU CAN DO IT IN 10 SECONDS. THE BULL CAN DO IT IN 10.1 SECONDS.

THE FARMER ALLOWS WALKERS TO CROSS THE FIELD FOR FREE, BUT THE BULL CHARGES

Fences aren't the only subject of construction on a farm. The story of barns is so complex that it needs its own history. Farming is a permanent form of construction and reconstruction—widgets that won't widget, doors that stick, and the designing of thingamajigs to hold whatchacallits in place—cams, links, gears, bearings, and gadgets. I love farming because it's all fuss and little finesse. You get it done with whatever is handy. In ancient days the technology was

wood, leather, and some home smithing. Now we reinvent
our world daily with gadgets of moulded metal, plastic, baling twine, and duct tape. One of the most common phrases
heard on a farm is "That'll hold it for now." This can lead
to some hilariously improvised devices. Fear of messiness
is a modern psychosis. Yet messiness is the badge of the
farmer's lifestyle, except for those few individuals with
a neatness fetish that leaves the rest of us standing at the
entrance to their workshop with our mouths agape. Their
sterile though very useful methodology has, unfortunately,
evolved into the factory farm, where technicians can now
operate in biosecure environments that belong more to the
laboratory than to the land.

Shortly after we bought Trauma Farm, I was driving my
aged father home for his first visit. He glanced out the truck
window and said, "That looks like a real farm. You should
get to know that guy." It was the Byron homestead, glorious in its unfinished fencing, sheep wandering across the
road, geese on the driveway, the sheds in various stages of
collapse and rebuilding, constantly changing, organic, alive.

We try to keep a neat house, except for my study, which
is a free-for-all of dreams and clutter. That's how I write.
Like the puppy in the yard, I need my fetish objects—on
the walls and the counters—bones, books, paintings, tools,
sculptures, and photographs. They bring me to the zone
where the words begin. The rest of the house is a different
matter. However, over the years I've watched with amusement the accumulation of junk in the barn and mud room,
attempting to invade the house itself where we are making our last stand, especially Sharon, who has good design
taste when it comes to a house and is determined to keep it.

But a farm has few tidy zones. Everything is in active movement. Sharon once brilliantly housed a hundred new-born chicks in an old playpen she pushed up beside the wood stove during an electrical failure. And over the years several struggling newborn lambs had the life warmed back into them beside the same stove. Although it's a lovely, enormous log home with a handmade thirty-foot-long adobe divider separating the stoves, emergencies always take precedence over house pride.

The barn workshop turns clutter into an art form. A farmer lives a magpie life, accumulating objects "just in case"—seduced by the harmony of gears, the simple intelligence of step valves. I've got irrigation sprayers, copper tubing, bags of lime, uncounted tools (wrenches, saws, files, drivers, hammers, nail cutters), Big 'O' connectors, screws, brushes, tar, sterilizers, fencing nails, electrical connectors, netting, brushes, Vaseline, udder unguents, organic fertilizers, soap solutions, mineral oil. Farmers thrive on this kind of junk and know that if by some chance they are missing a two-inch step-down pipe connector, their neighbour will have it. The only thing annoying me is that I still can't find my expensive fencing pliers in the mess.

MORE THAN A FEW tools are fondly cursed when you live on the land. A tractor is a universal instrument of torture for farmers. If it's not breaking down it's getting stuck, and when it's not doing that it's tipping over and crushing its driver. But I can't think of a tool that's enraged me more than the chainsaw, so necessary to our farm carved out of a forest only two decades before our arrival. After I went

257

through five second-hand chainsaws, I bought a new, small "professional" model, which was rated to handle our workload. It burned out in a year, and reduced me to tears. So Sharon bought the big model for me as a Valentine's Day present. Maybe she was hoping I'd fall on it and finish this farming dream once and for all. That saw has survived more than a decade.

Observing how much work firewood is, the fencing, the clearing of deadfalls and diseased trees in our forested acreage, I recognize the intrepid skills of our ancestors—their days spent chipping stone tools so cleverly, so distinctly that enemies could identify the makers of a spear tip pulled out of a corpse. Then I look at the spotty photographs of last century's axe-wielding loggers, standing on springboards, felling fifteen-foot-thick trees, and I understand why our species has so vastly increased the pace of its damage with its avalanche of new tools and weapons being created daily as our technology evolves faster than us.

Over the years I've removed a number of sick trees for various reasons, almost killing myself when an alder rolled over a fence after it kicked backwards off its stump. My neighbours watched in horror while I pretzelled my spine beneath the overhanging rail and the trunk rolled over me. If the rails hadn't held, I'd have been crushed. It was such an easy tree to fell that I hadn't paid due attention. The trick about felling timber is remembering that the easy trees can also kill you. When I was a logger in Haida Gwaii during the foolish days of my young manhood I witnessed several rogue trees in action. Monstrous widow-makers, they'd split up the middle, walk off their stumps, and chase you for fifty feet. Torque can create wild dances once you sever a tree from its roots.

258

THERE WAS A CEDAR blocking the tractor's route to the lower fence and the road, and I regretted having to slay it. This is all part of the circle. In order to pick up your firewood you need to make a road, and to make the road you have to fell a tree. It's an endless circle, the worm eating its tail. Construction and reconstruction. This tree had lived at least a century longer than me, but it had to go. There was no route around. It was almost five feet in diameter. Regretfully, I made my back cut. When I started my finishing cut, the trunk settled curiously on my saw. I hammered in a couple of wedges. They didn't make any difference. I trudged up to the house and roused the boys, who were busy lunching on a crown roast, a big jar of peanut butter, and a loaf of bread. I've long given up questioning what a hard-working young man will eat, and I didn't even grimace at the sandwich of beef slabs and peanut butter Jason was wolfing down.

I needed help. I'd met a strange tree.

For the young, challenges are what the world is about. Along with Roben we had four of them staying with us that summer: Paul, Jason, Seb, and Joaquin. They trooped down behind me to the tree, where I shot an arrow with a string attached through the branches near the crown of the cedar, and we drew up a thick hemp rope and cinched it tight. Four of them stood in line at the end, ready to yard on the rope when I gave the word. Meanwhile, I'd directed Seb to the road beyond the fence, where he could warn any neighbours if anything went wrong and the tree fell backwards while they were driving by. I sledgehammered more wedges into this fat cedar. It settled further, now leaning towards the road, threatening to crush my big new saw.

This wasn't supposed to happen. I've felled a number of trees in my life, and I've never seen one behave like this.

A turkey vulture glided across the pasture. Everyone watched in awe as this normally shy traveller of the thermals backflapped and landed gently on the crown of the tree I was cutting.

A vulture?

On my tree?

There was an unearthly cracking groan, and the vulture lifted into the sky as the tree reeled backwards. Seb was so enthralled by this piece of theatre that he forgot to check for traffic. My neighbours were driving up the hill as the cedar hit the road with a crash, taking out the phone and power lines of every house beyond our farm, only narrowly missing their car. The boys stood in the grass, mouths agape, the useless hemp rope yanked out of their hands, the vulture circling above us. "That was a show," I noted angrily, retrieving my chainsaw, miraculously untouched by the mishap.

"Wow," they kept repeating in their best stoner voices, impressed, as I thumped up the hills to call the power and phone companies to inform them I'd cut everyone off the grid. Worse, the tree had taken out the lines *after* they divided to go to our house and up the hill, so we still had phone and power. It was two days before my neighbours finally got their telephones back. BC Hydro, the power company, was quicker. When the Hydro crew pulled up we'd already bucked the tree and removed the pieces and cleared the road. I'd discovered the source of the disaster (aside from the fortune-telling vulture). Decades ago the cedar had been struck by lightning, topping it. A lateral branch then became the new leader, shooting ten feet away from the original trunk, on the side facing the road. The tree later regrew so bushy that it looked normal from the ground. The tree was also rotting from the mishap and was ultimately doomed, and there was no way I could have known it was off-centre, but that didn't make me feel much better.

The Hydro crew were annoyed, even though I'd saved the twisted crown to prove nature's duplicity. I took some serious abuse and financial threats but Hydro never billed me for the damage I caused. I had to stand on the road in front of my smirking gang of helpers and abjectly accept the lecture I deserved. I was told later that it's the custom to allow every islander one tree across the lines, at least if it's an authentic accident. I've used up my tree.

18

THIS NATURE
OF THE ABSURD

. . . . .

I'M USUALLY IN my study by dawn and outside in the afternoon, doing my chores, because I can't take the heat emanating from the attached greenhouse. The parrot loves the heat and his perch, especially because it commands a view of the road. If he sees cars approaching he starts shouting, "It's party time!" Tuco has been living with me too long. Twenty-four years now. Today I've returned, suddenly haunted by work, and slipped upstairs before dinner.

He was bored and I was wearing the letters off my keyboard, already sweating in the heat pouring in from the greenhouse, when I heard a buzzing while I answered a few overdue emails. I glanced up as the wasp zigzagged through the open greenhouse into the study, making an impressive dash past a snapping Tuco, although Tuco is so fast he can bite you twice before you realize you've been bitten the first time.

I watched these manoeuvres with a dumb curiosity, until the wasp made a sharp turn and dived into my open shirt, stinging me above the heart, before stinging its way down my belly as I leaped to my feet, cursing, ripping my shirt open, slapping at my chest and belly until it tumbled out and flew past the bird, now so impressed that he only glared balefully at it. The wasp exited the bright greenhouse while the stings reddened my chest and my heart started pounding.

"Where did that come from?" I whined to Tuco, numbed and throbbing.

It came from the world. The way it always does: like the day I was working on the coop while Sharon mucked about with her burn pile of blackberries, old prunings, paper feed bags, and broken-up lumber far beyond recycling. I use my wood thirty different ways until I finally give up and accept its ashes for the garden. She had an epic pile smouldering, but the fire wouldn't take, which was surprising, because Sharon is a closet pyromaniac.

She found me and said, "Why don't you heap it up with the tractor?" Give a man a tractor and a fire and you've instantly created a dangerous combination. Soon I was using the bucket to fluff up the pile and make it burn better. The smouldering mess caught and began to flame. Then the tractor died in the pile. There was an exquisite moment of quiet terror as the motor coughed out, counterpointed by the crackles of the growing fire under my bucket. "Oh shit," I gulped, after checking the fuel gauge. The tractor is so old and trustworthy and so seldom used that I couldn't recall when I'd filled it up. For a moment, I couldn't even remember where the gas tank was. The last time I'd lifted the hood I'd discovered a mouse nest on the filter. I had no diesel fuel anyway. The fire crackled louder, and a whoosh of flame erupted under the bucket.

"What's the matter?" Sharon shouted.

"I ran out of gas. We have to push it out of the fire." I set everything in neutral and climbed off.

Sharon looked at me with that kind of resigned contempt you never want to see on the face of your wife. "Push it out of the fire? It's too big!"

"Come on, it's almost downhill," I said, leaning into the big back tire. The thing wiggled slightly, which inspired her enough to lean against the other tire. I had the bucket lightly resting on the fire pile, and the hydraulics were holding. If the bucket was down we'd have been finished. I rammed my shoulder into the tire and shouted, "Heave! Fast!" The fire was growing larger by the second. There's nothing like desperation to triple your strength. The adrenalin was throbbing in my blood vessels, and the tractor inched backwards. "Heave!" Six inches. "Heave!" A foot. "Heave!" Two feet. Heave!" Four feet. We were on a roll! "Heave!" My backside was getting hot, and the fire six feet high. "Heave!" The tractor was out. We sat down on a couple of firewood rounds, watching the beautiful licking flames soar into the air. "That was a thrill." I beamed encouragingly at Sharon, while she looked at me with a bright-eyed, breathless astonishment.

"We actually pushed that big tractor out of a fire!" she said. Sometimes she gets a real thrill out of the hare-brained stunts I invent.

ABSURDITY HAS LIVED WITH the planet since the first cell divided. The mutations that led to the platypus and the nuclear bomb are the ultimate theatre of the absurd. That's why cultures need their tricksters as much as they need their heroes. Looking at the *American Heritage Dictionary* definition of *absurdism,* I discover its roots come from *ab* (away from) and *surdus* (silence). It's the noise of the world. "Ridiculously incongruous or unreasonable." And we all encounter it in our daily living.

Because I've been living in the impressively varied kingdom of Trauma Farm, I suspect I see more of the absurd than many people. Sometimes I think I've spent my life hauling hay in the rain. But human encounters with the strange and the nonlinear carry greater weight when lives depend on them, as any soldier or pistol-toting gang kid in the urban wastelands will tell you. Fighting with a computer for ten hours only to discover you failed to tick a software function doesn't carry the same visceral impact as a tractor running out of fuel in a fire pile, or a bull falling into an abandoned well. This could account for the rising need for extreme adventure tourism among urbanites.

Whether you're dealing with battlefields, computers, or tractors, the absurd is essential to life. What interests me is how we confront the absurd. When I consider honestly the two ends of the spectrum of modern farming, whether it's the reductionist methodology of agribusiness or the traditional culture of the small farm, I can only recognize how absurd both are. Each style of farming resembles what Samuel Johnson called a man's second marriage after a failed first one: "The triumph of hope over experience."

Albert Camus tells us in *The Myth of Sisyphus:* "The absurd is born of the confrontation between the human call and the unreasonable silence of the world." And he's right if you consider cosmic irrelevance to be silence. The noisiness of life confronts death. The absurd is what brings us to the deep well of traditional knowledge behind the tricksters in so many aboriginal mythologies. How do we face our need for order and answers in a world whose order has no answers, only differing systems of survival?

In our human arrogance we don't realize that animals have a lot to teach us about absurdity and desire. I see it every day as events unfold around the dogs and the sheep or in the uncanny manoeuvres of my parrot, contriving to figure out ways to surprise me. If you are a lazy thinker, and unobservant, you begin to believe that absurdity happens only to humans who drive tractors into fires. But if you contemplate the natural world you soon recognize stupid, blind fate and foolishness everywhere.

A couple of decades ago I was skiing a steep, snowy ridge when I saw something that brought me to a sudden stop. In a pine tree growing alongside the cliff, about five feet away, a handsome buck stared back at me with dead eyes, impaled on a branch fifty feet above the forest floor. He hadn't been hanging there long. Did he panic at a noise and take a wrong leap? The natural world is full of false turns, which is why I've gradually learned not to become so angry about the stupidities of the human species. Absurdity is a constant, whether it's two dogs bonking heads as they try to enter a gate from opposite directions or a gander attacking a horse. Guests at the farm often warn me with breathless voices that a lamb is limping. The truth is, the lambs are always limping. These frisky little champions of idiocy have perfected every conceivable technique for falling into holes. Nor is foolishness restricted to domesticated animals—the poor dead buck was proof enough that blind fate thrives just as freely in the wild.

SMALL JOYS ON THE FARM

Winter came weird this year, as it always does—
cool and wet—rain after rain, the ponds flooding,
the sheep limping on rotten hooves.

Then the cold snapped its brittle fingers
and a sheet of ice shielded the ponds
for a week before the rain came again,
leaving a deceptive film of water on the slick surface.

I was sitting by the window drinking red wine
in the afternoon, depressed, lost in my life,
losing money on a farm, thinking about the large
destruction my race has engraved into the earth,
when the flock of mallards whistled through
    the rock maples.

I was alone, except for the animals, the sheep
    and the horse,
the audience of winter crows dotted like black
    crescent moons
on the green pastures that were wearing me down.

The mallards hit the secret ice like a circus pouring
onto a stage, skulls driving into the earthen bank,

tangles of feathers, collisions, and sliding webbed feet,
a duck braking with its beak, leaving a white crease
like the track of a lost arrow leading to the shore as
fifteen mallards attempted to regather the honour
        of a flock.

Even the crows rushed to the shoreline
to witness the relics of this indignity
while the last ducks waddled gracelessly
off the ice like miniature Charlie Chaplins.

And for a slender moment in the furrow of time,
on a farm in nowhere, everyone stopped to rejoice
        and wonder,
horse and sheep and mallards and man and crows.

Yes, the ecology retains its own madness,
        attended or unattended by us—
this strange planet overflowing with
odd carcasses skating on hidden ice.

268

Because so many of us live apart from nature today, it's
easy to lose our place in the cosmic lunacy of existence.
Funniest-video shows on television are a riot, but they don't
carry the same otherworldliness as watching a mink cavalierly skip down the road while being stalked by a white
peacock. Nor does a photocopier machine that won't quit
zooming or a video that dies in the closing scene of a dra-
matic film have the same immediacy as an animal nativity.
Sure, we encounter daily drama and tragedy in ghettoes
and work accidents, but while I've had my share of riotous

times on the streets of our cities, I didn't begin to understand absurdity in its fullness until arriving at the farm.

I always thought the world was strange. Maybe that's why I can smile at the gonzo journalist Hunter S. Thompson's flippant remark "It never got weird enough for me." But it's gotten pretty close for Sharon and me—such as the time we decided to drain and excavate the biggest pond, enlarging and deepening it. With the increasing droughts of the recent decade the pond had begun to fall dangerously low by the end of summer. The loss of irrigation water in late August is no fun on a farm. Before the excavator dipped into the bottom muck remaining after I'd pumped out the last of the water, I grew suspicious. "I think there's fish in that mud," I told the operator. "Empty your bucket on the ridge between the ponds, so if there's fish, we can scoop them into the lower pond."

He hooked the bucket into the mud, and when he opened it above the green field a multitude of golden flashes poured forth in a muddy blob of slithering leaping, twitching goldfish up to a foot long and six inches deep. The dogs went crazy, snapping up the smaller fish, tossing them into the air, and swallowing the fish whole, while Sharon and I yelled them back and madly scooped fish into the lower pond. Even the quiet, dignified excavator operator was soon on his knees in the mud, scooping up fish (at $120 an hour, I might add) and heaving them into the pond.

I decided there could be money in these fish, and I didn't want to choke the lower pond with too many, so when the excavator dumped the next load we scooped them into water-filled garbage cans, hundreds of fish to a can. Goldfish can gulp air and, even though confined, could survive

while we finished the pond work. Only a half-dozen perished, but I was still desperate to get them out of their
overcrowded containers and either back into the pond
or sold. Naturally, we discovered there was no market for
pond fish in the fall months, and I ended up returning them
to the redug pond once it began quickly refilling. They're
still out there, feeding the herons and the ospreys, and me
occasionally, if I decide to scare a guest by serving up a
giant deep-fried goldfish with a sweet-and-sour sauce.

THE MOST ABSURD MOMENTS come suddenly. Mike and I
had been slaughtering pigs all morning, and we were covered with gore. We finally got the carcasses into the cooler.
While we were working we'd made a deal on five laying hens I wanted to take home. We were walking down
the roadway between the barn and his utility shed when I
slipped on a big clump of goose shit. My slide was stopped
by a rock. I glanced at my foot. It was twisted weirdly—
pointing left while my legs were straight ahead. We both
looked at it.

"Oh man," I said. "I twisted my ankle on that goose shit."

"Just like that?" Mike asked, befuddled by how quickly it
had happened. I hadn't even fallen. I lifted my leg. The foot
was practically hanging.

"This is not good," I said. "But I've never broken a bone
in my life except when I shot off my finger twenty-five years
ago." Since I wasn't worried about it, I just grabbed the foot
and straightened it out. The thing clicked into place. The
pain was tolerable, but I have a high pain threshold. "I better collect my chickens and get out of here."

270

Mike was confused. "You sure you're all right?"

"I'm fine. I must have ripped a muscle. Catch those chickens. I'm not leaving without them."

We got the five chickens crated and in my truck, but the leg was starting to throb. "It's hurting. I have to leave before the shock wears off." The truck had a heavy-duty manual transmission and clutch, and every gear change was excruciating. I managed to drive home, the last half-mile in first gear. At the inner gate I pulled up and stepped down from the truck. A lightning bolt of pain shot up my leg and hit my head. I almost fainted. I was on the ground. The shock had worn off. I wanted to vomit.

"Sharon?" I called like a child or a dying man wanting his mother. "Sharon?" I crawled through the gate because I couldn't stand anymore. The fifty-foot deck leading to the kitchen was now a mile long. "Sharon," I whispered. "Sharon, I think I'm in trouble." I vomited over the side of the deck, into the flower garden, where it wouldn't be seen, and crawled forward. By now my calls were only whispers. So much for my high pain threshold. "Sharon. I need help."

I crawled to the kitchen door and pushed my way in. 271
"Sharon? I've hurt myself." Finally, she heard me and rushed into the kitchen. She got me into a chair, where I lolled about in excruciating pain. "I think I broke my leg. We have to go to the hospital." She tried to touch the obviously damaged foot. But I wouldn't let her.

"I'm disgusting. I can't go in like this. Take my clothes off." Since Sharon worked at the emergency ward, she immediately knew what I was thinking. Pride is one of the absurd wonders of human life. I hadn't shaved lately and I was covered with pig's blood and guts and feathers. I was a spectacular sight, and I knew it would embarrass her among the people she worked with. Somehow we got my clothes off, and Sharon brought a bowl of hot, soapy water. Together, we washed and shaved me, and then I tenderly dragged clean clothes onto my carcass. I put my arm on her shoulder, and we limped out to the car. I was drooling with pain by the time we reached emergency.

They put me on a stretcher and hauled me in and X-rayed me. It turned out I'd broken my fibula on that goose-shit slide. But miraculously, I'd put it back into place. The doctor was impressed. "I've never seen anyone set their own broken leg so beautifully." Normally, with a break like that they'd have to carve me up and insert pins. However, the swelling had locked it into place. The doctor didn't need to do anything. I'd done his job for him, though I probably caused myself more pain. "Don't ever try that again, you lucky fellow." They slapped a cast on and shot some Demerol into me, and in an hour I was good to go. By then I was woozy and cheeky enough to ask for a doggy bag of Demerol, but they weren't amused. So I cheerfully waltzed out of the door with my new heavy-duty cast and my blood full of narcotics.

I was a lucky boy indeed. Farming accidents are not always so minor. On June 8, 1948, Cecil Harris was repairing his tractor when it fell on him. The old boy couldn't haul himself out and he knew he was messed up internally. He managed to free his pocket knife and carved on the fender: "In case I die in this mess I leave all to the wife." Then he signed it before he lost consciousness and eventually died. He had the presence of mind to recognize that without a will Canadian law would put the family assets into a temporary legal limbo, which would have hurt his beloved wife financially. The fender is now in the University of Saskatchewan College of Law library—as an example of a legal will, and a testament to forethought in the face of death and the absurdity of life. When I consider how weak and craven I had become after a mere broken leg, I'm ashamed of myself.

HOW DOES ONE LIVE consciously? Only with praise, I think—by celebrating the landscape of life that we don't understand and never will. What do you do when, as Camus discusses in *The Myth of Sisyphus,* you finally acknowledge your inevitable death, the death of all things? You can become a hedonist like Don Juan or a conqueror, seizing what you want before you die. You can hide behind organized religion and take instruction from preachers who insist there is a creator designing your life. You can accept defeat and commit suicide, perhaps the weakest of those choices. Or you can live with all your senses alert to the world. Live in beauty and then die an artist. That was the best answer Camus could devise, and it's a good answer. In the end Camus argues for neither science nor God, and despite being tagged an existentialist, he is one of the most optimistic of philosophers. He argues for existence. That's what he meant by existentialism.

For him the story of the Greek trickster Sisyphus provides a clear example of a man living life at his fullest, doomed by the gods to forever push a rock up a hill only to watch it roll back down, over and over again. For Camus, that's the moment Sisyphus is most alive—watching that damned stone roll back down. That's when he understands

273

the comedy of the world, and so he turns and goes to fetch the rock, fully self-aware and conscious of the comedy inside his personal tragedy. You could call this the story of farming.

⁂

WE WERE WATCHING A trashy Hollywood film on television. Suddenly, the cat went strange and began yowling. Tara, the black Labrador, was under the table sucking up the popcorn the parrot was throwing from the dish attached to his perch. They both stared at the cat. We tossed the annoying cat into the mud room.

After the film, Sharon put the dog out and started screaming. She saw what the cat had been sensing—it was a dead peahen, her bloody head resting on the doorsill. Lady Jane, sweet Lady Jane, had fought off a raccoon but her skull was fractured. She'd crawled from her destroyed nest in the bush to the greenhouse door before she expired. Her pathetic trust that we could save her made me want to scream at my world. While peafowl can fight off a raccoon, the hen is at a disadvantage on the ground, defending her nest, because she won't abandon her eggs or young. When a raccoon stumbles upon a nesting hen, it probably feels about the same as a young mugger discovering a drunk in a business suit staggering down a dark alley.

The next year, when nesting season came I was determined to protect Lady Jane's daughter, Lady. I had the good fortune to find her nest immediately—peahens remain still on their nests and are nearly invisible in the brush. I phoned around and discovered a farmer who had a broody hen resolutely attempting to hatch a porcelain egg, which he'd placed under her in case he needed an emergency hatchery.

Since I feared Lady would hate me forever, I decided to disguise myself. I found a pair of rubber gloves and some overalls. Sharon announced I'd look terrific in a feed bag, so she cut out eyeholes and slit the sides to fit it over my shoulders. Then she handed me a cute little basket with a bright red towel to wrap the warm eggs in. There I was, all two hundred pounds of me, with an empty hog-grower bag over my head, gloved and padded, clutching a tiny red basket, resembling either a deranged IRA gunman or a monstrous Red Riding Hood. In retrospect I now realize I was the victim of an elaborate practical joke by Sharon.

Restraining her laughter as much as she could, Sharon said, "I'll start the truck."

I nodded my feed bag and lunged into the woods, praying nobody would drop by for a visit. This would be the capper to my reputation on the island. I smashed my way through the brush, trying to be scary, which wasn't hard. It's tricky stumbling around dense shrubbery with a feed bag on your head and a delicate basket in hand. I practically fell on the nest. Lady regarded me with disdain as she backed away from the eggs, reminding me of my crabby grade-school teacher after a kid had vomited on her desk. Lady didn't even fight while I gathered up the eggs and threw some spiky debris onto her rudimentary nest, hoping this would be enough to keep her out of the raccoon's clutches. I'm convinced she knew exactly who I was but was so astonished by my performance she temporarily forgot about her nest. I fled through the bush, triumphantly holding the wrapped eggs in the basket, and leaped into the truck after tearing away my feed bag and other gear, feeling like a bank robber who'd just pulled off the big one. I said to

Sharon, "Let's get out of here." Those eggs had about thirty minutes before they'd lose viability.

As Sharon drove off, she turned to me and said, "If you'd told me ten years ago this was what farming was going to be like, I would have left you."

And we both started to laugh . . . hopelessly . . . hysterically . . . .

By the time we returned—the eggs now under a slightly annoyed hen who would soon be hatching the strangest chicks—it was dusk. In a month we'd pick up those chicks and raise them. But tonight we walked down to the lower pond. The moon had risen behind the half-dead big maple reflecting on the sheet surface. Myriads of small bats skimmed the water, ghost-flying for insects, dipping once in a while to shiver the mirror of water.

Ajax gave his long nerve-tearing scream from the maple, and distantly, behind the house, high in the cedars, Lady replied, a little sadly I thought, but safe, at least for tonight.

⁂

276   NOT EVERY FARMER ENJOYS the absurd. You have to be a bit deranged to even consider taking up farming. As the old farmer said, farming is tough because it's so close to the ground. Faced with dead birds, the progress traps of human culture, the vagaries of weather, intransigent government regulators, clueless customers, and insane income tax forms, farming cultivates a dry wit and patience, an almost Buddhist ability to accept the fortune of the natural world. What did the farmer say when he won the lottery? "I guess I'll just keep on farming until it's all gone." He understood living in beauty.

One of our south island farmers leased a neighbour's field and used the elegant heritage barn to store the hay after he mowed and baled it every year. Recently, the uninsured, empty barn burned to the ground.

Less than a month later, under a threatening sky, I was phoned to pick up the hay I was buying from him, but I couldn't make it until later that day. I drove onto the field, noting my load was safely under a tarp. The storm had come and gone by then, drenching the field. The farmer was on his tractor, contemplating hundreds of uncovered bales still in the field, ruined by the rain. There hadn't been enough time to get them all covered.

He just sat there with a wry smile and said, "I guess if the weather had been better last month and the tractor hadn't broke, I could have got all the hay into the barn before it burned down."

19

DINNER LIKE A BELL

. . . . .

*I*T WAS A feast. Spontaneous dinners occur often in this big log house when friends arrive. There were a dozen of us, mostly in the galley kitchen—washing and preparing the salad, carving meat, plating dishes, setting the table—drinking wine, whisky, tea, water, or beer—talking too much and too loudly.

We sat ourselves at a table so overflowing with food it was embarrassing: boiled black potatoes and a plate of Yukon Gold potatoes roasted with garlic and basil and oregano; free-range chicken; parboiled young chard, cooled and drenched with oil and balsamic vinegar and sea salt; a stuffed leg of venison; a stir-fry of Chinese greens, snap peas, noodles, seeds, and nuts; a salad garnished with edible flowers. Almost everything—except the noodles, some of the condiments, the nuts, and the seeds—came from the farm.

We were laughing and shovelling food onto our plates until a shriek jarred us into silence. Our eyes turned to Mary, and the long pink worm escaping from her salad. Then the laughter erupted again as I picked the worm out of her oakleaf lettuce and returned it to the garden where it belonged.

Another good friend had washed the greens and, being from the city, hadn't been as thorough as Sharon and I are. Even though our friend seeks real produce, the world has changed. There are no bugs and dirt in stores anymore, unless you can find a real farmers' market—salad greens are generally already cut and washed and sealed in carbon-dioxide-injected plastic containers.

The loss of insect life in our greens has long been a source of concern for those who still respect the natural world and reject a culture that believes it can extinguish bugs and bacteria. Though many methods for destroying insect life and fungi and bacteria are clever and harmless, the logic of the chemical assault chasing the illusion of bug-free iceberg lettuce is too dangerous. And along with the other dangers I've discussed—specialized plant breeding, monoculture, and the demands of globalized transportation industries—it's why supermarket food has managed to become both tasteless and easily contaminated on a large scale. Dinners like ours have become rare events.

I am the child of a diminishing generation that accepted a little grit in its lettuce and never thought much about bugs in the water unless it was foul. I grew up in various backcountry communities where the old-timers threw live newts into the well to clean up the bug population. Today the horror of salmonella and every other natural terror would get that well padlocked, but in those years of wood-cribbed, spider-and-woodbug-rich, leaky-lidded wells it was a good idea.

YOUR BLOOD IS LIKE soil, living and learning and thriving on the wealth of invisible creation. The body learns as much as the brain does. According to Frank T. Vertosick Jr., author of *The Genius Within*, "The immune system must learn and recall billions, perhaps trillions, of different molecular patterns. Our lives depend on its ability to make instant discriminations between friend and foe, not an easy task."

There's much talk lately about how our antibacterial fixations and the fetishism of pill culture is endangering us. Since a controversial article appeared in the *British Medical Journal* in 1989 there has been increasing interest in the "hygiene hypothesis," which claims that our futile attempt to separate ourselves from bacteria has led to childhood immune system disruptions and a surge of allergies and other immune disorders. Incidentally, these disorders are much less common in farm children. Natural living is proving less dangerous than unnecessary sterilization. This is why traditional "raw milk" dairy farmers insist that those who run modern dairies, knowing their milk will be pasteurized, are not always as scrupulous about contamination.

DIRT IS GOOD. EVERYTHING comes out of dirt. Farmers know this, which is why so many old gardeners still eat their soil. The tongue tells the truth when it's not twisted by a culture that has cut off its own roots. You can taste soil's texture, its acid balance, its life. Eating soil is like eating life, and that's why it's tough to stomach for some. I've never been good at it. I'm thinking this as I begin preparing tonight's dinner. I'm peeling a basket of Pontiac potatoes—a favourite. Crisp fleshed, they make for magnificent baby potatoes, and fully grown they're excellent fried, mashed, or baked. They don't go sawdusty like the modern early-season varieties when cooked a minute past their prime. But they have a fatal flaw: deep, dirt-collecting eyes, and I begin to wonder if I'm also developing a dirt fetish as I meticulously scrape the eyeholes clean.

Modern addiction studies tell us the brain takes thirty days to form an addiction and a lifetime to overcome such dangerous chains of synapses. I probably wash my greens more meticulously than the average person because we have plentiful water and I've met what can come crawling out of our garden, and I'm not fond of eating cutworms or grit. Common sense is the answer for food handlers, not the paranoia promoted by industrial farming and the advertising campaigns of cleanliness-addiction industries.

Dangers in food are a fact of life. Parasites, protozoa, bacteria, viruses. A myriad of creatures. Everything from *Salmonella* to *Listeria monocytogenes* to *Campylobacter jejuni*, from *Escherichia coli* O157:H7 to parasitic worms. These days we've all learned to be more careful, but traditional behaviour and general cleanliness are less invasive than dangerous factory methodology. A few years ago a single infected steer in a multinational slaughterhouse contaminated thousands of tons of meat that appeared in places as diverse as Guam and Nevada within days. This, as I've explained, is why the local-food movement was born— out of the common sense of people who want to purchase their food from producers known and respected in their community. Those willing to take their chances with natural food, whether it's real milk, organic produce, or traditionally slaughtered livestock, should retain that right. Eventually, Western society needs to make sane decisions about what is safe and what is not, because the increasingly sterile hygiene levels our government is driving us toward are becoming more dangerous and unhealthy than living with our feet and fingers touching dirt—and more environmentally expensive.

Lately, all local farmers have been required to take a FOODSAFE course before we are allowed to sell our produce in supermarkets. Sharon got the short straw and attended. The woman giving the course displayed a classic case of too much science and too little common sense. Sharon and a clutch of local organic farmers had to sit there suffering a lecture about how manure is bad for the garden "because it's full of bacteria," along with other such useful information. The instructor's paranoid list of dangers even ended up implying all water should be boiled before drinking. When one farmer finally asked her what was healthy to drink, the woman replied, "Soda pop is safe." On this island, she was lucky she wasn't tarred and feathered and set adrift in a rowboat.

EVERY DISH HAS ITS season. Spring is rich with greens and strawberries and asparagus. My favourite crop is the early seed tops (scapes) of the hard-necked garlic, which appear at the same time as our Chinese snow peas. I steam-soften the scapes, then pan-fry them in butter with the snow peas, rock salt, and freshly ground pepper. As simple and clean as you can get. We have an abundance of garlic tops because people don't know how delicious they are or how to use them. So they don't buy them. Western society's indifference (or even fear of) nontraditional food constantly surprises me, though that attitude has been changing during the last thirty years as ethnic cuisines sweep the world, riding the globalization wave, introducing cappuccinos to Beijing and rice noodles to Idaho.

Another late spring dish is fresh fava beans, which most people consider winter food. I find them too dry and lumpy then, though they might have been cooked for hours in a broth, but when they're green and stir-fried they'll melt in your mouth, and they remind me of those tender white butter beans of Greece. Equally delicious are the fava and snap-pea flowers that we add to our spring salads. Mixed with *mizuna,* romaine, spinach, tiny beet tops, green onions, and spidery pea-leaf tips, they keep us going until the more substantial and complex salads of summer.

Then we gorge on tomatoes and cucumbers and the *tromboncino,* or Tromba d'Albenga, which resembles a twisted baseball bat—a summer squash-marrow that's delicious raw, steamed, or fried. The artichokes also arrive in full, big bud, and we steam them and dip their leaves in garlic butter and swoon over the hearts. Summer is also the season for flower and seed salads. Entertaining gives us the opportunity to play in the garden, picking an assortment of blossoms for a garish and tasty plate. I'm especially fond of nasturtium and day-lily flowers.

We cook according to the season, and I eat less, more simply, and later in the day. Often, we find ourselves out in the garden at eight in the evening. My stomach will start growling as I realize I haven't thought about dinner, so we tend toward quick stir-fries and raw fruits and vegetables.

During the fall the dehydrator comes out and the harvest fills our storeroom and freezers. Cooking meals becomes more extended, especially on the days cool enough to justify lighting the kitchen stove. We begin soups we can leave simmering all day on the cast-iron surface. This is also the season when Sharon and our friend Gerda have a big antipasto day, making enough for the year, and sometimes pesto, which they freeze in ice cube trays, then dump into freezer bags for use in the winter.

Winter is our season for long, slow, hearty dishes. The wood cookstove is roaring and we raid the freezer and storeroom to make stocks to freeze for quick lunches and dinners in summer, when we are too busy to cook. Sharon or I will cook up large batches of tomato sauces. The iron of the stove clangs daily once again as we rustle about in the kitchen and the storeroom overflowing with onions, squash, shallots, cabbages, potatoes, and several varieties of garlic. Here, in our temperate climate, the garden goes on through the winter, filled with winter greens and Chinese (jade *choi, mei king choi*) and Japanese (*mizuna*) vegetables, leeks, kale, overwintered beets, and parsnips. We have a large kitchen with three ovens (including the wood stove). Sometimes we need them when a dinner party erupts.

"Some of us eat to live, and others live to eat." That's the theory of the American poet and novelist Jim Harrison, who also invented a new school of journalism—gonzo cooking columns. We eat both ways at Trauma Farm. Food does sustain us, and yet we delight in its rich opportunities.

I GREW UP IN a kingdom of local food. Fraser Valley suburban cuisine—mashed potatoes, overcooked beef roasts, canned mushy peas—I exaggerate, but it was determinedly plain, except for the cooking of my Italian relatives. In my early twenties, for no reason I can understand—maybe because of the psychological fluctuations caused by my dicey medical state, my love of Vancouver's Chinatown and a beautiful young woman whose family owned one of the tastiest restaurants in Chinatown, and an omnivorous mind that insisted on reading everything—I underwent what's known as a "click." One morning I woke up curious about what I ate and why. That's when I began my adventures with food, discovering the diversity of local cuisines around the world.

Jane Jacobs, in *The Death and Life of Great American Cities*, argues that the variety in our cities sprang from a thriving, untrammelled, almost microbial civic core—a human eco-system that naturally extended to the rural world feeding it. Published in 1961, her book was treated with contempt because it opposed the dominant planning theory of the era—the logic trap of the Radiant City, promoted in the book of the same name by the modernist artist and architect Le Corbusier. He insisted that we design mechanical, reductive environments such as traffic grids, malls, suburbs, office-tower grids, environmental green spaces—all the claptrap of modernist planners, who also see nothing wrong with factory farms feeding the factory cities. This philosophy not only contaminated urban planning but contributed to the growing pressure on the small farm. It eventually devolved into a view of food as flavoured nutrient molecules.

The Radiant City concept ignores the organic magic of people living together and treats the home, culture, and food as merely gears in a "machine for living." Thus the boring dinners of my youth, which I soon rejected.

A half-dozen years after my first investigations into food, and the week after meeting Sharon, I invited her to one of the two surviving sushi restaurants in Vancouver during that era. The relationship nearly ended when I ordered a plate of sashimi (sliced raw tuna) and an *ikura* (salmon roe on rice in a seaweed wrap). But she fell in love with the tempura, and fortunately the restaurant served substantial whisky sours (called cherry blossoms), so she soon forgot the raw fish, and we remain together nearly thirty years later.

Although we were both raised at plain tables, over the years we have become companion adventurers in the world of food.

One of the first things we discovered was that we could resolve our expanding social debts by throwing an epic feast every couple of years and inviting our neighbours, relatives, and friends—all those whose dinners we had not reciprocated. We called these "pig parties" because we'd impale a pig on a spit and roast it whole, or sometimes we substituted a couple of lambs. The main dish made the vegans and vegetarians a little queasy, but since we provided more than enough vegetable and fruit dishes, they survived, and a few even discreetly sidled up to the carving table for a taste of crackling or tenderloin once they learned it was "happy" meat, the local term for livestock raised naturally.

If you have close to 150 people of all ages and politics wandering around stuffed with food and drink, things can go sideways very fast. And after a couple of kegs of beer the crowd gets a bit loose. At one pig party there was far too much Scotch and probably island herb smoked out in the bush, where the young rowdies wouldn't get caught

286

and lectured by their elders. I was fairly distorted myself, and one of the last things I remember, around three in the morning, was a large, hairy biker saying, "I've got thirty oysters in the shell." We kicked up the fire in the field and roasted them in their shells. Once they popped open we forked them into a pot of melted butter, chopped garlic, and cilantro—then swallowed them whole. Only old Howard and a couple of the skateboarders hung in there with me and the biker, who announced he was known as Pigster because he used to raise pigs for a living.

Around dawn I was lying in bed with a crashing headache and what felt like a pound of congealed butter in my belly. A racket erupted below our bedroom. "That rooster sounds awful close," Sharon muttered. Her tone indicated this was my problem. I staggered out of bed onto the walkway overlooking the main floor and realized that not only were there sleeping bodies of expired partygoers everywhere but the doors were all open and we'd forgotten to shut the coop. Gertrude the hen, being a leader and not a follower, had invited the chickens into the house. Charlie was standing atop a pile of expensive art books on the front-room coffee table, crowing his heart out while Gertie observed fondly.

287

I pulled on my pants and scrambled down the stairs, shooing the chickens out before they shat on the fancy books and rugs, waking a few unhappy and hungover guests. Outside I noticed Pigster crawling from under a willow tree. He strode around the house without a goodbye, tucking his shirt in, climbed on a big, black bike by the house gate, and cranked it over. It had no muffler and the roar echoed through the house. Then he revved it up and rolled down the driveway, past the field of guests who'd brought tents for the weekend, no doubt waking them all.

The bike's thunder faded, and then, as if in a Clint Eastwood spaghetti western, it grew louder again. He drove back past the sleeping tenters and parked by the house, strode off to the willow tree, stuffed a pair of polka-dot boxer shorts into his leather jacket, and returned to the house. By then I was sitting on the front deck with a few friends. I was so wrecked I had a bottle of Maalox in one hand and a beer in the other. This time Pigster silently nodded goodbye.

He started up the bike again, and the hapless tenters got another concert as he roared by and was gone. I never did find out who he was, or who invited him to the party, but the oysters were great. I chugged back a good shot of my hair of the dog while the chickens pecked about our feet, cleaning up the spilled food from the night's festivities.

ONE OF THE MORE curious phenomena since the seventies is the shift in our attitude toward food in North America— the ascendency of nutritional hysterias and fad diets, the cults of exotic dishes and ethnic cuisines. Cultures generally have complex, ancient traditions of diet, yet for various historical reasons, including the modernist, mechanistic attitude to community inspired by Le Corbusier, the majority of North Americans (apart from the Québécois) have lived in ignorance and relative unconcern about what goes into their bellies. Today, overcooked meat, boiled potatoes, Southern fried chicken, and mushy veggies don't cut it anymore, except for those whose taste buds and neural synapses have been redesigned by the artificial flavours and advertising of the fast food industry. These people—and you can see them waddling down any American street—are programmed addicts of adult-sized flavoured Pablums fortified with sugar, fat, and salt.

At the same time, food fetishism is sweeping through our society and we are discovering what only a few gourmets or world travellers once knew. Never before have people experienced such a bonanza of exotic produce. Even while thousands of tomato and cabbage varieties are disappearing, the supermarkets are displaying dragon fruit and plantains and truffles. Food shows and magazines and reviews are now ubiquitous. Dinner guests can knowledgeably discuss everything from ratatouille to the Japanese art of *kaiseki*—the ultimate combination of art and dining in which everything from the view through the window to the flower arrangement to the serving dishes is designed to express the totality of the food and the theme of the meal.

In this new and crazy universe I found our refrigerator overflowing for several years with alien produce and condiments from around the world. Now I've begun limiting myself to simpler meals and local food in season. There are those who glamorize the small-farm diet. But as I've noted, the real rural diet is not always so pretty—especially if you're poor and have just spent a year living on potatoes. If I stop and consider the local food of millions of people trapped in isolated communities where it's millet for breakfast, millet for lunch, and millet for dinner, I'm grateful for the feasts I've embraced, even though I'm too aware of the damage caused by the population explosion and the demands of my refrigerator.

Food fetishism also includes health bores and vegetarians, who can rattle off their diets and colon cleanses interminably, and, worse, the pill freaks who still don't eat their vegetables but thrive on vitamins and nutritional additives. There are disturbed people out there, I'm sure, who spend more on their vitamin and health supplements than on their food. Meanwhile, organic-lettuce eaters can be as obnoxious and insanely righteous as nonsmokers and their counterparts—exotic food cultists wired into the Food Network with its unreal "reality" shows and what's often referred to as food porn. Food has always been a jungle.

DINNER! ISN'T IT AMAZING the changes it has gone through over the centuries? Whether you're contemplating a stuffed lobster, a feed of mushrooms sprung from decaying trees, a New Age vegetarian hamburger, lettuce grown in that age-old standard—composted manure—or flesh slaughtered by hook or gun, it's the endless, mysterious cycle that matters. According to Stephen Sondheim in *Sweeney Todd,* his play about the mad barber of London, "The history of the world, my sweet...is the story of who gets eaten and who gets to eat."

As the small farm faces its greatest crisis, it also celebrates its greatest glories—on the land and on the table. When I recall our feasts and those I've encountered everywhere from Beijing to Morocco, I wonder if our greed will ever end, even as I stand in my garden among the arugula, yard-long beans, chicories, radicchio, cantaloupes, artichokes, and the gaudy Swiss chards while enormous chickens lumber like dinosaurs after cutworms in the

290

pasture and the lambs gambol under the willow trees. The foreign has become local. We have too much, and someone will eventually pay for our gluttony. Somebody already is paying. People and landscapes all around the world have fed this feast that is our small farm, and I know we can't go on forever.

That's why, like a recovering addict, I am trying to wean myself from the banquet laid out on the increasingly empty table of the planet, eating what I can grow, eating what is at hand, eating the garden. We have learned to love arugula and coriander, although both are introduced greens (but local now), out of the garden. They've become ours. They've joined the tasty bones of our lamb shanks and the broth I can braise them with, along with other herbs. The lost art of organ meat is returning. Liver and kidney and heart and intestines and tripe are re-entering the diet as the slow-food movement introduces new attitudes toward food and revives traditions. At last we can enjoy once again the real fat of real animals—the healthy smoothness of that fat and the gelatin of cooked bones warming the tongue. Like our dogs, I love the good bones in my dish, their marrow well herbed. Lots of vegetables, root and stem and leaf, and the fruits of shrubs and trees—sweet apples and luscious plums, hard pears and raspberries. The old foods. They thrive in our fields and they are our true diet. They don't need all the condiments of Vietnam or Provence. You can cook them straight and ungarnished, and their ambrosial essence is obvious.

Every year I find more delight in less. And maybe, at last, I have learned one small thing about consuming the world— take everything in moderation, including moderation.

20

A TOUR IS GOOD
FOR THE DIGESTION

. . . . . .

*A*FTER I'VE EATEN heaven in our dinner a sleepiness falls upon me, usually while I'm drinking my tea. Walking is the finest cure for lethargy. I've always been a walker, and in the fire of my youth I could walk the shoes off my feet. At the age of twenty-two I walked across Mexico City in a single day.

As soon as I'm at the door and pulling on my shoes, a thrill goes through the dogs, and they lunge to their feet with anticipation. I wish I still had their eagerness for such simple pleasures. Bella is bouncing high on the springs of her young legs, while Jen watches her with suspicion. Olive, black and glistening, her legs bowed, her back painful with arthritis, is still game. The puppy will turn back when it's evident there's no sheep herding or raccoons in the trees. The others will follow to see what surprises I stir up.

Walking our small orchard, I stop at the magnolias we planted on the perimeter for the pleasure of our neighbours, who drive by the pink cuplike blossoms every spring. The trees are of varying sizes, ranging from four-footers mauled by deer that pushed through the fencing to fifteen-foot-tall young trees. Already, though it's barely summer, their leaves are losing vibrancy. They need watering. Fifteen years to reach fifteen feet, and that's the best of the lot. When I planted the same variety in our front yard in White Rock nearly three decades ago it took only six years before it was half the size of our house. The difference? Water. Healthy plants seldom need more than the environment they belong in, but after failing to provide them with the simple essentials, people will bombard them with fertilizers and pesticides instead.

Our farm, like most small farms, is abundant with the hedgerows that nourish the birds and small mammals which have lost vast swaths of their natural habitat as human development dismantles meadowland and wilderness. On Trauma Farm the hedgerows are a mess and thus rich. In small farms around the world hedgerows remain like ours. In Europe they became more formal as the forests disappeared, turning into topiary hedges and rock or wood fencing of property lines. The disappearance of the margins has spread to North America and even to regions of Asia and Africa. This loss of habitat can be devastating. The North American grosbeak population has declined 78 percent in the last forty years, and much of that loss is blamed on habitat destruction.

We have been lucky here, because of our benevolently neglected hedgerows and determined planting of trees, shrubs, and flowers that provide shelter and food for birds in the gardens surrounding the house. The "birdvine" soon spread the word, and although our summers are particularly rich, the shrubs of Trauma Farm vibrate all year with juncos, quail, towhees, finches, wrens, bushtits, and sparrows, augmented during the summer by flocks of migrating warblers, crossbills, grosbeaks, thrushes, tanagers, goldfinches, waxwings, and whatever. The world is impressively resilient, given the chance.

IF FARMING TEACHES ANYTHING, it's tolerance. My tendency in garden design is toward the Oriental rather than the classic "garden rooms" philosophy of European gardeners. And I haven't the patience for the repressive linearity of a manicured garden like the geometric knot garden. But Sharon and I have the greed of the average North American, so we often plant too much too close together, which demands greater maintenance. Our display gardens combine English cottage gardens with Zen stylings, achieving the success of neither.

I've never favoured row planting, even with vegetables, which we generally plant in our raised wide beds to allow more dense, often nonlinear plantings. Nature has few straight lines. I always smile at flower gardens where the tulips resemble soldiers on parade days. This is a mechanistic sensibility enjoyed by municipal gardeners, who prefer linear arrangements, especially along roadsides—the flowers marching like little leafy drummers to the tune of the idling cars locked in rush-hour traffic. In their few concessions to the natural world, shopping malls feature evergreen shrubs in stiff cement islands or rows separating parking stalls.

To plant our bulbs we dig out the area and then throw the bulbs up in the air and cover them where they land. This technique inevitably provides a more natural formation. We hardly ever plant in twos and fours, preferring the Japanese bonsai-grower philosophy of odd numbers. For various reasons even-numbered plantings, especially in flower gardens, irritate almost all observers except those with control issues. Even-numbered plantings work only in a formal design, and a missing tree or shrub can be jarring.

In a spirit of anarchist defiance I planted our orchard in crooked rows, thinking foolishly that as the trees aged it would take on the look of an ancient orchard. All I got was a crooked orchard, which is a pain to mow and water, and that doesn't impress Sharon, who you'd think by now would have gotten used to my wacko ideas. Sometimes I think my history on this farm is one of tradition, education, and idiocy. Then again, that might be the history of the average small farm. All that said, Sharon grudgingly admits the orchard now looks old and picturesque.

A lot of our failings at Trauma Farm stem from the scarcity of teachers. Fewer than a dozen farmers with a rich past, like the Byrons, remain working on the island, along with a greater number of talented and self-educated amateur gardeners and perhaps a dozen horticulturally trained master gardeners. Traditional knowledge is dying, the community is breaking, and because of that, knowledge is now coming more from books or government agriculturalists informing farmers about good practices such as "Don't put the corral above the well." If you had done that fifty years ago, you would have been laughed out of the local coffee shop. Today such information seems original and is sometimes frighteningly necessary.

Our pasture is still green, though drying in its open, sandy heart, where the sun strikes it hardest. In another few weeks there won't be much nutrition left in the grass, and by the end of the summer, instructed by the sheep's grazing pattern, I will know which soil is weakest and needs liming or tilling or reseeding. When the sheep see me they rush up, led by the big ram, Jesus, named by a waggish friend because he was "resurrected" after a rough birth on Easter, and because that's what I usually swear when he sneaks up behind me and tries to bang the food bucket out of my hand. Jesus is a beauty among rams, docile and gentlemanly, except for his occasional desperation at feeding time. He can be intimidating when he charges the food trough with the single-minded dumb hunger of a sheep. He caught Sharon once when she wasn't looking and hurt her back. Almost all injuries with farm animals are the result of a distracted moment's inattention, which can be rewarded as harshly on a farm as when driving down the road.

Trust in dealing with animals is hard to explain; it can be learned only by contact. When our grandchildren were young every one of them would break out in wails as soon as they saw Olive galumphing happily out of the house. Ajra was particularly frightened. She'd been visiting and living with our animals for a few years, you'd glance out the window and see this tiny girl hilariously shooing the big ram away from her flower collection, while Olive dutifully followed.

Working with animals can be scary at first because relationships in the natural world usually involve a combination of trust, power, and the pecking order. Only once all that is established does the relationship fall into place. The livestock understand that we are demanding obedience, and natural rebels that they are, they want to push for their freedom. It's a bizarre relationship, if you think about it. Once our livestock and dogs realize that the rules are not onerous, that we are gentle and firm and want to work with them, they come over. Then they start to listen and often take delight in having direction. The sheep nature is inside every animal, including us. Good relationships are also tactile. I constantly touch them, but casually. I have no illusions about my power relationship with them.

And I must also admit I've taken the occasional perverse pleasure in watching our livestock startle a friend. A good surprise every now and then teaches us to recognize when to run and when to stand—a skill generally neglected in city living. A friend, a Native artist from back east, once dropped by for a visit, and while we were touring the lower pasture Jackson caught wind of us and charged in our direction, no doubt hoping to mug someone for a sugar cube. My friend took one look at this big black horse barrelling at us and from a standing position leaped the six-rail fence into the neighbour's llama yard. I was impressed. He quickly scrambled back over the fence, away from the hissing llamas, while the horse eyeballed us cravenly, wondering what had happened to his sugar cube. I've always enjoyed a man who can move quickly.

THE FARM PROVIDES A great opportunity for kids to develop country skills. Our city-raised grandchildren spend at least a week at the farm every summer. They arrive fresh-faced and eager and immediately fight over who gets the better bed; then we send them out to explore. By the end of the first week they've been eaten alive by mosquitoes, got sunburned, run screeching out of the bush after encountering a wasp nest, discovered a dead chicken crawling with maggots that's been dragged away by a raccoon, picked flowers for the house, eaten peas from the vine, and casually nibbled fennel in the flower garden. They scrape their backs falling off swings over a creek, ride the horse, peel the garlic, and are sent back to their terrified parents a little bruised and beaten but almost islandized. Their parents recognize that this experience is essential to their upbringing, like violin or dance lessons.

Grotesquely few children encounter the natural world these days. A few guilty, dutiful parents send their children to "park experiences," where rangers complain that the kids carry antibacterial sprays so they can sterilize themselves after touching a leaf or a slug. A writer has named a syndrome, "nature deficit disorder," after these unfortunate and deprived urban children. While it's natural for a parent to fear every poisonous bug, falling branch, and imaginary cougar behind the trees, it's also natural for a child to experience these events and fears, and the loss of this experience is a danger to our civilization. People often phone and ask us if they can bring a friend's children over to the farm, because they have never encountered a live chicken or sheep, or picked vegetables from a garden.

I WANDER DOWN BY the willows, at the edge of the first pond, in this eighteen-year-long day of the time-shifting,

endangered, yet eternal farm. Chloe the goose is convers-
ing with LaBarisha, the Arabian grey. Horse and goose have
a curious relationship. They meet almost every day at the
water's edge, and I wonder what mysterious conversation
travels between them. Chloe will swim up to the shoreline as the horse sips meditatively from the water. Then she
will lift her head and they remain motionless, beak to nose,
sometimes for several minutes, soundless, at least as far as
I can tell from far away. Over the years I've watched similar conversations. Jackson loved the pigs and Jesus the ram.
Animals talk, they die, they're born, they die again, until all
the stories fold into a long summer's day of memories.

A giant, shimmering goldfish leaps into the air and lands
on its belly with a slap, disturbing the tableau of horse and
goose, and they separate, the horse eyeing me as I approach.
Then a cluster of mallards crash into the air and wheel several times overhead before deciding I am going to stay, and
they leave, no doubt disgusted. In the far rushes of the
lower pond I see the red-headed merganser slip through the
reeds and evaporate into the foliage. Mergansers are clever,
and this one has the knack for raising broods from eggs
laid in the muddy bank in this semi-public pond, miraculously shielding them from eagles, raccoons, and my dogs
in the night.

The ponds are still high, but as summer drives its hot
fingers into the earth the water level will drop, and the
big pond we use for irrigation will soon resemble a bomb
hole in a field near Baghdad. As the water tables fall with
global warming, I have twice had to bring in an excavator to deepen and enlarge the pond, and only now are my
water plants starting to fill in. These are artificial ponds. It's

tougher than it looks to create a natural ecosystem. And my plantings are often shredded by the geese, wild ducks, the horse, and sheep when the water level drops.

Yet somehow the life is moving in, aquatic plants arriving as seeds in the excrement of overflying birds or on the feet of ducks—insects from the unknown. There are water boatmen and fascinating stick bugs that resemble dead branches underwater, big fat toe-biters like aquatic cockroaches and leeches—both of which can make the grandchildren studiously avoid the water. Contemplating our ponds, as immature as they are, I understand that I could spend my life researching them and still know very little. My gaze sweeps the farm, and I am struck by the inadequacy of my years of studying and practising the art of living on this tiny parcel of land.

Like the pond, like myself, like the changing and surprising world, the farm is countless events occurring simultaneously—an organism, a mycelium sending out threads in every direction. When we "rationalize" and narrow the diversity in the name of greater production efficiencies, we diminish it, although we may produce more yields initially. The fatal flaw of the infamous "green revolution" is our failure to comprehend that the more we expand our production abilities, the more we diminish the quality of both farm produce and rural life. Natural laws are a lot more complex than they first appear. And the natural world is always slipping through our fingers.

We have a tendency to reduce this complex world to simplistic, systematic, and superficial formulas. The scientific method is our greatest asset and our greatest failure. It applies reductionist, linear logic to a nonlinear world. This

300

can work spectacularly in specific cases, but it slides into muddier ground as we witness with growing horror the results of this reductive logic in factory farming. That's why so much of our land and ecological management has been disastrous. The more bureaucrats manage fisheries, the fewer fish we have; the more we "scientifically" regulate our livestock practices, the farther we drift from good health and good nutrition. If our science fails to take in the lessons of traditional knowledge and its intuitive skills, we doom our science. Nature doesn't create factory environments, with good reason. We create them at our peril. Jane Jacobs points out that natural organisms thrive in conjunction with thousands of stimuli, not just one. If you consider the immensely complex world of the small farm, reductive and linear practices generally work, but all kinds of nonlinear approaches also work.

Running a farm or cultivating a garden means accepting life within a cat's cradle of fertility and rain and sun and weeds and deer. The insistence on perfection is the habit of the human mind. The drive to make sure that each crop is as good as or better than the last is the direct route to artificial fertilizers, pesticides, single-cropping, and GM seeds, even though they eventually diminish the entire system.

These measures have not only led to desertification and poisoned fields where our food is grown; they've also affected the flower industry. Store-bought roses carry a legacy of ruined gardens, toxic greenhouses, and ill workers in the Third World, where environmental and labour regulations are nearly nonexistent. A few flowers from a local field or greenhouse sold at the corner store have been replaced by an enormous $40-billion-a-year multinational industry in which the flowers have travelled far more than the young couple buying them at the corner market.

To combat this phenomenon a wave of environmentalists have been working on the ethical and ecological flower trade. You can avoid the whole issue by either growing your own flowers (what an innovative idea!) or, if you can't because of your living circumstances, buying real flowers from local growers at farmers' markets. Common sense is most uncommon in our species. Meanwhile, Valentine's Day has become a toxic festival. Fifty million greenhouse roses wilt around the world each year in order for us to celebrate this day. Ninety percent of them are purchased by men. It has been calculated that more than £22 million is spent on flowers for Valentine's Day in England alone. This news made me stop and consider the madness of our society, gearing up for an annual extravaganza of supply-and-demand globalized economics at its kookiest excess. The majority of sales are geared toward perfection on a single day. Imagine the cost of the lighting, heating, fertilizers, and pesticides necessary to force a flower into reaching its prime on a single day. The rest of the world might be collapsing from starvation and AIDS and ecological catastrophe, but we are putting our romantic shoulders to the wheel, keeping that skewed economy blossoming.

On Trauma Farm we soon learned about that cat's cradle weaving together many fingers and criss-crossing patterns of string, and learned to celebrate it. I start cutting firewood. I have to get the sheep out of the field so that I don't drop a tree on them, especially if it's a maple, because they're mad for the sugar in the maple and if they see me with the chainsaw they will follow me in hope of maple leaves.

To get the sheep out of the pasture I need to fix the cross-fencing, which involves splitting a couple of new cedar rails or removing them from another fence. Then I need to mow the field before the broken branches make a mess. With all that done, I discover some of the junk wood is very beautiful filigreed maple—a crime to waste for firewood. It needs milling. But by now I can't get the mill in until fire season is over. It's a multidimensional chess game always in process. There are no solutions. Farming is life itself: the means are more important than the end—the means *are* the end. As Oswald Spengler noted: "Godhead is effective in the living and not in the dead, in the becoming and the changing, not in the become and the set-fast."

The natural world is a miracle: mystery after mystery. Though it is full of wonder, it's not necessarily wise or nice, as the Gnostic heretics noticed. I wouldn't call liver disease, tooth decay, anal maggots in sheep, and stillbirths wise or nice, even as I recognize the natural systems and the evolutionary beauty of how they arose. Though I'm amused by the teleological argument—that nature is like a watch designed by a watchmaker—or its new variation, intelligent design, I would have wished for a more kindly designer.

Nature actually is the complicated watch of teleology, only one designed not by a god but by blind and amoral natural forces. And though I worship its beauty I recognize it's just as twisted as we are. Living inside an ecology and meditating upon it deeply—the gore, the parasites, the gorgeous birthings, those green leaves after a rain, the rusty nail in the foot, a nasturtium blossom close up, and the babies born headless while a tidal wave approaches—we can only suspect that if this is intelligent design, the designer

303

is a devil indeed. That's not my kind of god. But maybe the god is the energy to break away, the energy behind the whirlpool, the need to perpetuate itself, breeding and changing—entropy—and that's why we recognize and worship the insanity of diversity and why I've long admired the cosmologist Brian Swimme's remark "You take hydrogen gas, you leave it alone for 14 billion years—and it turns into rosebuds, giraffes and humans."

Besides rosebuds and giraffes, you also get succulent strawberries at the height of their season, and that's how I end up back in the garden, remembering that we haven't picked any for a few days. We have to cover them with netting or remay cloth to keep away the birds. We grow two varieties, the fat, one-shot wonders of early summer, and the perpetuals, which really aren't that perpetual. They just have a second burst of fruit later in the summer. They are smaller, not as lush, like little jewels compared with the tasty fat boys of this time of year. The taste of either is so superior to those big woody things in the supermarkets. This has been a good year for strawberries. We fended off the birds and the slugs, and the weather was perfect. But sometimes the farm takes away our dreams. We wait for crops all winter and then they die on us or don't fruit well during days of rain, or they shrivel and burn under a malicious sun. Farming, like foraging, is as much about hope as about accepting what you receive.

Sharon and I engage in our share of good-natured, amusing disputes in the garden. They are usually all about memory, which is why we keep a gardener's log to resolve the extended differences of opinion. My short-term memory is so bad I can never remember where I left the garden hoe, which frustrates her no end, yet when she announces the lemon cucumber is useless I remember that it was spectacular last summer, and it was only a late planting and poor weather that made it perform so badly this season. Over the years, like all domestic couples, we have learned the benefits of banter, and also when to quietly ignore a disagreement. Her one habit that still breaks my heart is when I'm facing the imminent demise of one of my thirty-year-old bonsais, which I've accidentally moved into some corner where it didn't get watered for a week. Sharon will look at it and tell me, "It's getting better." This remark, I've long ago learned, is the kiss of death. She unconsciously has that nurse's knack for recognizing when death is near. There's a brightness in the dying human eye and the struggling leaf—just before everything gives up and the life fades. That brightness in the dying leaf always gives her hope.

Tonight the flowers are humming with butterflies, and the slanting, golden light of the late afternoon is bringing out the luminosity of flowers. The bumblebees are working them as if there will be no tomorrow, though the honeybees are already bedded down. I prefer my flowers in the garden. Sharon loves them both in the house and in the garden. I always have a moment of horror if I see the decapitated stems of slaughtered delphiniums, but I know they will appear on a table or a counter in the house in an elegant vase, surprising me again, and making me look closer. Despite living in this jungle of colour I keep forgetting to stop and live with beauty. Sharon's spectacular talent as an arranger, her true calling in life, reminds me of the beauty I sometimes miss.

We bought an elegant little ikebana dish, which we keep on the table in the sunroom, where we usually sit in the evening. This allows us to show off a small flower and interesting leaves. The art of sparsity in flower arrangements is not a tradition of the West, which prizes overflowing bouquets. Big and more is always better here, until you go farther west and encounter the Oriental philosophy of less.

One of the delights of the farm is that we tiled our bathtub surround white. This gave Sharon the opportunity of a corner where she can arrange small bouquets out of range of the hot spray of the shower. A couple of times a week she changes them, so that every bath or shower has a little surprise to encounter and contemplate. I've often thought of photographing that corner of the bath enclosure over the years, recording the seasons and the changes in her sense of design with time. Beauty is as close as that, observing original displays of flowers you have known all your life.

Contemplating these beauties reminds me of the Zeigarnik effect, the thesis that the human brain is better at remembering incomplete tasks (naturally) than it is at recalling completed ones. This is all for the good when living simply in a simple environment, but faced with the overwhelming information and distractions of today, the brain falls into a miasma of unconcentrated energy, addicted to stimulus shock, lost in cognitive dissonance. As a result a growing number of people have rebelled and joined the recent drive toward simplicity. We have to shut off the news and look at the single flower again. And that's why it's our daily duty to wander our garden from spring to winter, searching for a flower or leaf or branch that suits the day's arrangement.

BENEATH THE BIG STUMP crowned with the small stone
Buddha peeking out from a huckleberry shrub, the voodoo
lily has fallen over, and I go to the barn for the stakes I left
by the table saw. Suddenly I am confronted by the fledgling
swallows in the nest above the saw. At least tonight I don't
need to cut a board, but they're still indignant at the interruption, and they fly chattering through the door after
buzzing my head several times. One of them bangs against
a wall and temporarily stuns itself. This is the scary time of
the year for birds, as nestlings take their first flights, bouncing off walls, crashing into each other, performing goofy
acrobatics. This is also when the newly hatched nighthawks
come down off the mountain—the electric whir of their
wings startling us as they hunt the insects above the ponds,
completing the circle of the garden where we live.

21

REGULATING A
REBELLIOUS UNIVERSE

· · · · · ·

I WAS SEATED IN a rickety chair at a Farmers' Institute meeting one evening with thirty other annoyed farmers, drinking coffee that tasted like tar infected with particles of artificial whitener. A trio of government managers were lecturing us about the steps they were taking to help us, but these three blind mice couldn't comprehend that, despite our protests, it was their help that was killing us. Bored, I made a few calculations based on what I knew of my neighbours, and I realized the combined salaries of those officials, none of whom had ever run a farm, was probably greater than the net earnings of all the farmers in the room. That's when I felt the numbing sadness of someone being trampled by his government, and I finally understood what Karl Marx meant when he said that human labour had become merely another commodity doomed to increasing specialization and alienation from

308

the human condition and that modern economics was producing "its own gravediggers." In this faceless room, we were being lectured by our gravediggers.

Max Weber studied the expansion of bureaucracy and, more importantly, its inbuilt dysfunction. He understood that rational systems, implemented by bureaucracies, can't deal "with individual particularities, to which earlier types of justice were well suited." In other words the tribe would always be more flexible than a federal trial. According to Weber, the "iron cage" of bureaucracy would prevent us from ever living in the Garden of Eden, where we were born, a garden we still crave, even as the natural world comes crashing down around us. These three managers facing the crowd were that iron cage, and it was difficult not to feel glum as they lectured farmers about farming. We all knew they were here to shut us down, yet like sheep we sat in the room and attempted to learn why—hope is an impressive instrument of control.

Listening, I understood why every year Sharon and I spend days filling out forty-three pages of income tax documentation for a farm with a gross income of half the national poverty level, and why we are forced to spend hours filling out compulsory census forms designed to promote the agribusinesses crushing us. I am a poet, and Sharon is a nurse. Together, we earn enough money to feed our farming habit. Even though I consider poetry one of the highest callings, I think there's something bizarrely wrong with our economy when writing poetry helps sustain traditional farming.

Farming, they say, is the only occupation where you buy retail and sell wholesale and pay the freight both ways. Mike Byron told me that in his early days of farming there were

309

several years he was grateful to sell his apples for enough money to buy apple boxes for the next year. How do you make a small fortune at farming? Start with a large fortune.

The rural life has weathered many a storm from pests and plagues to blights and scorched-earth warfare, but it has never encountered anything like the outlandish experiment in food production that began with the Industrial Revolution and the shift from small farming to the globalized factory farm—an experiment with few safety measures, where the term "precautionary principle" is regarded by the likes of these bureaucrats as a threat concocted by ignorant vegetarian cultists and scummy environmentalists (not that there weren't a couple of them in the room).

These officials were all victims of what Ronald Wright, in *A Short History of Progress,* has called progress traps, which I mentioned earlier: they're failures in logic or, more aptly, products of failed reductive logic—tunnel vision, in which an idea, a trail, is followed because it appears to be progressive, only there's a big bear waiting at the end of the tunnel. An example Wright uses is the development of weapons technology through the centuries. Each improvement, from the stone point to the spear thrower to the high-calibre scoped rifle of today, allowed the easier hunting of game, but the end result is the extinction of game and, finally, the creation of the atom bomb. This is what's also occurring with agriculture, with the loss of tens of thousands of small farms, livestock and plant extinctions, and, until recently, the abandonment of rural communities. Will the eventual destination of agriculture become strips of meat grown in trays in laboratories, and vats of algaelike soups or dried cubes for vegetables?

Progress traps are what happens when scientists and health officials convince themselves they can control the natural world whose glow we walk within, though nature has always been reluctant to accept our regulation. Hence our inept attempts at "wildlife management." We have a cultlike belief that we can ultimately improve ecosystems that didn't need much improvement until we came along. Technology has had millions of fabulous successes, obviously, but these successes have blinded us to our many failures, which have harmed our environment, ourselves, our children, the food we eat, and the communities we create.

Friedrich Nietzsche notes that since the Renaissance, Western society has become possessed by "optimistic rationalism"—a pathetic obsession with the myth of progress.

Gone is the companionship of the logical and the ecstatic worlds. The Dionysian and the Apollonian, the yin and yang. Logic, rationalism, specialization, individualism; all of these are extremely useful but they need to be balanced with instinct, intuition, tradition, ecstasy, community, a healthy distrust of authority, and, most of all, the patience of an old farmer. Sometimes our scientists and economists just need a good dose of common sense.

This kind of thinking will give agricultural and health bureaucrats lizard eyes and send them to sleep. I know; I tried to point out to my three blind mice at the head table a few of these issues. "Aren't your health regulations destroying small farms while promoting toxic factory farms, which are spreading infections on a massive scale?" I watched their eyes glaze over, as if I'd dusted them with pesticide.

THE MODERN CORPORATE AND governmental knack for destroying environments by trying to fix them also comes from a generally confused understanding of evolution. Darwin titled one of his books, perhaps too aptly, *The Descent of Man.* He wasn't kidding. He understood what "progress" meant. Most creatures that rose out of the brew of evolution have gone extinct. Things change. Blind alleys are created, as when we inbred the turkey into a creature so deformed it can no longer mate naturally. It's entirely possible the human race is another evolutionary blind alley. It might make our behaviour more understandable if we considered our evolution a form of devolution.

Alfred Russel Wallace, the co-discoverer of natural selection with Darwin, theorized that natural selection operates as a kind of feedback mechanism, diverting creatures into either evolutionary blind alleys or successful adaptations to protect general ecosystems over the long term. "The action of this principle is exactly like that of the centrifugal governor of the steam engine, which checks and corrects any irregularities almost before they become evident; and in like manner no unbalanced deficiency in the animal kingdom can ever reach any conspicuous magnitude, because it would make itself felt at the very first step, by rendering existence difficult and extinction almost sure soon to follow." If this is true it doesn't augur well for our relatively short-lived species. In fact, in a weird way, Wallace might well be saying that the avian flu is nature's answer to the factory farming of chickens.

Evolution has nothing to do with "survival of the fittest," a term more suited to the social system propagated by the industrial tycoons of the Victorian era than to the natural world. Many creatures survive in mutually supportive social structures. In his book *Mutual Aid,* the great anarchist philosopher Pyotr Kropotkin claimed that mutual aid was also a driving force for natural selection of landscapes and creatures—it's about adaptation more than competition. Evolution, like farming, is an interactive way of life, not a goal.

THERE'S A SLIM BOOK by Homer W. Smith called *Kamongo: The Lungfish and the Padre,* where I first encountered the concept of entropy, which can be loosely defined as a measure of the transfer of information of all life, or its "degradation"—but you have to think of degradation in its scientific sense, not as a negative. You can think of it as a measure of degrees of freedom. It can also lead to complexity—diversity, the thrill of the world so many of us worship and strive to protect; and that's why, when looked at in this way, it's known as evolutionary entropy—what gave us those rosebuds and giraffes and opera.

The thin plot of *Kamongo,* a 1932 bestseller, consists of a scientist and a minister, both unable to sleep, meeting at the rail of their steamer ship on a hot night as it navigates the Suez Canal. The scientist explains his research on the kamongo, or lungfish, and meditates on the meaning of life. The kamongo has reached an evolutionary dead end. It's slowly going extinct, and he wonders if the human brain is merely another development similar to the fish's lung. He believes that we are like the lungfish—evolved into our own progress traps or feedback mechanisms—and that evolution consists of creatures breeding in the spinning eddies of a stream flowing to the sea. The two men debate this, but the minister is not convinced the world is so mechanical and remorseless. He believes in the need for mystery, for magic, the ineffable, a guiding hand, even though the scientist insists entropy is that ineffable, guiding hand—the whirlpool is the mystery the minister demands. Then they go their separate ways.

Smith is talking about not only natural selection but the second law of thermodynamics: the law that tells us energy is not lost. It merely flows to a more degraded, more diffuse form, or a more complex form in a closed system. Evolutionary entropy is the spinning whirlpools in the stream—the will to diversify and procreate in order to fill an ecological niche in a flowing environment. Understanding entrophy might be as close to knowing God as we're going to get.

Most environmentalists worship the products of the second law unconsciously. Diversity! It's the wonder of the small farm and the ocean deeps. How can we not love the exotic, enormous variety of the universe? One evening I was talking to the artist Robert Bateman about how diversity grows, and he mentioned that he considered life a river—of arts and animals and music and plants—flowing out of key tributaries along this river, until everything reaches the delta where it spreads like countless grains of sand. In many ways this is the evolution of science. Beginning with a number of simple and beautiful theories and natural laws, science has evolved into discoveries so complex only experts in the field can understand them.

⸻

WHAT DOES THIS HAVE to do with small farming and my three blind mice? Everything, of course. There's good reason for believing that the factory farm is our version of the lungfish. The distance between our mouths and the farm that grows our food has telescoped exponentially. We have gone from munching on an edible vine, to Mendel's discovery of genetics, to genetic modification and the industrial production of rice on another continent. Sometimes it seems like we've raced straight from the digging stick to the combine-harvester.

As ugly as it can be, globalization is also a wonder of human ingenuity. First came the spinach, then came the varieties, then came the hydroponic factories thousands of miles away, and the mechanical sterilization and packaging in plastic containers injected with carbon dioxide so you can eat a "fresh" spinach salad—untouched by human hands— that is forty-three days old. With or without the salmonella. Then the packaging is shipped to China for recycling.

Such an intricate food system needs regulations respectful of the whole environment, not just the multinational agribusiness industry. Since our regulators are unable to see beyond this system, the ordinances, whether health or agricultural, are approaching an evolutionary dead end. The lungfish meets the feedback mechanism of Wallace, the progress trap of Wright. This is why small farming is being legislated out of existence, despite an inspired guerrilla war by the defenders of small farms and real food. So far our legislators can't see beyond this progress trap we've inflicted upon ourselves. One of the main reasons why is that our species hasn't evolved as quickly as the tools we have created. We're gorillas with machine guns riding a fast train to oblivion.

Thus the farm joke about regulation I once ran into. According to this joke—whose accuracy I doubt, though I love it—the Lord's Prayer is 66 words, the Gettysburg

Address is 286 words, and there are 1,322 words in the Declaration of Independence, but the U.S. government regulations on the sale of cabbage take up 26,911 words.

This is the world of my three blind mice at the head table. They belong to the school that designed the laws that define the cabbage.

CONSIDER HEALTH REGULATIONS RELATED to farm production. Each is individually good, all implemented for rational reasons, but incrementally they are unhealthy. Now we have health cops shutting down community barbecues or seizing the eggs from a farm stand or some old lady's muffins made with real farm eggs. All sense of proportion has been lost. It used to be that a few people got sick at a picnic. Now 7 million pounds of potentially toxic meat or truckloads of infected spinach can cross nations within days. Yet this is what health and agricultural officials and the designers of manufactured food regard as progress. Since 1994 meat factories have recalled on average 8,500 tons of meat annually. The recalls are generally issued long after the food has been eaten. This is because there is none of the immediate feedback that occurs with local produce.

Meanwhile, because of the power shift in government, health regulators can harass small farmers, but in some American states meat inspectors assigned to visit agribusiness slaughterhouses actually have to make written applications for permission (which has been refused more than once) to inspect on a specified time and date. This explains those many tainted-meat scandals.

ANOTHER PROGRESS TRAP IS the so-called green revolution. The use of new hybrid seeds and pesticides and fertilizers and monoculture allowed many Asian nations to increase cultivation of crops from rice to cotton for decades, but now as the land becomes sterile, the insects immune, the chemicals too expensive, and traditional farming unviable in the era of globalization, the bankrupt farmers of India are suffering an epidemic of suicides as the farmers drink their own pesticides, illustrating too well what ruined them.

Our regulatory infrastructure can lead to the saddest consequences. In Poland swallows are symbols of good luck and favoured in barns, where they eat flies and insects with gusto. Yet entry into the European Union entails obeying its health regulations—and one of the edicts is that swallows must be exterminated in the Polish barns, since birds are potential disease carriers. The farmers are instructed to hang special plastic bags filled with chemical toxins that flying swallows will stick to and die, poisoned, thus creating the modern, healthy Polish barn.

Agribusiness originally assumed cheap food would attract customers, which it did, but as information spread about the production technologies and their dangers, consumption shifted toward organic produce, which also tastes better. Once organic produce grew into a major industry, it began transforming into what's become known as "Big Organic"—mass-produced organic food using the factory methodology. That's why people have lately taken up local food, bringing us full circle to the nutritious, more environmentally friendly, tasty diet provided by the local small farm in season. The trick is to not lose sight of the goal—good food.

317

Every agrarian society has traditionally offered what's now termed farm-gate sales. On Salt Spring, until the last three years, farm stands were a booming trade. Islanders are environmentally conscious and fans of organic, local food. Unfortunately, the regulators have begun systematically targeting traditional community food. First they pursued our pie ladies, banning all bake sales and homemade pies. After the near-rioting died down they limited the ban to cream pies, but we know they'll be back.

During the great forest fires in Kelowna, on the British Columbia mainland, several years ago, a small army of beleaguered firemen fought back the flames and saved hundreds of homes, orchards, and vineyards. An outpouring of thanks erupted from our elders, and thousands of homemade food items were mailed or delivered to the firemen, everything from pies to cookies to sandwiches. All of this food—truckloads of it—was dumped because it hadn't been inspected and wasn't prepared in approved kitchens, and was probably made by little old ladies who hadn't taken a FOODSAFE course. That's how a community is strangled. Whether it's local barbecues and benefits, pie ladies, or candy apples on Halloween, we're witnessing the alienation of ourselves from our neighbours.

Personal responsibility, relationships with your neighbours, and the traditional defences of small communities against bad practices have been replaced by food manufactured in thousands of countries from China to Mexico and a byzantine regulatory structure restricting real food and promoting factory farming. It's taken North Americans several hundred years to begin learning to respect the traditional cultures of aboriginal peoples. Yet our governments have lost their respect for the traditional cultures of our own farmers.

These three blind mice were ostensibly sent here to protect us and our livestock. Their regulations ended up destroying us by banning all traditional slaughter. Within two years of this meeting, the most famous gourmet market lamb in the world, Salt Spring lamb, was effectively destroyed. Gone. The few surviving sheep farms have to book their slaughter off-island and four months in advance, paying more for the slaughter than for all the other costs of raising a lamb, guaranteeing its unprofitability. Nor can we provide the cuts our customers desire, and almost all local farmers fear that their babied, organic lamb is going to be switched and come back from a distant slaughterhouse as some scuzzy commercial lamb from a factory farm. We're finished. Just about wiped out. Today, for now, we're the lambs. Hopefully, not tomorrow.

And what of my three mice? They were changing in front of my eyes, morphing.... The anger began to flow like a infection through my blood as the discussion went around in circles, so I got up and left before I could utter words I would regret. Sometimes, you just can't argue with a lungfish.

22

LOCAL LIVING, LOCAL COMMUNITIES

· · · · ·

"WHO'S THAT?" SHARON asked as I lifted my finger off the steering wheel in the standard country wave to an unfamiliar pickup truck passing us on our dusty gravel road. We'd just finished dinner and were rushing our produce into the Farmers' Institute before the deadline closed on the annual fall fair competitions. He waved a finger back.

"I have no idea," I said.

"So why did you wave?"

That's not hard to explain. If he was on our road, he was likely a neighbour who'd bought a different truck, or a new neighbour, or someone visiting a neighbour, or a tradesman coming back after dinner to finish some project for a neighbour, or a lost tourist. In any of these cases he deserved a friendly wave.

I enjoy living on an island where we greet each other, where not saying hello can get you lectured for unneighbourly behaviour—though a stroll between the bank and the hardware store can cost two hours in small talk and drive me wild with desperation to get home. Yet how outlandish is today's urban world, where people walk past people every day without even acknowledging their presence.

People working together will work things out, as Jane Jacobs noted. You only have to watch the wonder of the human interactions at ferry time in our tiny village of Fulford Harbour during summer: the ferry overflowing with cars disembarking and boarding, locals picking up milk or a video in the small store or jawing about a bear sighting as they sip a soy cappuccino, while tourists stroll through the cluster of unorthodox shops that sell everything from Balinese mirrors to beads and wood-oven bread. It's chaos, cars and foot traffic wandering in every direction, yet hardly ever do I see glass from a broken tail light. Everyone knows the place is a hazard, and they watch out for each other. It's a kind of choreographed conversation among the community, performed with grace and good cheer.

Once I honked at a man's car straddling the parking lot entrance. Then a neighbour hollered at me, "Hey, Brian, he's only waiting to get gas!" I immediately understood why the car was trapped in its awkward spot. I turned red with shame at my rudeness. Another time, a friend of ours got stuck in a freak snowstorm and managed to block both loading and unloading ferry traffic, creating a fabulous jam-up, which soon had everyone in the harbour guffawing, while a crew of Fulford irregulars shoved her car into position in the icy snow.

321

Tonight was another community event. The fall fair is the culmination of the forging of relationships between musicians, farmers, car enthusiasts, bakers, growers, cooks, bead stringers, and blacksmiths. We all show up. When we arrived at the fair and began organizing our produce I noticed Sam, the border collie, in the back seat with a guilty look on her face and what appeared to be a bean stem dangling from her muzzle. Sure enough, there were only eleven green beans in the basket that was supposed to hold twelve, so as soon as we entered the hall, not even having enough time to wonder why a dog would eat a raw string bean, I rang up Bev Byron on the pay phone and explained the crisis as the deadline for entry neared. I knew she'd soon be on the way with her own produce. So she drove up to our house and picked a half-dozen of our pole beans. Once she arrived we found a bean that matched our specimens and finished our entry. Those cobbled-together beans won the trophy for grand champion of vegetables. That's what community is all about.

LAST CENTURY, AS THE mixed farms were rolled over by the banks, the corporate bone collectors picked them up for a song. The towns began fading, their population migrating toward the cities, as they have done throughout history when small farming collapses. Our great web of little towns winked out like bedroom lights at night. Yet recently, there's been a reverse flood of often wealthy immigrants, connected electronically and more educated about local living, finding themselves in conflict with the developers eager to cash in on the outer regions and ruin the communities with success. Salt Spring Island is a forward-looking community where people demand local food from their shopkeepers— yet we don't supply 10 percent of our own food today.

Living locally, you soon learn that at least the his- toric modes of exchange of labour and goods still thrive, annually at the fall fair and weekly at the local craft and farmers' market in Ganges, which shuts down only in the winter months and is a fine conduit for supplies, culture, and eccentric community conflicts. Our island newspaper estimates it has received more letters to the editor about the market than about any other subject. There also may be hundreds of farm-gate stands. Small farmers are an integral link in the rural social structure, whether pulling cars out of mudholes with their tractors, providing land or buildings for community gatherings, or scaring local hooligans up to no good in the fields or woods.

Gifting and helping flow around our island like water. There's a subtle ritual attitude to debt—a pass-it-on men- tality that can grow deliciously eccentric as oddball instruments like a burdizzo (a tool used for gelding male livestock) or a honey extractor travel the island. Although the extractor, donated to the community by a couple who'd given up bees, has become an increasing challenge to track down every year during its migrations.

Tool- and help-swapping can lead to a complicated, amusing, lively web of debts between neighbours—rela- tionships built upon mutual need and mutual gifting, and sometimes mutual annoyance. This is what Pyotr Kropot- kin talked about with his argument that mutual aid was necessary for evolutionary survival. The trick about get- ting caught in this cycle is to remember that giving is more

323

important than selling. You give tools or help—safe in the knowledge that they will return someday. Theoretically (hey, every system has its failings). If your neighbour needs something, you give it to her. It doesn't matter who it is. You give, and you keep on giving, never expecting a return. In *The Gift*, Christopher Hyde contrasts the market economy, which has made acquisition the core of society and led to the manufacturing of wants that can never be satisfied, with a "gifting economy," where, as in Native communities, especially of the coast, self-worth is measured not by what you have but by what you have given.

As Hyde points out, now we have entered the kingdom of the consumer—a kingdom easily manipulated by the manufacturing of wants, so that our economy succeeds only if we are continually wanting, and thus unfulfilled. Gifting rarely goes off the rails, as it did with potlatches for a brief, confused period before they were banned. It's true that an escalating pattern of gift giving bankrupted chiefs. They also knew that most of the gifts would come back, one way or another, for that is the way of potlatching, which the government officials couldn't comprehend; and I love how my Native friends rely on the ceremony for community good order. Several times I've heard the remark "He won't complain. I've potlatched him more than he's potlatched me."

But the "gifting wars," as I call them, have their drawbacks—such as figuring out who has that honey extractor, which can cost time spent on social calls and lead to excessive dinner invitations or requests for community service, like weeding all those invasive Scotch broom plants from the nearby park. You can also inherit monumental social debt from generous individuals. Farmers have long learned that the more help you give another farmer, the more help he will owe you, and help is always needed on a farm. So I grow twitchy when I realize I'm falling behind, because there are certain farm chores you'd do anything to dodge, like helping clean out a plugged septic system or castrating baby pigs.

If gifting doesn't always work, there's barter. Before you know it, you can find yourself in a complex mixture of debts and barter where you end up trading your cow (there goes Betty) for a truck and a load of hay, or an old canoe for five broiler chickens. It's the glory of a rural community that such dealings remain possible.

WHEN WE FIRST ARRIVED Salt Spring was still a place where parents could send their kids out with the ancient phrase "Be home by dinner," which translated into "Don't come home before dinner." Often they would be gone to their friends for days, with parental approvals exchanged, of course. But every year I notice a growing number of suvs lined up where the school bus stops, because parents are afraid to let their children walk home in the brightest weather. I suspect more children in the cities are smashed by the hordes of harried moms driving big suvs into today's schoolyards than are snatched by crazed maniacs.

325

I WAS DRIVING HOME past the Stowel Lake swimming hole when a wannabe junior baseball pitcher hucked something at the passenger door of my pickup. It struck with a bang. This is a hazardous curve above crowds of swimming and suntanning families and children, and locals drive slowly past it. His dangerous act instantly enraged me. I braked, turned the motor off, and leaped out, running after the miscreant, who was about ten or eleven and impressing his friends. There was no escape route, and he stared at me, aghast. The beach was packed and everyone watched with amusement as I captured our little terrorist. It turned out he'd thrown an orange at the truck. If it had hit me through my open passenger window there could have been a serious accident. I asked him who he was and where his mother was. He looked blankly at me, the little brat. The rest of the crowd soon lost interest in the incident, since the offender had been quickly apprehended, and they all knew me. Learning where he lived, I told him I was taking him home so I'd be sure he told his mother what he did. By then traffic was backing up behind my truck and drivers were growing annoyed. Then a young woman drove in from the other direction, parked, and rushed toward us. She was his older sister, and asked what was the matter. After I told her and the boy agreed he'd done the misdeed, I explained that I wanted the boy to tell his mother what he'd done. The sister obviously thought this was a good idea and said she'd take him home right away and tell his mother. I thanked her and said goodbye to the boy, jumped back into my truck, and drove off.

That night, at dinner, I mentioned the incident to Sharon, and since she has a much better sense of social politics, she was aghast. "You could have been arrested for kidnapping!"

"Kidnapping? I was just gonna take him to his mother. He was lucky. If he'd done it to somebody's fancy car instead of my old beater, they'd have called the cops."

After a few minutes of Sharon explaining the new reality to me I grew paranoid. I'd assumed that because of the community nature of the island, multiple parenting was still practised, but of course that's not necessarily true in our age of fear and victims. So I picked up the phone, with no idea who he was, since I'd already forgotten his name. It was so very island that with a few phone calls I could track down this child I'd never met before. I phoned his mother, identified myself, described the incident, and started to apologize, but she cut me off and informed me that he was a good child but excitable when he was with friends and needed to encounter authority on occasion. We ended up having a lovely chat and I felt redeemed, but Sharon was still nervously drinking her green tea, while I wondered what kind of children will grow up in this new age where they can't walk freely or get harangued by strange elders.

FOR A HUNDRED YEARS local markets, the central core of villages, edged toward oblivion; then they began reappearing. Instead of fishmongers, blacksmiths, vegetable and fruit merchants, stalls with meat hanging on hooks, bear tamers, copper-pot makers, and fortune tellers, the markets were soon repopulated by handcrafters, and then the farmers moved back. Salt Spring has a market that's so packed on Saturday mornings the town becomes near-unworkable. There are musicians, jam and soap makers, potters, wild-mushroom stalkers, felt-hat and basket makers, flower sellers, and people offering decadent pastries, Chinese potstickers, whacked-out fair-trade coffees that'll make your hair stand on end, world-renowned local cheeses,

327

and garlic braids. Years ago, if I had a big crop I'd haul it to
the market at dawn and sell out by ten in the morning. Now,
Trauma Farm's produce is bought by local greengrocers, so
we don't go anymore, but I miss the dawn bustle and clatter,
the overloaded trucks, the jokes and banter, those steaming
coffees while admiring the sheepskin rugs and the welder-
artist unloading a twelve-foot dinosaur skeleton made out
of leftover rebar rods.

As always, we have to be watchful that someone isn't
selling wholesale commercial apples as organic locals, or
other scams. But the eyes of your neighbours are more
invasive than secret police. Gossip can equal a bureaucracy's best efforts at enforcing good practice. In a small
neighbourhood everyone knows everyone else's business.
Sometimes this can be suffocating, yet it usually works.
The market is self-policed in the way that most local living
is. Thus the terroir of the goods is protected and our market
has become famous across Canada, like a growing number
of other local markets offering an alternative to globalized
food and goods.

Not long ago the health Gestapo arrived and seized an
unsuspecting farmer's eggs because they were "unsafe."
Legal eggs must be candled, washed (which removes their
protective down and makes them able to absorb organisms like salmonella), inspected, and refrigerated—in other
words, they demand a factory farm with sealed biosecurity
sheds, complex technology, regular inspections, costly egg
quotas, a mechanized packaging operation, and extensive
shipping routes in order for a farmer to sell "fresh farm
eggs" locally. This is hilarious science fiction when you're
running fifty hens and selling maybe three or four dozen

eggs a day during the peak laying months, but it's the continuing saga of the horror story I discussed in the last chapter. The assault caught the community by surprise. But when the inspector came back the next week, the market was waiting for him, and everyone gathered into a clump; hundreds of people surrounded the endangered farmer. They were so packed and so aggressive that the inspector needed a cop. The RCMP officer, wisely recognizing the situation was only going to get ugly, suggested the bureaucrat make a tactical retreat, which he did, threatening, "I'll be back!" The food police always come back.

The 2005 Salt Spring Egg War, as it soon became known in headlines across Canada, turned into an epic dust-up, and to everyone's surprise the inspection agency capitulated temporarily, granting a dispensation to Salt Spring eggs, as long as the eggs were kept in coolers and clearly marked "uninspected." Creative islanders took up this challenge and produced their version of the appropriate stamp: THESE EGGS HAVE NOT BEEN INSPECTED BY ANY GOVERNMENT BUREAUCRATS.

One of the glories of small communities is that, left alone, they tend to regulate themselves, utilizing community approval and gossip and traditional community behaviour. Jane Jacobs, Canada's doyenne of civic interactions, often illustrated how functioning communities can exhibit even better control than distant bureaucracies. On our island, anyone producing bad food, whether wilty greens, mouldy garlic, or unhealthy sheep, is eventually boycotted or driven out of business. This causes citizens to take the high road (except those inevitable sneaky few,

329

buying factory eggs wholesale and selling them on their "organic farm stands"). But no community is perfect, and good neighbours can be circumvented, which is why the injured demand regulations and administrations, gradually flooding the world with laws and police, because laws tend to encourage more innovative crimes, which demand more laws, and that's how we ended up with all those regulations on cabbages. Strangely, agribusiness also has an affinity for regulation, because it helps eliminate small competitors, while globalization allows a thousand ways to dodge regulations or else pressure governments to alter them to benefit the larger corporations.

Globalization doesn't care about customer satisfaction or community reaction because there's no human contact between maker and buyer. It's not a true free market. Classic examples are small tools and appliances: returning faulty ones is often more expensive and time-consuming than just throwing the junk away and buying another. Meanwhile, immoral corporations will put a bureaucratic firewall between their service departments and their customers, because they know people will give up after a while. It's a wasteful, ecologically disastrous, dangerous-to-the-health global market we have constructed. You can't get away with that kind of stuff for long at the local market. The opinion of a community can be more powerful than any regulation.

Our market is also an important social hub. Once, our eldest granddaughter saw a girl playing guitar—busking—so Kylie begged for permission to take her guitar down there next weekend. We thought it would be fun and off we went. We soon discovered the market had considered the role of child performers, and the rules appeared restrictive and weird. Each child was permitted to play for only one hour. When our cute seven-year-old Kylie strummed a few chords and money began flying at her basket, I immediately understood why. The cuteness factor was difficult for the wealthy tourists to resist, and they poured money onto the children. She made more than a hundred dollars—an outrageous amount of money for such a young child to earn in an hour. The market organizers didn't want children to play too long because they didn't want kids to compete with each other, or have greedy parents learn to rely on child labour. Also, more than an hour of some screeching wannabe superstar flautist would scare too many customers away from nearby stalls or drive the marketers crazy. As Kylie grew older, her income diminished, while her younger, violin-playing sister, Jenna, began raking in the cash. We teased Kylie that she'd grown too old and would have to retire by the time she was fifteen.

ALMOST EQUAL TO MARKETS as social events are the community fairs. At our first fair, we were thrilled, as newcomers often are—and out of control. We entered the "family farm harvest" competition, which gave us the opportunity to display our collected wares. We brought in multicoloured chicken eggs and glass jars layered with varieties of colourful beans, peacock feathers, hand-turned pottery vases of dried flowers, canned jams, bottled wine, apples, late plums, corn, artichokes. We even had our son Roben design a rustic open basket of alder branches so we could heap everything up in the thirty-inch-square space we were allotted on the table. There were grapes and a dozen varieties of squash, the twisted ornamental willows we grow for florists, and rising above all, smiling benevolently down on the display, a spray of gaudy sunflowers.

I was going back for the second wheelbarrow load (I'm not kidding when I say our display was out of control) just as the garden coordinator stepped up to Sharon and said something like, "Oh, I'm afraid you've got this all wrong, dear. It should be displayed like this." And she pointed to the entry beside ours—six tiny clusters of miniature garden fruit and vegetables meticulously lined up on a paper plate. There wasn't enough food there for my dinner, let alone a family display of the annual harvest, but judging at these events swings toward the retentive, and the fall fair can unleash the pretentious, the neurotic, and the vicious.

The majority of judges are scrupulously fair, yet a few often seem to take delight in insulting their neighbours. Display coordinators, generally dedicated and enthusiastic, may also become so rigid, exhausted, or loopy that you want to throttle them. This woman, we later learned, was a tireless community worker, but she was having an off night. Trying to shepherd a pack of ignorant but excited competitors in a two-hour period is stressful, and she was taking it out on Sharon. By the time I returned with the second instalment poor Sharon was weeping over the waste of all the work we had gone through, while the horrified organizer looked down her nose at my second wheelbarrowful, topped with an extra-large pumpkin. The look reminded me of a sadistic elementary teacher who used to slap my fingers with her pointer forty years ago. I can't remember exactly how the conversation went, but here's the general idea:

"Oh, this is just not going to do," the woman said.

Sharon said, "We're doing it all wrong! It's supposed to be like those." She waved her arm at the wimpy displays down the table and broke into a fresh round of tears.

I glanced at the pathetic paper plates with their measly clusters laid out by compulsive minimalists and made my decision immediately. "Are you a judge?"

"No," the woman said, "I'm the display coordinator."

"Good." I began heaping the rest into the open framework of the basket, tamping it all down with the pumpkin.

That got her colour up. "And you'll just be disqualified anyways, because you can't exceed your space." She was eyeballing the sunflowers, which were overhanging our neighbour's paper plate.

I reached out and gave the sunflowers a yank, twisting them so that the flowers hovered directly above our cornucopia. "There, is it legal now?"

Sharon, recovering, had shifted quickly from tears to anger. Defiance was in her eyes. The coordinator looked at us cheeky newcomers, standing proud side by side, and shook her head in despair. "Yes," she harrumphed, walking away.

Our cornucopia won the grand championship display trophy of the fair, and along with the silver cup came a gaudy ribbon we stapled to the back of the door of our pantry. It has been joined over the year by numerous ribbons and more than a few disqualified entry forms with acidic comments by judges about our more spectacularly dumb entries. That cornucopia became the talk of the fair and was even mentioned on an off-island radio show.

In the rural communities of British Columbia the fall fair has begun to blossom again, a gesture of defiance against globalization as well as an act of community. According to the local-food grapevine this is also happening across North America and England. I love watching the children chomping on candy apples or practising their archery, the cheerful firemen talking passersby into buying corn on the cob for a good cause, the bikers grinning benevolently in the beer tent. Then there are the competitions. Every jar of preserves is like tasting your summer, but my legendary peach jam, so sweet it gave you a headache, was disdainfully rejected for being too sweet. I had my revenge when my photograph of a flower blossom won first prize even though it was hung upside down. We won first prize for twenty-four perfectly uniform hazelnuts, but I miscounted the zinnias (sure winners) while rushing an artful display, which was disqualified, of course, and then I managed to forget the scissors in the prep area—earning the remark "I thought you could at least count to five."

People engage in these competitions with a lunatic ferocity, and store-bought pickles have been disqualified by discerning judges at fair competitions. Sharon determinedly challenged the flower events and lost every year, disqualified for the most picayune mistakes. Then one year she practically swept the board and she was stunned. It almost seemed too easy after all the years of rejection.

The fair brings out everyone's energy, and absurd events erupt when too many enthusiastic volunteers get together. There was the year the swine people and the goat people feuded over space in the barn during set-up day until they ingeniously solved their problem by shuffling aside a painstakingly crafted display by the cattle people, who had gone home. Returning later to discover this misdeed, the cattle people packed up and left in justifiable outrage over the cavalier mistreatment of their hard work—taking their cattle with them. The animal coordinator reputedly repaired to the bar to drown his sorrows and was nowhere to be found for hours. Ah well, these things happen. They are also part of the community. By fair time I gather everyone was friends again (more or less).

SINCE HE HAS WORKING herd dogs, a livestock hauler, and a classic case of public spirit, Mike usually volunteered to haul people's livestock to the fall fair. While he was hauling one year—on the other end of the island—a pair of pigs escaped from their owner. Mike and his dogs were called. He soon had the rogue pigs herded into his truck, but because he was so busy and had no idea who the owner was, he left them in a spare pen at the fairground until everything was sorted out. Upon returning to the fair he discovered he'd won second prize for them.

THE VARIETY OF LIFE is what we live for; it's all here, even more than at the market—the good, and a little of the bad. There's the apple grower with 120 kinds of apples, offering everyone a taste. The seed savers. The salmon stream keepers. The woman who makes dolls like angels, basket weavers and wine makers, and the lonely politicians at their booths. The scarecrow that wouldn't scare a mouse. The cute rabbit with immense ears. The little girl crying beside the road after she scraped her knee. Famous islanders—rock stars, lawyers, artists, writers, politicians—cheerfully washing dishes in the recycling booth. Hidden away upstairs a clan of women elders count the fair's proceeds with a moral accuracy that's daunting.

The market and the fair and the miraculous movement of gifts flowing through us like water in a creek are what make me love my local culture. Real communities are held together by just that, the community. The hand-crafters, the artists, and the skilled tradespeople—from cabinetmakers to clothes makers to backhoe drivers—are the core that attracts and civilizes the rest of the rural community. Sometimes it's merely everyone meandering down to the park beside the bay, wearing silly Halloween costumes and eating junk food while the children run ragged among us, and we sip hot chocolates sneakily laced with a touch of rum. Later, the fireworks fall in cascading fountains over the blue-black waters of the bay and all of us go "Awwwwwwwww...."

23

THE LAST ROUNDUP

*D*YING IS THE way we live, and as night approaches I often find myself recalling our losses—the dimming of light can do that. Without death, the world wouldn't be alive. Some years ago I was at an Ontario farm with a young farmer who happened to glance over my shoulder and see that one of his ewes was dead under an apple tree, a half-eaten apple in her jaws. She had choked on it. The unhappy farmer gazed at his once-prime ewe and remarked dryly, "If you've got livestock, you've also got dead stock."

"IT'S ONLY AN ANIMAL," my father said as I stood on the deck, weeping—hard words I've replayed in my head for fifty years. I'd been scouting in the bush like any good kid on the edge of the urban world when, in a thicket of salmonberry branches, I glimpsed the corpse of our white cat, its jaws drawn back in the grimace of a hard death. It was ancient in cat years, and it had crawled into the bushes to die. I began wailing like a child with a hammered hand. Everyone who's had a dog or a cat knows what I'm talking about.

My thesaurus tells me that the antonym of *human* is *animal*. Whoever came up with that definition did not grow up with a dog or a horse or a cat. If you've got a nervous system, you've got a personality, and we're suckers for personality. A biographer once claimed a literary friend had a pet clam when she was a child—which she denied. However, I can understand how the rumour began. She has a mind capable of seeing the beauty in a clam's life. Whenever a creature we know dies, animal or human, we weep for it, and, greedily, we weep for ourselves—the lost possibilities of a golden future with our companions, the way I wept for my cat.

There are numerous reasons why a child should grow up with animals. For companionship, of course, and the discipline their care entails, but also to learn about loss when the creature dies—a crucial moment in childhood, yet one we never totally comprehend, as I discovered the day Stonewall Jackson, our proud, ancient gelding, had a stroke and died in my arms. If you can picture a horse dying in your arms, that was exactly what it was like. How outlandish to live with a creature so big and handsome, a real dancer in his prime, then watch him grow old and die.

It happens fast with animals, the descent from glory to the rag-and-bone shop. He looked ancient the last few months. People walking down the road beside the pasture would stop and stare at him. I wondered if they suspected we were mistreating him. Perhaps we were by not putting him down. Yet he had nothing but heart and a stubborn desire to live, checking our pockets for sugar cubes or ripping open a bag of feed as soon as I wasn't looking. He had an unyielding righteousness that would bring him shambling to the deck every afternoon, demanding his daily carrot.

We knew it was coming for a long time, but we were never expecting it. Denial and death are companions. We were lucky enough to go for a walk in the lower field at the right moment. Did we sense the moment? As soon as I saw Jack down, I knew this was no rolling scratch of an itchy back. It was a stroke. As he tried to rise I grabbed him around the shoulders and somehow heaved him, almost supernaturally, to his feet. It was a stupid thing to do, but once a horse can't get up that's the end; their digestive systems will kill them if they go down for too long. He was so scared, leaning into me, shivering, sweaty, losing muscle control. I managed to hold him upright for about five minutes while he glanced, forlorn and knowingly, over his shoulder at me.

Then he collapsed. I had to leap out of the way as he had a second stroke. We could only brush his head while he shivered and gasped. We told him it was okay to go, but he wasn't buying that. Not ever. Despite being paralyzed on one side he kept trying to get up, and it became a terrifying, slow, repetitive dance.

Sharon ran back to the house and started phoning. Mike took the call as he was halfway out the door of his house. She asked him to bring his gun. Though I've killed many animals in my life, I knew I couldn't shoot Jack. Then she managed to find Malcolm—the vet with "the touch." He must have roared down the island, because he arrived a few minutes before Mike. I suppose he'd encountered enough anguished horse owners to understand the necessity for speed if a horse is dying. He gave Jack a needle to relax him before the killing injection, while I cradled Jack's head in my arms and Sharon stroked his neck.

Since we had to bring a backhoe in to bury Jack, we made sure he got the biggest headstone under the willow tree. The stone gives the farm the patina of an old western film, an island version of Tombstone, and I often smile wistfully when I glance out the window at his stone. I buried him with my favourite raku tea bowl. I always give our companions pottery I've made, offering a fragment of myself to their grave. There's a growing collection of ceramics buried under that willow tree now, an archaeological record of our lives together here at the farm. We almost need a bigger cemetery. Two old dogs, two cats, one ancient canary, four geese, and two peafowl murdered by raccoons. They are Stonewall Jackson's bedmates. Since then they've been joined by the Arabian grey, LaBarisha, and Samantha. Sharon scattered yellow rose petals around the grave after we covered Jack, so it was luxurious for a few hours. Then the sheep ate the rose petals.

Some days I go down there and sit on his headstone for a few minutes.

340

SEVERAL YEARS LATER LABARISHA died, and I had to make the same round of choked-up phone calls to the answering machines of backhoe operators. Almost all our original machine operators on the island have small farms or were raised on them. They understand the tragedy of a dead horse and consider it a civic duty to temporarily abandon a big-paying job to bury a family horse. Ken Byron had one of his boys down at the farm by lunchtime and we buried her next to Stonewall Jackson, under a large sandstone fossil rock a good friend had discovered behind the house. Another one of my pots went beside her beneath the willows, and a vase that contained some of Sharon's father's ashes so that he could also become part of the farm. Because of the growing number of graves under the willow tree, we had to lay her facing the field, her ass end to the house, which is the way she often treated us in her vain and beautiful arrogance. The kindness of the young backhoe operator made me recall the elaborate rituals that tribal cultures, and even some organized religions, have conjured to describe the birth of death and how we must treat it.

Our two sons were surprised upon learing Sharon had put her portion of her dad's ashes with LaBarisha. She just told Chris, our older boy, that her dad wanted to be near us, and besides, she thought her dad would like the company of the horse. I could see the boys were a little confused by the unorthodox burial, but I admired its wonderful gesture.

It strikes me that in the early days of our species death was usually immediate, often brutal, and always magical. If you study tribal societies, it's apparent that a thread of reverence toward death, human or animal, inhabits the majority, as it generally does on small farms, though a vein of mistreatment also runs like a cancer in all communities. Most small farmers are gentle with their animals, and while slaughter might appear grim, they tend to respect livestock and pets. As in tribal cultures, rogue practices have

continued since history began, whether it is the cruelty of
Native buffalo jumps or mean farmers beating stubborn
livestock.

Our species, fortunately, has empathy, one of the qualities that make us human—the ability to inhabit another
mind. Our imagination takes us there in an eye-blink. Imagination can save us from cruelty. To be cruel we have to
break the imaginative bond, distancing ourselves from our
victim—thus, we refer to the slaughter of animals as "har-
vesting," and the animals become "products" or, worse yet,
"units." Then we can tuck into our platefull of pork spareribs
and not feel the pain of the pig. This is also why writers tend
to sanitize farm life, glossing over gruesome deaths, and
why it's difficult for so many to read or watch documentary
accounts of slaughter or accidental deaths of livestock. We
are living amid modern myths, whether they're the free-
enterprise propaganda of agribusiness products basking in
glowing fields, or the sunshine vision of small farms extolled
by eco-urbanite enthusiasts blind to the dirt, mindless labour,
gore, and dangers of a real mixed farm.

342   While urban people tend to hold a bucolic view of rural
life, but the idyllic farm of children's tales has also had a
long history of barbarity and ugly practices; the difference
is that the small farm never had the mechanistic qualities
and plant-endagering scale of corporate agriculture.

Still, even eras of small farming have affected world
climate, mostly because of population explosions but also
because of foolish practices. Burn-and-plant periods of civilization around the world often accelerated climate change,
followed by cooling periods after plagues and famines. Ice-
core samples show that the epic worldwide slash-and-burn

farming era that peaked around 1000 BC denuded most of China, India, the Mediterranean region, the lowlands of Central America, and the highlands of Peru, leading to population explosions and gradual world warming that was counteracted only by what scholars now believe was a volcanic eruption, an atmospheric veil of dust that caused sudden global cooling. Mayan corn culture suffered its first major crash, and in the sixth century AD the already over-stressed European population encountered the Justinian plague, which led to further global cooling when deforestation and burning decreased. The Roman priests might have dragged a lot of entrails out of living roosters and owls, but their divinations still couldn't predict their culture was its own worst enemy.

Once the European populations rebuilt and became overcrowded again, the Black Death that climaxed in the 1300s was followed by another round of global cooling, which likely encouraged the collapse of both complex and simple civilizations such as the Khmers and the Greenlanders. It's now clear that traditional agriculture, though not as potentially dangerous as our Oil Age, is capable of affecting the world's climate.

343

Despite these climate change episodes, our populations continued growing, and the animals died in ever-increasing quantities. However, with the dawn of industrial food production we learned how to hide animal slaughter behind locked doors. Death is now relegated to films, books, distant wars, car accidents, and our own ghettoes. It's the last great taboo of modern society, an event discreetly hidden since we began moving away from the land and the animals. Europeans and North Americans not only conceal death behind factory walls, they've also erected walls of gushy sentiment—the trusty pet mourned with much ceremony and tears. But most of all, we want it out of sight, even when it comes to our relatives and loved ones. Grieving with the corpse has been shrunk to a single ceremony for the community, with very little time for the actual relatives. No more the body laid out on the table or the uncovered coffin in the home.

However, death walks openly and commonly on every mixed farm. There's not only the loss of the trusty dog, the horse, and the ancient, much-loved hen or ewe. There's the slaughter of the chickens, the lambs, the cows, the pigs. Then there are the surprise deaths—the attack of a cougar or wild dogs, or the ewe that delivers a lamb and just walks away, uncaring about her crying offspring. What twists me up most is the startling way death can arrive, like a mystery guest at a party, wearing a different suit or dress each time.

One day a friend, the poet Patrick Lane, and I were sitting in the sunroom, drinking Scotch, several years before he went dry. We were being bad in the afternoon and enjoying it, until a tree swallow darted in through the open door. Recognizing its mistake, it made a sharp turn and tried to exit through the window beside Patrick. It bounced off the glass with a fatal *ka-thunk,* landing dead in his lap, while he sat there, stunned, whisky glass half raised to his lips.

"Does this happen to you often?" I asked. "Or was it a special performance just for me?"

YOU TURN YOUR BACK and fate arrives, usually at the most awkward times, the dead ewe you have to perform a Caesarean on in the pouring rain, with barely seconds to save the chilled lamb, and then you do save it, and it revives, coughing in the wet grass while you desperately towel-rub it, bringing warmth and blood circulation into its newborn limbs.

The dead lambs—they made me understand how delicate and precarious the miracle of life is. There was the terrible year a lamb died being born. Suddenly, in the next stall, an older ewe perished giving birth, yet her lamb survived. Sharon, determined to save the living lamb, tried to give it to the ewe who had lost her baby, but she rejected it, pushing it away from her udder. So Sharon skinned the dead lamb and tied its hide around the rejected one. The mother was suspicious of the gore but recognized the smell. She didn't reject it, quite, though she didn't accept it. We kept her chained for the day to the wall of the birthing room so she wouldn't trample the lamb to death if she did reject it. Then suddenly Samantha darted into the room, and the ewe, seeing the dog, converted into an instant mother, ripping the flimsy chain from the wall, chasing the collie out of the room, and herding the suddenly accepted, disguised lamb into a safe corner. I always considered this episode the goriest in our history on the farm, maybe because I didn't have the willpower to do what we both knew had to be done. Only Sharon, who'd worked her entire adult life as a nurse, had the strength to save the lamb. Out of the gore another life leaped, a lovely lamb that went on to become a prime ewe in the tribe.

WHEN I LIE WITH THE DYING LAMB

When I lie with the dying lamb
in the manger, I desire so little,

because life is already
more than I can take,
nestled in the hay, listening
to the gasps of tiny breath—the hiss
of the propane lantern hanging overhead.
The mother is dead in the corner,
and soon death will follow death
as it has done for the millenniums
since this unholy mess invented itself
in a chemical fog that should
make any thinking creature bitter.

How our blood surges for the newborn,
the gorgeous miracle and enigma—
even though we will slaughter this lamb
for meat in four months if it survives,
which it won't. Death is seconds away.
I look into its eyes, seeking the mystery,
but they are already filled with the secrets
of the other side, the place
where we can't go, until we go.
And I lie still in the hay, holding the black hoof
of a dead lamb—feeling left behind once again,
uninstructed.

The strangest thing about raising sheep for meat is that
you will weep for them, fight for their survival; and then,
when their time comes for the market, you will kill them.
Mike Byron slaughters in his field, the old way. I've field-
dressed deer and moose and eaten bear in the bush and
thrived for nearly forty years eating raw fish and sometimes

raw meat, but I was taken aback the first day I helped him slaughter a lamb and saw his gore-covered killing platform in the field behind his house. Then, after watching him carefully, and following his instructions, I learned his techniques for killing as many as a dozen lambs a day (during his most productive years) and his way of keeping the flesh clear of contamination. He moved his killing site so that contamination wouldn't build up and handled the hide with one hand while skinning it, thus preventing his knife hand and knife from being soiled by the hide. Then he winched the lamb up as he finished skinning and gutting so that the cleaned lamb wouldn't contact anything foul. During his forty years of slaughter he's never heard of anyone getting sick from his meat. Traditional slaughter is a lot safer than it looks. However, it's still a shock to city denizens, who appear to believe that meat is born prewrapped in plastic on Styrofoam platters.

Sharon and I were visited by friends from Montreal and their two children, Jacob and Isaac. The boys were twitchy at first, but like most children they soon began to enjoy farm life—until the day we dropped in on the Byrons to pick up extra eggs. Mike was in his field, wrestling with a recalcitrant lamb as we drove up. "Here, hold this lamb," he instructed in his no-time-to-waste voice. I was so used to working and talking with him that I just held the lamb and he slit its throat, then efficiently drove the knife into the neck vertebrae, quickly severing the spinal cord and ending its suffering. His standard technique. The lamb's corpse flung itself into its final convulsions, bleeding out on the grass. The youngest boy began hyperventilating. Slaughter was so much a part of our life that it never occurred to me, in that brief moment, to recognize how harsh it would appear to a city kid. This was the moment I realized how distant I had become from the urban world. I went red with embarrassment and guilt while Marie-Louise led the sobbing boy away. It would be a long time before I heard the end of this affair. "What's the matter with him?" Mike asked, handing me the knife and dragging the lamb toward the skinning trough, where we swung it up onto the platform so he could begin the skinning and gutting. Then I quickly returned to the car with my friends, apologizing profusely and endlessly.

Over the years I've learned to respect the traditional slaughter of animals, along with age-old growing techniques for vegetables and fruits. Modern concepts of hygiene and cleanliness can be even more dangerous than the "dirty" practices of our ancestors and the animal world, as the now-immense scale of meat recalls and food poisonings reminds us. I've known a few deaths in my time and slaughtered my share of game and livestock, and usually I want to weep when I look at the body. It's claimed that the dead instantly become three-quarters of an ounce lighter: the weight of the soul. That's too little, in my book—death is much heavier.

Usually, we don't know death unless we know the victim. Bloodbaths in Zimbabwe, or suicide bombings in Jerusalem and the customary reprisal that inevitably kills children in Palestine, are distant until we see the distraught faces close up, and then our heart unravels, as it does when we lose a relative, a friend, or a pet. Whether it's Old Yeller or Lassie, dogs especially grab our emotions—maybe because they can be among the sappiest creatures on earth, or because their world is based on the pack mentality's need to please. Cats aren't far behind. When ancient Egyptians lost a cat, they shaved off their eyebrows, and if their dog died, they shaved their entire bodies. Who doesn't feel sorrow reading the story of Odysseus coming home after nineteen years? His ancient hound, warming its old bones on the dung heap where it had been relegated, recognizes him immediately, raises its head, and whimpers before it falls back, dead, having fulfilled its obligation—waiting for him to come home. Dogs love us unconditionally. I wish I could be as good a person as my dogs think I am. They can love you more than you can love yourself. Maybe that's why the French say the best thing about a man is his dog.

For several years we kept two dogs on our farm. The border collie, Samantha, to round up the sheep, and Olive, to fight off the raccoons that prey on our chickens. Samantha was such a good shepherd that you hardly noticed her working. We used to delight in sending people out for walks in the fields. A motley, rambling crowd would leave and then return in a tight cluster, tripping over each other's feet, not realizing the dog had invisibly, patiently grouped them. She looked at you with eyes that said: "I can get around you." And she could. Everything they say about the intelligence of border collies is true. Her partner, the giant, galumphing hound Olive—as black as an olive and as graceful as Olive Oyl—has about three brain cells, and not all of them are switched on at the same time. One of her favourite tricks is to drop her ball in the pond and then mourn its disappearance after it sinks—staring at the water, sometimes for hours, hoping someone will rescue the ball.

Sam died before dawn at Malcolm Bond's new pet

349

hospital. Pancreatic cancer. It was sudden. We thought she'd eaten something bad, but when Malcolm opened her up she was full of cancer. We never had the chance to say goodbye. Dead dogs stick to us like ghost limbs. After my first dog died I locked myself in my room for two days with a bottle of whisky. Leonard Cohen knew the feeling exactly when he sang about fathers and dogs dying.

Olive was so sickened at the sight of Samantha's body in the wheelbarrow that she drooled. She refused to come near the grave and say goodbye as we buried her. Olive sat on the far side of the pond, staring at the water.

At least Samantha had a good week before her death. She and Olive had driven a marauding deer off the property. The next night we came home with a quarter of beef and they had a feed of scraps. The dogs must think we're the ultimate hunters. We go out for a few hours and return laden with bones.

Then they treed the biggest raccoon they'd ever fought in their lives. It was almost as big as Sam. It took both Olive and me to kill it during another one of those brutal, five-in-the-morning fights. Sam loved it. Everybody was bleeding by the end. She always tracked the raccoons and then let Olive move in. In her youth Sam actually used to climb the fruit trees after them. We buried Samantha in the late morning with twin lambs that had been stillborn in the night. We were too distracted to notice them until we were burying Samantha. Then we realized one of the ewes was calling. Her calls led us to the dead lambs.

So now Samantha has two lambs to shepherd under the willow tree where we buried her with a lovely little black-and-white, Oriental-looking stoneware lidded pot that I turned on my wheel ten years ago. We dragged up a quartz-crystalline rock for a headstone and Sharon transplanted some flowering snowdrops next to it. Later in the afternoon Olive slipped out of the house, alone, took her favourite ball down to the willow tree, left it on the grave, and returned to the house, silent with the private sorrow only a dog understands.

24

CREATURES
OF THE NIGHT

· · · · ·

*A*ND NOW THE day has come to its liquid end, the sky as blue-dark as deep water—another of the many blues that our sky has given us over the years. At dusk the peafowl make their regular night flight to the maple, using our upper deck as a launching pad. Perched on the rail, they pump themselves up like Thai kick-boxers preparing for a match. Building a rhythm, their heads bobbing before they leap, the birds pound their wings against the air until they rise like helicopters into the high tree, where they perch, faintly silhouetted among the leaves.

In the gathering darkness the dogs are desperate for a night walk, so we go down to the gravel intersection beyond our farm. Our footfalls echo in the relative quiet, accompanied by the frail and querulous cry of the killdeer and a couple of crickets. A lonely tree frog makes itself known by the pond. Our spring "wall of frogs" is muted now, and we will nervously await their return next spring. Like so much of the world, they are endangered. Out of 6,000 known amphibians, 1,900 are threatened with extinction from the chytrid fungus. Already 170 have gone extinct. All we can do is provide habitat for our gang, planting more shoreline reeds and willows to shelter them from the fish, herons, and raccoons.

Sharon and I decide to relax in the hot tub. It's a wasteful, monstrous thing, our tub—an energy hog. I've got to devise a solar supplement. But when it's given to you free, it's difficult to resist, especially since I'm tortured by osteoarthritis, a by-product of my genetic condition. My bones have crumbled. They hurt. An evening soak temporarily relieves the pain and gives me the opportunity to consider the elasticity of the day.

The barred owls across the road launch into a territorial war that startles us. We undress and sink into the hot water. A shooting star flares overhead. It's early—meteors occur every night of the year, but they're best in August, during the Perseid shower at its zenith, and they flash right and left and thrill us. Although our tiny valley blocks sunsets, it makes for good darkness and star viewing because the forest obstructs the glow of Vancouver on the northern horizon. The Milky Way is a wide gauzy river that cuts our sky in two, and we often use star charts to refresh our memory of the constellations.

The meteor reminds me of my wilderness years—when I wanted to hike every mountain I met, and the stars seemed so bright I could almost reach up and touch them. How original the world is in your youth! The joy I found in staring at a fire for hours as if I had invented it. I couldn't get enough of my night fires—like a ten-year-old jumping off a dock into a lake, over and over. I wish I could always live within that delight, at perfect attention, but the moments seem to grow more rare, though they still happen—like the day I was lying on my back in Blackburn Lake's cool water, motionless as endless clouds passed—so still that a dragonfly landed on my nose to rest before flying off again.

Those mountain campfires many decades ago saved me from the street-kid world I also toyed with then, taking me away from a lifestyle that would have killed me. The campfires gave both flame and shadow, and the glowing eyes of deer lurked in the shadows. Sometimes I built fires at cave mouths and watched the shadows they cast on the walls, and sometimes I would dance alone between the fire and the wall, creating personal shadow-puppet mythologies, as old as the Thai *Ramakian* or Plato. They were my mystic alternative to the hardness of urban shadows and the electric glow that dims the stars above cities. If you look deeply at a fire you can understand how alien the world is and perhaps remember the astonishing moon of your childhood. The mind loses its sense of mystery when mystery is ignored—or, worse, when earnest people insist that every mystery must have a meaning, and therefore a human use, the rationale we use to justify saving the Amazon or the great trees of Haida Gwaii. Yet their magic lies not in how they can be used, but in what they are. Our greatest mysteries are great because they are mysteries. Sometimes it's that simple.

The sky above the pond is shape-shifting with bats, and we admire their eerie fluttering. In an early year on the farm Sharon and I were sitting close together on the deck, watching a moon rise, and she grew jumpy about the bats. I told her that the story about bats getting caught in people's hair was a myth, and as soon as I finished speaking one darted between us, so close it touched both our heads, before it somehow flipped up without crashing into the wall and darted away. Sharon hollered one of her famous "Gawww" screams, which the parrot so loves to imitate, and I had a hard time holding back my laughter.

Tonight she decides to leave early and make tea. She departs with much fluttering of her towel. She's still twitchy about the bats. As she passes the guest room window I notice the chewed-up corner where Bonnie, a black Labrador, went through it years ago, and I immediately think, "I have to fix that window," knowing I won't for a long time, because there's an enormous backlog of other projects that are more important. The fifty-year plan, as we call it.

No, I'm not optimistic about our prospects. My health is a mess, my joints below the waist are corn flakes, my liver is shot, and my blood pressure is through the roof. Sharon and I are both as high-strung as piano wires, and that can make for a chancy relationship. Our finances are dicey because of our farming habit. I'm growing old, but I shouldn't have that privilege—considering the misadventures of my birth—so I call myself a lucky child of the world, as we are all lucky children of the world, being born into this whirlpool. I wouldn't have the nerve to ask for more. I'm embarrassed by how much we've taken, and when I witness the sense of entitlement of people around me I can only feel ashamed of the angry members of my First World culture.

355

All of this brings me back to that damned window. It got wrecked on the day we last renewed the mortgage, increasing it for the third time in ten years—a standard business practice for a farmer and another hazard of expensive island living. A friend of ours had a black Labrador, big and gentle tempered. A sudden series of medical tragedies left this dog blind and deaf. The vets weren't sure it was permanent, and our friends had previously booked a skiing holiday for two days, so we agreed to take Bonnie while we all awaited her diagnosis. There is nothing sadder than a blind, deaf dog. Bonnie also had a character flaw we weren't warned about; she didn't like to be left alone, especially in her present condition.

We were gone only two hours, signing the papers for the mortgage, but it was dark by the time we returned. Another of those black raincoast nights. During a recent one Sharon and I actually bonked heads as we crept home from a cheerful dinner with the neighbours that extended beyond the dusk hours.

As soon as I entered the house I saw the damage. Bonnie had started on the door, chewing the cedar trim. This is not as depressing as it sounds, since another friend's dog had already chewed the same door, so we were old hands in the dog-chewed-door lifestyle of the islands. Then she'd leaped onto a bed, sucked up a few mouthfuls of windowsill, forced the window open, and escaped. Glancing at the damage, I rushed out to look for her. A block away, at the roadside trailhead to the neighbourhood forest park, in near-perfect darkness, I met our neighbour riding her horse.

Islanders, out of necessity, develop a tolerance for interesting behaviour. After a few close encounters in the night between my truck and her horse, I'm less skittish about her riding habits and I know to keep an eye out for her. So when this big, dark gelding's nose appeared out of nowhere and started frisking me for treats, I was more interested in hearing his rider warn me about a black dog lurking in the forest. I started calling back to the house for more flashlights and for Sharon to phone the other neighbours and warn them we had a lost dog.

I'd be the first to admit that humping through the forest on a recently installed artificial knee, using a bad flashlight to search for a blind, black, deaf dog, is not intelligent behaviour. At the same time, if the human race waited around for its intelligence to catch up to its technology, we'd still be living in caves (where we'll probably end up anyway). Besides, I'd recently gone cross-country skiing during a freak snowstorm, so I figured I was already toast with the doctors. I never paid much attention to their instructions, which might explain why my health is shot.

By the time the night mist settled to chest height, we had our cars lined up, high beams illuminating the forest's edge. Our stalwart equestrian neighbour hoofed the trails, and Sharon and I crawled through the cedar swamps, attempting to trace the occasional plaintive howl that Bonnie released.

The only way to know wilderness is to lose yourself in it, let yourself be captured. I've spent enough nights camped alone in untravelled forests to understand that haunting. I could only imagine what a blind, deaf dog thought of it in her lonely agony. Isn't that what we all are? Blind, lost dogs in a forest? We set our own dogs after her; however, because they knew her, they wouldn't bark, and they couldn't lure her back. They kept returning, panting, desperate for further instruction. Gradually, I caught glimpses of her shadowy form and figured out where she was heading. Alongside her, our own black Lab's eyes glowed green among the primeval ferns, wetly reflecting my lamp.

I wondered if Bonnie had some residual sight and the dim beam of my flashlight was scaring her, or maybe it was my thumping human vibrations in the forest. She was terrified. She was fleeing! I began shouting out directions to Sharon, trying to get her to double back on the road. Sharon kept mishearing my directions in the echoing cedars and stumbled into her own swampy misadventures, while I slashed through a jungle of ferns and crawled over waist-high logs sprouting mushrooms bigger than wheelbarrow wheels.

I'm now screaming, "Bonnie, stop! Bonnie! Lie down," hoping she might be able to sense my booming voice. Meanwhile, I'm alternating this with instructions to my working dog—"Bring her in! Bring her to me!"—and hollering directions to Sharon, still slogging through the swamp: "Get on the road! Go around the back of the park." If Sharon could double back, we'd have the dog between us. But of course, at this point, I've got the search party completely confused with my contradictory instructions. I'm in a panic that we are going to lose this dog in the night, a dog so old and ill she'd die of exposure. I'm banging my bad knee on branches and stepping in holes, cursing like a trooper in battle—it never occurred to me that Bonnie was also the name of a neighbour on the other side of the park.

I finally latched onto Bonnie's tail, and she stopped walking, throwing her head against my thigh, inhaling my odour—releasing a huge, trembling sob of relief as she realized it was me—the despair of a dog gone blind and deaf. Thankfully, our neighbours were away that weekend, so we never had to explain the swearing and strange instructions to Bonnie from the bush across from their house.

Two days later we learned the dog had a terminal brain tumour. She's now cold and mouldering in her grave, and my knee doesn't feel any better these days. Aside from the numbness her death left behind, I'm grateful I abandoned city living for so many years—that I had the opportunity to receive that blind dog's gift of another rich night in the nearly primeval cedar forest that dwells beyond our farm. It makes me remember the words of Wallace Stevens: "The greatest poverty is not to live in a physical world."

Yet we are living in what scientists call the Holocene extinction event, the greatest era of extinctions since the Cretaceous/Tertiary extinction event 65 million years ago. And "the wild" is becoming an idea, not a place. The physical world has become a tourist destination for the exploding urban populations. Our delights have shifted from being spied on by tiny owls to coveting shoe brands endorsed by basketball stars.

The Inupiat people have a word, *uniari*, that means the nervous awe felt in the face of an overwhelming encounter with a natural phenomenon. It's a disappearing word and emotion.

359

LATELY, MANY ENVIRONMENTAL THINKERS have speculated that when civilizations reach a tipping point they can't recover. Writers as diverse as Ronald Wright, Jared Diamond, and Margaret Atwood have suggested that we're fast approaching ours. We are exhibiting the mutant behaviour of the creatures we have caged in overcrowded, sensory-deprived conditions. We have factory farmed ourselves. The accelerating scale of our looting suggests that, recognizing our damage to climate and wilderness, we have collectively begun to grab the last from the gutted stores in the hurricane city we have made out of our home. In *A Scientific Romance*, Wright points out that the human species has stripped off the top fossil fuel and mineral layer of the earth, and if any kind of environmental or major economic collapse occurs, rebuilding will be inhibited by our inability to reach any deeper resources. Atwood also notes this danger in *Oryx and Crake*.

All this great tumult has happened since we discovered the portable memory bank called writing. The first clumsy markings of symbols for moons and seasons and game animals became hieroglyphic variations for keeping track of goods that led eventually to the alphabet, which enabled us to leap beyond our ecological niche and move so quickly from hunter-gatherers to small farmers to global looters, and to inevitable collapse, the way a slime mould culture in a petri dish will begin with a few cells, build cities, collapse, and explode, creating other cities until the petri dish is filled and the whole mess melts down. But nature abhors vacuums. Once we are gone the environment will fill with other spawn.

360

We are only a mote in the eye of time—laughing and weeping and exterminating and being born. Though it will be a terrible era when the dominion of humankind collapses, as eventually it must, it seems to me that if there is some unified field out there to this universe, it will be the law of the whirlpool in the creek bed—entropy—the enormous ability to create and diversify. That's why, as much as I admire the single-celled amoeba, I love the deer of my fields and even the dangerous, distressing, almost erotic, yet grim and joyful confusion of Beijing.

HUNTER-GATHERER CULTURES WEREN'T any more eco-logical than us. Their damage was usually only less because of smaller populations and either a cultural rejection of technology or a lack of it. Is that an answer? In my worst moments, I believe we are approaching our ecological destination—scraping the earth's surface clean of minerals and metals before returning to our hunter-gatherer niche.

You can't practise "traditional" whale hunting with high-powered rifles and harpoon cannons; that's the world of shellfish-headed spears, rope, and seal bladders and a few crazily intrepid individuals in a canoe, individuals who could return one day. Cluster bombs will become rocks again, missiles will be spears, and we will revisit the caves and huts where we might belong, gathering roots, perhaps small-farming a slash-and-burn garden patch, chasing a few mammals and lizards about, eating grubs, watching the shadows of our fires on the walls.

MAYBE MY THOUGHTS GO this way because I'm in my dec-adent tub, and able to enjoy the luxury of the night. The stars are fading as the moon breaks above the cedars. I hear a noise by the back gate and remember the chickens are not locked up. The dogs are in the house with Sharon. I get up, dripping, step into my sandals, and seal the tub, pre-serving the heat with my homemade double cover. Then I'm padding around the house to the gate. Everything is quiet, the chickens murmuring in their coop. I lift the ramp and drop the latch to lock the coop tight, as the moonlight shafts through the trees in silver bars. My whole world is going primeval again. I exit the outer run, careful I don't take a slide on any loose mound of chicken shit. I look at the woods beyond, and start to imagine them rustling with dinosaurs, until I hear a clickety-click in the nettles. Oh no, here we go again—and the dogs are inside. I double back to the road behind the coop while the sheep shift tentatively toward the lower field.

It's magic time.

I guess this sounds as if I often wander naked in the dark. I don't. However, there are always those inevitable moments when the world goes sideways. We have to respect them as well in this long day of storytelling. Everything in moderation, including moderation. I still can't see the creature in the silver pouring over the nettle patch by the field, but the sheep are unafraid and have moved up to the soft, shaded grass by the fence. A branch cracks and I sight him. He's enormous. The big buck that's been lurking in the woods behind the farm. Last year he startled Sharon and me, leaping out of the salal and across the trail in front of us.

Big-chested with a wide, long rack, uneven, four points on one side, five on the other. Maybe the largest buck I've seen on this island of small deer. He skips over the rail fence with the ease of a teenager hopping a mud puddle. I can't cross the nettles because I'm only wearing my sandals, so I continue down the road and slip through the gate to the lower pasture and back toward the field, where he's mingled with the sheep, browsing. The animals shine like platinum in the moonlight. I come around the bigleaf maple until I face him barely ten feet away. He's unconcerned. And I realize with some sadness that he's joined the herd of deer being fed by my neighbour. This has made him lose his fear of people. Dangerous.

The sheep recognize me and continue eating. I can tell he's deciding whether to run; then he returns to grazing the lush, early-summer grass, yet keeping his eye on me. I back away. Tonight the field is his.

By now, Sharon will be wondering why I haven't come for my tea, but it's warm outside and the moon is upon me in the pasture beside the big, linked ponds, and I feel thrilled. I am being washed clean by the moonlight, all my senses alive, the breeze on my skin, the bats like fluttering shadows, the ripping of the grass by the sheep. I'm flooded with the happiness of knowing that I am here, that I don't own any of this. I am merely present, linked into the absurd chain that goes back to Gautama delivering his fire sermon to a thousand monks at Gaya Head, and further...

O my priests, everything is on fire. And with what is everything on fire?

The eye is on fire, form is on fire, awareness is on fire, the eye's glance is on fire. Also everything that is pleasant or painful or unpleasant or painless to the glance. They are aflame with what? They are on fire with the fire of passion, the fire of hatred, the fire of delusions. I say the mind is on fire with birth, with age, with death, sorrow, weeping, pain, grief, and despair.

The ear is on fire. Sound is on fire. The nose is on fire. Smells are on fire. The tongue is on fire. Flavours are on fire. The body is on fire. Touch is on fire.

Yes! And I guess this is why I could never be a true Buddhist. I love the fire too much that Gautama warns us against. Like Camus, I can only adore the absurd in all its glory—the high-speed run to the inevitable grave—performing the

363

living dance of death—celebrating the river, diving in it, diverting it, flowing in it, lusting naked with my companions in the current. Celebration and struggle. In quantum physics, effect can occur before cause. Time and events are the tangle our minds live within—this eighteen-year-long day at Trauma Farm that stretches back to Babylon and into the future. This is our only victory. The only way I've been able to move beyond my desires and distractions is by being immersed fully in the world—by paying attention.

⚓

IN *On the Origin of Species*, Charles Darwin writes of the richness around us and how it all arrived.

> *It is interesting to contemplate an entangled bank, clothed with many plants of many kinds, with birds singing on the bushes, with various insects flitting about, and with worms crawling through the damp earth, and to reflect that these elaborately constructed forms, so different from each other, and dependent on each other in so complex a manner, have all been produced by laws acting around us... There is grandeur in this view of life, with its several powers, having been originally breathed into a few forms or into one; and that, whilst this planet has gone cycling on according to the fixed law of gravity, from so simple a beginning endless forms most beautiful and most wonderful have been, and are being, evolved.*

We go through long periods of self-hypnosis, sandwiched between sublime incidents of attention (awareness) and stupid, boring labours. But existence is a surprise, the real questions we haven't figured out, so that suggests to me we should learn to treat our planet gently. According to the Dakota proverb, probably first spoken by Black Elk, "We shall be known by the tracks we leave behind." That said, it's clear factory farming is dangerous, but it has fed many people economically. We have to learn how to harness it, and reduce our addiction to its defiled products. Traditional farming is good, but it's caused mayhem as well. We need to find a balance. I don't know if that's possible.

Meanwhile, eat your local vegetables and fruits and take long walks every day. After that, everything becomes dicey, especially when we start making laws. It's difficult not to be ironic if we consider our history of solutions.

⚓︎

I ARRIVE IN THE night with fewer answers than when I began. The most I have learned is that living in these moments, close to the land, is good, and behaving with as much common decency as I can muster is also good. The Tetlit Gwich'in tribe have no word for wilderness. That's because it was not out there for them until recent years. They were living inside the wilderness. You can know an ecology only if you are inside it. I question all authority and the twisted by-products of reductionist logic, and I rise on a summer morning to the haunting song of a thrush, live with the birds of the day, and sleep to the random vocalizations of the night.

The plaintive call of the killdeer erupts again from the field. She's on her nest. I almost stepped on it the other day while rounding up the sheep. The male had been doing his broken-wing trick a few minutes earlier, near the pond, but

I'd ignored him. The nest is four speckled eggs in a pasture. Hidden in plain sight. They make it most of the time. We've seen a few hatches. According to Audubon, people consider the killdeer "a noisy bird and restless," but I've always found it beautiful, and its cry in the night is haunting. A companion to the frog chorus of spring. It's a noise against the silence of fate.

I'M OUT WANDERING AGAIN, in the blue warmth of a night silvered by the moon—I am only another maggot laughing inside the ecstasy of my community. The high cedars are trembling in the breeze. Ajax shouts me out from his perch in the maple, while Sharon has drunk her tea and gone to bed. I leave this story as I entered it. Confused and enthralled—in the world—naked again, and still alive. I look around me in the dark and I know it's a joke, but it's a good joke. I think I'm home, living on the land. We're in this together—the wild, the domestic, the wormy, the laughing ones and the weepers, black dogs and Buddhas, all of us divine in our diversity—our orgiastic, gorgeous confusion—all of us dancing in the stream of everything.

SELECTED
REFERENCES

*A*LTHOUGH A LIFETIME of reading went into *Trauma Farm*, the books listed here were most essential to its creation. They are also recommended reading. Several of the books quoted in the text are not included, such as the epic treatises of Darwin (along with a great number of reference books and Internet sources), because they don't make good general reading, although I couldn't resist including a couple of "difficult" classics in this list. The editions cited are the ones I used, and they are often not first editions. I listed subtitles only where I thought them relevant to understanding the nature of the book, and I have tried to keep to the spirit of *Trauma Farm* with the format of this unorthodox bibliography.

Edward Abbey. *Desert Solitaire: A Season in the Wilderness*. New York: Ballantine, 1985. A lyric, raucous collection of essays by the naturally rebellious naturalist and author of the original American eco-terrorist novel, *The Monkey Wrench Gang*.

Wendell Berry. *The Unsettling of America*. San Francisco: Sierra Club, 1997. One of his many books about rural life. A poet and philosopher of the land, Wendell Berry was among the first and best at warning us about the destruction of the rural world and its glories.

Kathleen Norris Brenzel, ed. *The Western Garden Book*. Menlo Park, CA: Sunset, 2001. The editor calls this "the ultimate guide to Western gardening." She might be right. A comprehensive list of nursery plants and their requirements that can also be useful to gardeners in North America and England.

Albert Camus. *The Myth of Sisyphus*. New York: Vintage International, 1983. An adventure into the absurdity of life. Camus was an original-thinking explorer of meaning as well as social behaviour and ethics (especially in *The Rebel* and *Resistance, Rebellion, and Death*).

Rachel Carson. *Silent Spring*. New York: Fawcett Crest, 1964. The book that alerted North America to the dangers of pesticides.

Rosalind Creasey. *Cooking from the Garden: Creative Gardening & Contemporary Cuisine*. Vancouver: Douglas & McIntyre, 1988. Pricey but essential for gourmands of the garden.

Christopher Dewdney. *Acquainted with the Night*. Toronto: HarperCollins Canada, 2004. The joy of darkness.

Jared Diamond. *Collapse: How Societies Choose to Fail or Succeed*. New York: Viking, 2005. A recent wordy but impressive examination of the dangers facing human cultural evolution. The chapter on the extinction of the Greenland farming communities is fabulous.

Annie Dillard. *Pilgrim at Tinker Creek*. New York: Harper's Magazine Press, 1975. A luminous, nearly precious naturalist observes the world around her. A lyrical updating of Walden.

Selected References

Loren Eiseley. *The Immense Journey, The Star Thrower, The Night Country, All the Strange Hours.* Any of his books is a poetic adventure. Science meets literature. A "wood child" whose haunted writings are venerated by naturalists worldwide.

Carla Emery. *The Encyclopedia of Country Living.* Seattle: Sasquatch, 1994. An insanely inclusive ongoing book that started out as how-to newsletters sold at craft fairs in 1970 and a twelve-page table of contents, and ended only with Emery's death in 2005. A quirky, massive effort, it got very little wrong during a lifetime of compiling traditional knowledge. If you are going to be left alone with one book while maintaining a farm, this is that book.

Ron L. England. *Growing Great Garlic: The Definitive Guide for Organic Gardeners and Small Farmers.* Okanogan, WA: Filaree Productions, 1991. This book is pretty well what it says it is. For the true garlic fetishist.

Jean-Henri Fabre. *The Insect World of J. Henri Fabre.* New York: Dodd, Mead, 1949. Everything you wanted to know about dung beetles and more. A collection of essays by the prolific and eloquent nineteenth-century god of entomologists.

M.F.K. Fisher. *The Art of Eating.* New York: Macmillan, 1990. The high priestess of cookbook writers, a great cook, stylist, and eccentric. Five of her most noted books collected in one volume.

Wayne Grady. *Bringing Back the Dodo.* Toronto: McClelland & Stewart, 2007. Or just about any of his other books. The former editor of *Harrowsmith* in its glory days, Grady is a hard-working, no-nonsense naturalist who is always interesting.

Graham Harvey. *We Want Real Food: Why Our Food Is Deficient in Minerals and Nutrients—and What We Can Do about It.* London: Constable, 2006. Sometimes simplistic yet substantial exploration of the effects industrialized farming is having on food and the ecology.

Bernd Heinrich. *Mind of the Raven.* New York: HarperCollins, 1999. The mind that explores the mind of the raven is also fascinating.

Hesiod and Theognis. London: Penguin Classic, 1976. Hesiod's eighth-century BC poem *Works and Days* is the earliest writing on farming I've encountered. Most people today would consider his vision of small farming terrifying and unacceptable, but it has its moments of common sense.

Lewis Hyde. *The Gift: Imagination and the Erotic Life of Property*. New York: Vintage, 1983. My copy was given to me by a friend. It's a real gift.

Daniel Imhoff and Jo Ann Baumgartner, eds. *Farming and the Fate of Wild Nature: Essays in Conservation-Based Agriculture*. Berkeley: University of California Press, Watershed Media, 2006. A fine collection of essays.

Verlyn Klinkenborg. *The Rural Life*. Boston: Back Bay Books, 2002. He's also written the lovely *Making Hay* and other memoirs. According to a review in the *New York Times* this book is "luminous...a brilliant book." The review is correct.

Brewster Kneen. *Farmageddon: Food and the Culture of Biotechnology*. Gabriola Island, B.C.: New Society, 1999. A well-wrought rant against the green revolution and globalized farming and its technology.

Aldo Leopold. *A Sand County Almanac*. New York: Ballantine, 1971. "A thing is right when it tends to preserve the integrity, stability, and beauty of the biotic community. It is wrong when it tends otherwise." The master naturalist and his greatest work. This is the book where he first observed how the removal of a keystone species can wreak havoc on the entire ecosystem in what's now known as a trophic cascade.

John A. Livingston. *Rogue Primate: An Exploration of Human Domestication*. Toronto: Key Porter, 1994. Chilling thoughts from an incisive thinker.

William Bryant Logan. *Dirt: The Ecstatic Skin of the Earth*. New York: Riverhead, 1995. An enchanting exploration of soil.

Barry Lopez. *Of Wolves and Men*. New York: Scribner, 1978. A book that is informative not only about wolves but about our relationship with the "wild."

Konrad Z. Lorenz. *King Solomon's Ring*. New York: Mentor, 1991. Animal behaviour innovatively examined.

Richard A. Nelson. *Heart and Blood: Living with Deer in America*. New York: Random House, 1998. By the author of the much-admired *The Island Within*. This landmark study is the definitive book on how the deer plague is remaking vast swaths of the North American environment.

Andrew Nikiforuk. *Pandemonium: Bird Flu, Mad Cow Disease, and Other Biological Plagues of the 21st Century*. Toronto: Viking Canada, 2006. Nikiforuk is a penetrating researcher into environmental issues.

Raj Patel. *Stuffed and Starved: Markets, Power and the Hidden Battle for the World's Food System*. Toronto: HarperCollins Canada, 2007. For those who like their agriculture buttered with statistics. An ominous picture of food economics and market manipulation.

Angelo Pellegrini. *The Unprejudiced Palate*. New York: Macmillan, 1984. A deliciously prejudiced and opinionated memoir about growing up with real (though scant) food, and then relearning the art of its preparation.

Michael Pollan. *The Omnivore's Dilemma*. New York: Penguin, 2006. A classic work on the modern diet. His *In Defence of Food* is also a must-read.

Irma S. Rombauer (with Marion Rombauer Becker). *Joy of Cooking*. New York: Bobbs-Merrill, 1964. After my first copy fell apart I practically had to fight three people off to buy this eclectic, supremely sensible collection of traditional recipes at a garage sale. The 1975 edition is reputedly the best. The New Age Heart Smart "professional" revision of 1997 by hired authors is a notorious disaster in book publishing. I believe the newest edition returns to many of the traditional recipes and original voice of Rombauer.

Candace Savage. *Curious by Nature*. Vancouver: Greystone, 2005.
A charming collection of naturalist essays by one of Canada's hardest-working environmental writers.

Eric Schlosser. *Fast Food Nation*. Boston: Houghton Mifflin, 2001.
A devastating book about the fast-food industry and the monopolistic monstrousness of the new American food empires. Required reading (along with Michael Pollan) for those who care about what they eat and what their children eat.

E.F. Schumacher. *Small Is Beautiful: Economics as if People Mattered*.
New York: Harper & Row, 1975. A groundbreaking book on reverse thinking.

John Seymour. *The Self-Sufficient Gardener*. Garden City, NY: Dolphin, 1980. The best book on wide deep-bed gardening. Straight-talking, succinct, common-sense gardening, and highly recommended.

Scott Slovic. *Seeking Awareness in American Nature Writing*. Salt Lake City: University of Utah, 1982. Thoreau. Dillard. Abbey. Berry. Lopez.
A collection of essays on five great American naturalists.

Alisa Smith and J.B. MacKinnon. *The 100-Mile Diet: A Year of Local Eating*. Toronto: Random House Canada, 2007. The rallying cry for the champions of local food.

Steve Solomon. *Organic Gardening West of the Cascades*. Seattle: Pacific Search, 1981. A somewhat New Age West Coast organic text, but also full of common sense and straightforward gardening advice that would apply worldwide.

Don Stap. *Birdsong*. New York: Scribner, 2005. Charming. A look at birds and their songs. Packed with engrossing trivia and important information.

Robert Sullivan. *Rats*. New York: Bloomsbury, 2004. A fascinating obsession for the writer. Full of facts though a little too obsessive for this reader.

Jiro Takei and Marc P. Keane. *Sakuteiki Visions of the Japanese Garden: A Modern Translation of Japan's Gardening Classic.* Boston: Tuttle, 2001. Includes a translation of the *Sakuteiki* (Records of Garden Making). Written a thousand years ago, it begins with the evocative phrase "the art of setting stones" and works its way through the garden. Only for those compulsive gardeners interested in the arcane and deep Japanese aesthetics.

Henry David Thoreau. *Walden, Journals,* etc. Almost everything he wrote. After young Thoreau accidentally set the local woods on fire, he made it his life's work to understand the world around him, and did a mighty fine job of it.

Ronald Wright. *A Short History of Progress.* Toronto: Anansi, 2004. The inspired Massey Lectures that succinctly examine cultural evolution.

In addition I can recommend the magazines *Organic Gardening* and *Small Farm Canada,* and the early editions of *Harrowsmith* magazine. The various *Harrowsmith* books are usually excellent on an assortment of rural subjects, along with the *Foxfire* books. The same with the numerous editions and titles of *The Whole Earth Catalog.*

Websites like Wikipedia are often unreliable, although Wikipedia is a good starting point for research on the Internet. As almost everyone knows by now, the Internet can be a treacherous but juicy source of facts and factoids and opinions; just be aware of the agendas of the websites, and look for confirmation of any facts elsewhere.